T0305144

Trade in Health

Also by David Reisman

Adam Smith's Sociological Economics
Alfred Marshall: Progress and Politics
Alfred Marshall's Mission
Anthony Crosland: The Mixed Economy
Conservative Capitalism: The Social Economy
Crosland's Future: Opportunity and Outcome
Democracy and Exchange: Schumpeter, Galbraith, T.H. Marshall, Titmuss and Adam Smith
The Economics of Alfred Marshall
Galbraith and Market Capitalism
Health Care and Public Policy
Health Tourism: Social Welfare through International Trade
The Institutional Economy: Demand and Supply
Market and Health
The Political Economy of Health Care
The Political Economy of James Buchanan
Richard Titmuss: Welfare and Society
Schumpeter's Market: Enterprise and Evolution
The Social Economics of Thorstein Veblen
Social Policy in an Ageing Society: Age and Health in Singapore
State and Welfare: Tawney, Galbraith and Adam Smith
Theories of Collective Action: Downs, Olson and Hirsch

Trade in Health

Economics, Ethics and Public Policy

David Reisman

Edward Elgar
Cheltenham, UK • Northampton, MA, USA

Published by
Edward Elgar Publishing Limited
The Lypiatts
15 Lansdown Road
Cheltenham
Glos GL50 2JA
UK

Edward Elgar Publishing, Inc.
William Pratt House
9 Dewey Court
Northampton
Massachusetts 01060
USA

A catalogue record for this book
is available from the British Library

Library of Congress Control Number: 2013949871

This book is available electronically in the ElgarOnline.com
Economics Subject Collection, E-ISBN 978 1 78254 721 1

ISBN 978 1 78254 720 4

Typeset by Servis Filmsetting Ltd, Stockport, Cheshire
Printed and bound in Great Britain by T.J. International Ltd, Padstow

Contents

Acknowledgement

The author and publishers would like to thank the New Silk Road Research Fund of the Nanyang Technological University for its generous support. They would also like to thank the representatives of hospitals and other organisations for their willingness to provide information and answer questions.

1. Medical travel: the nature of the beast

The link between international travel and medical attention is not new. The sheikhs, the sultans, the princes and the plutocrats have long been going to Harley Street, Johns Hopkins, the Cleveland Clinic, the Mayo Clinic for their health. Before them there were the Roman hot springs, the pilgrimage to Lourdes, the sanatorium in the Alps and the powdered rhinoceros horn that made old people young. What is new is not the existence of medical travel but its extent. In earlier times it was only the very rich who went abroad for medical attention. Rising incomes have put paid to the privilege. Transnational care has become a topic in inclusion and democracy. Like pepper, camphor and bananas, what was once a minority interest is becoming a widespread expectation. North–south, south–north, north–north, south–south, it is not a one-way street or even a two-way turnpike so much as a spaghetti junction. We are all increasingly mixed up.

Cuba was the first country to promote mass healthcare travel. In the early 1990s, turning the United States trade embargo to its own advantage, it targeted the Spanish-speaking nations in Central and South America and did so at a profit (Goodrich, 1993). Other countries followed suit, often specialising in affordable cosmetic surgery for North American clients. There are currently between 70 and 80 countries, highly diversified, that are actively competing for the market. There are at least as many, mainly emergent, economies in Asia, Eastern Europe and Latin America with a token presence. They are challenging the first movers for a significant profile.

The motive has been survival as often as expansion. The Asian economic crisis in 1997 forced Thai hospitals like Bumrungrad, faced with a fall in demand at home, to leverage on the baht devaluation to source additional customers abroad. The private hospitals in Malaysia faced a similar need to look abroad for throughput after the recession-ridden middle classes had fled back to the public system and bankruptcy loomed. By the next upswing the process had acquired a momentum of its own. It was not always smooth sailing. As with any bandwagon effect, for some players it was a licence to print money but for others it resulted in oversupply and poor returns. De-territorialisation need not mean high profits from scale.

This book is concerned with the de-territorialisation of the medical contract. It is divided into ten chapters. Chapter 2, 'Number, weight and measure', asks what information is needed, what sources are available and what black holes remain. Chapter 3, 'The preconditions for trade', says that affluence, information and consensus are the ingredients that make possible a global marketplace in prevention and cure. Chapter 4 on 'Price and quality' and Chapter 5 on 'Difference' examine the three main reasons why medical services cross the political divide. Chapter 6, 'Trade: the outputs', discusses distance facilitation and patient displacement. Chapter 7, 'The inputs: commercial presence', turns to the international flows of capital, equipment and business acumen. Chapter 8, 'The inputs: labour', extends the discussion of inputs to the migration of medical manpower.

Chapter 9, 'The ethics of medical travel', shifts the focus from expediency to absolutes. A patient dies because the specialist has gone to California. A hip is not replaced because the doctoring stock has moved into aesthetic surgery. Morally, something may have gone wrong. That leads to the final chapter. Entitled 'Conclusion: commodification', Chapter 10 states the obvious, that some things are economic tradeables and some things are not. A pineapple lends itself to the calculus of gain and loss. A wife may not so legitimately be arbitraged into a higher-return investment. Healthcare may be a commodity or it may be an entitlement. Different people say different things. This book proves that some of them or even all of them have got it right.

Before that, however, it is necessary to build a wall around the city. The present chapter is entitled 'Medical travel: the nature of the beast'. It is the most difficult chapter in the book. It seeks to identify the boundaries of an elusive service that has many names and passports. It tries to describe the nature of a beast that is in truth a veritable zoo.

On this at least there is agreement. Medical travel is intended and not accidental. It is not emergency care while on holiday or continuing care for major surgery. Rather, it is elective treatment for a non-acute condition where the patient can travel without prohibitive discomfort and where follow-up for complications will be possible at home. A deliberate and deliberative element is central to the definition. Thinking things through provides the link to rational choice. It limits the scope of the industry. Only a minority of procedures lend themselves to medical tourism.

Medical travel has many names. It has been called health travel, health tourism, healthcare tourism, holistic tourism, transnational healthcare, international patient business, international medical services, extra-national health-seeking, overseas care, medical treatment abroad, cross-border medical attention, medical value travel exports, medical tourism exports, travel for medical procedures. Inter-country patients form part of 'a global medical marketplace', 'a global medical commons', a network of 'interlinked nation-states' inhabited by 'national or global citizens' (Kangas, 2010: 344). A stay of at least one night might be involved. It is not necessary to be too pedantic about the name. 'Medical travel' will do. It is an umbrella term which, like a dictionary, brings together a good cross-section of words.

Travel for health may be planned in advance: well people must be prevented from falling ill. Travel for illness may be a reaction to circumstance: sick people must be restored to full possession of their faculties. It is an artificial distinction. Whether a routine check-up or an elective procedure, health status is better because the patient makes the trip.

Medical travel is Third World to First (the traditional Harley Street model), First World to Third (USA to India), Third World to Third (Myanmar to Thailand), First World to First (Britain to Belgium). The equator is no longer the line that defines the mobility.

So much so that intra-national mobility should logically be included in the definition. The United States is a big place. Medical travel can occur within the confines of a single country. It takes five times as long to go from Seattle to Fort Lauderdale as it does to go from Jakarta to Singapore. It is medical travel. Yet it is displacement within a single cultural, linguistic, economic and political entity. Rural women might prefer to give birth in an urban hospital. Regional dispersion exists in the price of drugs and appliances. Insurance status is not disrupted. Coordination with the family doctor may be easier. Non-portability at home is an unexpected problem. Many provinces in federated jurisdictions like the USA, Canada and Australia do not automatically release funds from social insurance for care in other parts of the country. That said, intra-national movement resembles international movement in that it makes competition more intense, has a dynamic effect on managerial efficiency and keeps the prices down.

In the UK, despite the claim of a National Health Service (NHS), patients often find it difficult to obtain treatment out-of-region. One nation can be more than one nation. Borders might be more porous if the patient went to Bangkok instead. Even so, NHS patients are already being placed in the over-bedded private sector. Support services are already being contracted out. Medical travel may be seen as a continuation of a home-grown trend.

Medical travel is nonetheless taken generally to mean a foreign dimension. Allowing for national insurance and national regulation, the terminology is becoming obsolete. The implication is that the individual belongs to a specific geographical territory. No one would say the same of the consumer who buys Dutch cheese or Portuguese wine. The boundaries themselves are becoming more permeable. A Scot is a member of Scotland and of the United Kingdom and of the European Union. Nationhood is political. Health is not. A term like 'outsourcing', the tendency to speak of patients 'going abroad', implies an original position. In fact, global disequilibrium and unimpeded search might be the better window on to the world market.

Kangas speaks of 'medical exiles' and of 'transnational therapeutic itineraries' (Kangas, 2010: 344). Song uses the term 'biotech pilgrims' (Song, 2010: 384). Arguing for a broad definition as well as a worldwide perspective, Song says that wellness does not begin and end in the doctor's office: 'Faith intertwines with technology, travel, and the political economies of health care and medical research in a global era' (Song, 2010: 384, 385). A hip transplant is medical travel. So is a facelift or a skin treatment which gives the recipient a better quality of life, self-perceived. So is a bracing *onsen*, a temple retreat or a visit to a holy place. Obese people are more exposed to diabetes. A weight-loss clinic may be as much pro-health as a hospital bed.

Wellness tourism in the form of a spa, a gym, a massage or a diet is not healthcare narrowly defined. It is, for all that, conducive to good health. Relaxation pays. Prevention pays. Spa tourism is worth US$255 million annually (Hudson, 2011: 44). It is a part of the good health production function. Spas should not be ignored. Nor should nursing homes, retirement villages, biomedical research, often globally integrated. Some observers would include the complements of transport, accommodation, travel insurance and meals. Good food is an important part of being well.

Medical travel, broadly defined, is more than sick people travelling abroad while they can. It is not just the restoration but also the preservation of function. It is as open-ended and as multidimensional as good health itself – which the World Health Organization defines to be 'a state of complete physical, mental and social well-being and not merely the absence of disease or infirmity' (World Health Organization, 1962 [1946]: 1). An all-encompassing definition like that means that anything can be counted as cross-border care. An apple grown by foreigners keeps our own local doctors away.

Sick people scour the earth for a miracle cure that will buy them salvation. Faith springs eternal. Recreation is re-creation. It is regeneration. The concept of search is an integral part of the human condition. In China Buddhists and Daoists say '*chao shan*' (Song, 2010: 308n). They believe that going to the mountain will regenerate and rejuvenate them. The mountain will make them fully themselves.

Beachy tourism is health. Hot yoga is health. T'ai chi is health. Hot mud is health. Time away from the stress of work is therapeutic in itself.

Medical travel may be seen as a joint product. It is for that reason less expensive than the medical component alone would suggest.

It is by no means easy to pin down the essence of the cross-border experience. Yet an attempt must be made and the General Agreement on Trade in Services (the GATS) provides a useful rubric. It identifies four modes: distance facilitation in forms such as telemedicine and outsourcing; consumption abroad because the patients demand imported attention; investment abroad because the businesses go where the opportunities are; and finally, mobility of labour because professionals like businesses are rational and purposive. The second mode is the mode that most closely corresponds to the popular perception of biomedical travel: 'Medical travel is defined as the activity of seeking medical treatment outside the borders of one's own country, and requires a patient to travel to a destination country, including making necessary arrangements (akin to a tourist) such as entry visas/permits, transfers and accommodation' (Frost & Sullivan, 2012: 12).

Health tourism is niche tourism. It is focused travel, on a par with golf holidays, battlefield tours and bird-watching abroad. It is on a par with meetings, incentives, conferences and exhibitions, collectively known as MICE. Niche tourism is always taken seriously: 'Perhaps the most obvious characteristic of niche tourism is that the niche is more important than the tourism' (Connell, 2011: 161). No one goes on a MICE purely for the beach.

Health is like MICE. Tourism suggests enjoyment. It was the journalists and the travel agents rather than the scholars and the patients who first began to speak of health tourism. Sickness, like MICE, is not leisure or hedonism. Invasive surgery or root-canal dentistry is not pleasure. At best it would be possible to speak of a mixed package, tourist attractions in combination with healthcare services. It is all a question of words. Foreign students are not called education tourists. Whatever they are called, everyone knows what they do.

A conclusion is required. It is that health travel in the global world is by no means as simple as the textbook Englishman who has a holiday in Cannes. Consider an Albanian who travels to a hospital in Costa Rica that is owned by a Thai–Russian consortium registered in the Bahamas and managed by an American born in Poland who had trained on-the-job in Macao. Once in the hospital the patient is seen by an Indian with a degree from Australia who is using equipment imported from Germany and is assisted by a Bangladeshi whose previous posting was in the Gulf. In the new global order we are all very mixed. The same country both sends and receives. It is the basis for harmonious interaction and the gains from trade.

2. Number, weight and measure

The evidence speaks for itself: 'The truthful answer: Nobody knows' (Youngman, 2009). The evidence is unreliable and it is inconsistent. As Lunt and his colleagues pointedly observe: 'We can narrow down the number of medical tourists worldwide as lying somewhere between 60 000 and 50 million' (Lunt, Smith, Exworthy, Green, Horsfall and Mannion, 2011: 15). Surveying the data-sources, Johnston is right to conclude that there is no reliable hard data on patient numbers, patient flows, treatment types and success rates. Even 'clear and unified definitions of the phenomenon' (Johnston, Crooks, Snyder and Kingsbury, 2010) are thin on the ground. Speculation abounds. There are theories and assumptions. Empirical evidence is more difficult to obtain. It is not even certain that the market is growing.

Not enough is known. Yet something is known. This chapter is about what has been established and what more there is to find out. Section 2.1, 'The questions', provides a check-list of important topics. Section 2.2, 'The sources', asks where information can be obtained to map out the international flows. Section 2.3, 'The facts', shows that the gaps are huge but that at the centre of the darkness there is nonetheless research.

2.1 THE QUESTIONS

A starting point would be world trade. Imports and exports are growing more rapidly than world value-added itself (Figure 2.1). The downside is that in periods of recession (1975, 1982, 2001, 2009) the fall in the rate of growth of world trade is more rapid than the counterpart decline in world gross domestic product (GDP).

Comparable data from international organisations allow investigators to distinguish between countries at different levels of national income and with a different mix of primary, secondary and tertiary activity. In each case the data on gross domestic product must be corrected for purchasing power parity to obtain a measure of what money can buy.

Within total trade, invisible trade is growing at a faster rate than the aggregate. In spite of that, about two-thirds of world trade is still trade

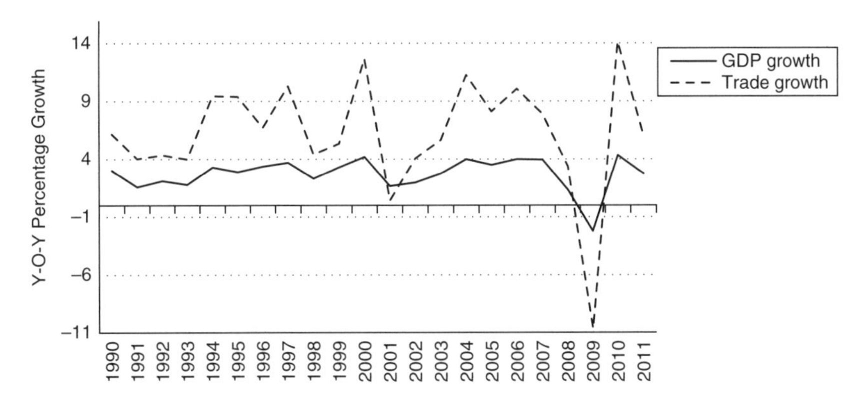

Source: World Bank (2013).

Figure 2.1 Comparison of world GDP growth and world trade growth

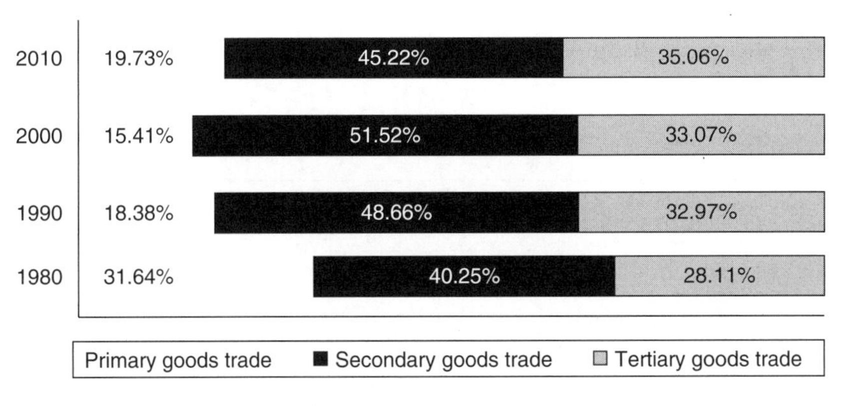

Source: World Trade Organization (2012).

Figure 2.2 Breakdown of world trade into primary, secondary and tertiary components

in manufactures and primary produce. Services (public and private) accounted for 35.06 per cent of world trade in 2010 (Figure 2.2). In 1980 the figure was 28.11 per cent.

The share has risen even if not dramatically. Investigators, extrapolating, believe it will rise more rapidly in the future: 'Trade in services has been the fastest growing component of international trade since the early 1990s, with average annual growth rates of close to 10%' (Breinlich and Criscuolo, 2011: 188). Lennon says that trade in services increased by a

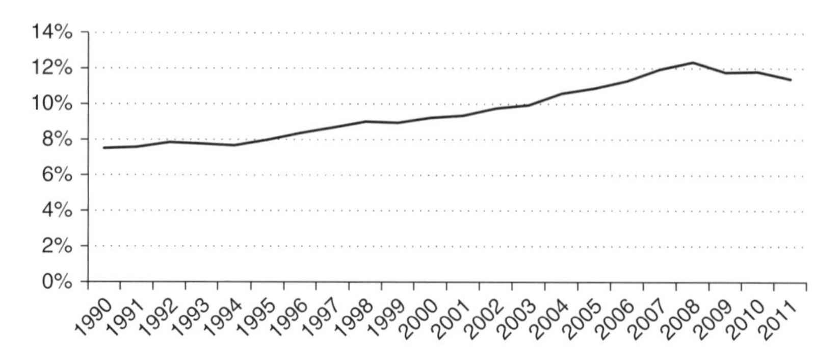

Source: World Bank (2013).

Figure 2.3 World trade in services as a percentage of world GDP

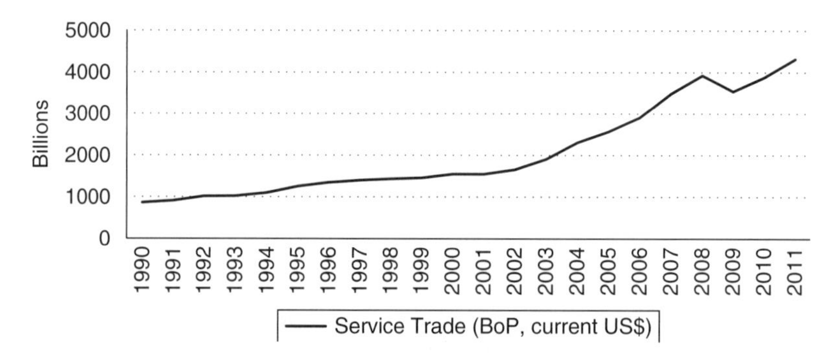

Source: World Bank (2013).

Figure 2.4 World trade in services in current US dollars

factor of five while trade in goods increased by a factor of only 3.5 over the two decades from 1989 to 2009 (Lennon, 2009: 1). Lautier expects that services will account for 50 per cent of world trade by 2020 (Lautier, 2013: 2). The growth rate of services is shown in Figure 2.3, while the absolute amounts are shown in Figure 2.4.

The principal components of world service trade are shown in Figure 2.5. Health services are included in Travel. The proportion of Travel represented by Health is not known. Travel has grown at approximately the same rate as the whole of service trade. The rate of growth is shown in Figure 2.6.

Invisibles are differentiated by quality, image, location and taste. Heterogeneity has not been an impediment to trade. Growth in skill-

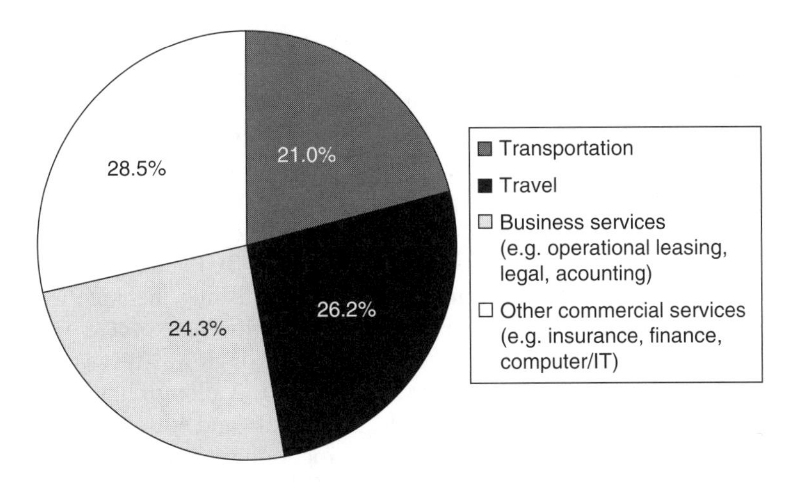

Source: World Trade Organization (2012).

Figure 2.5 Breakdown of world service trade components, 2012

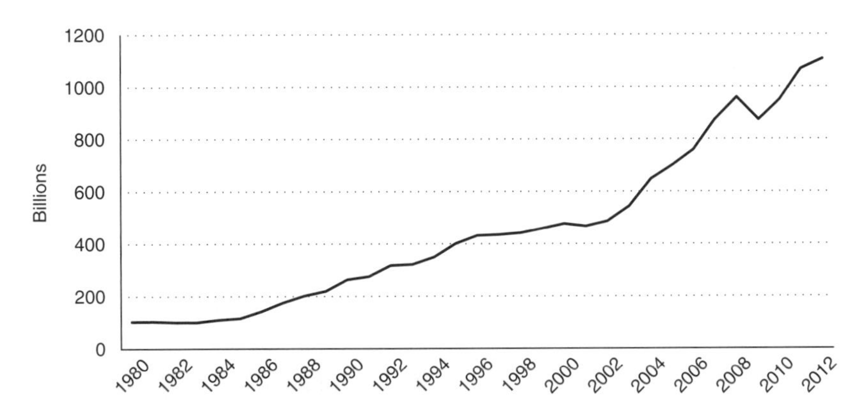

Source: World Trade Organization (2012).

Figure 2.6 Trade in travel services in current US dollars

intensive services such as business consultancy has been especially rapid within the sector. These are services where the buyer as well as the seller is in possession of specialist knowledge. Furthermore, there is substantial concentration in the invisible trade. In the United Kingdom, around 2 per cent of the firms account for over 80 per cent of UK service exports and imports (Breinlich and Criscuolo, 2011: 193). A small number of market participants have a good overview of the whole.

Trade in services is inherently more resistant to quantification than is trade in goods: 'The term "*services*" covers a heterogeneous range of intangible products and activities that are difficult to encapsulate within a simple definition. Services are also often difficult to separate from goods with which they may be associated in varying degrees' (United Nations Department of Economic and Social Affairs, 2002: 7). Even manufactures may be seen as services delivered over time. A washing machine is purchased not as an end-stage consumable but for its flow of expected washes.

More generally, some services are defined through abstract concepts rather than by any physical attribute or function. A plough has an internationally recognised commodity code. Healthcare and education do not. The United Nations Central Product Classification spells out what should be included under human health services (CPC 931), veterinary services (CPC 932) and social services related to health (CPC 933). The categories are arbitrary and by no means comprehensive. A number of trade-related services are excluded, including health education and health insurance. Nor is the United Nations schema universally adopted.

Investigators will want to know the service totals. They will also want to know the breakdown. Tourism accounts for one-third of all international services. It is the largest single item. The growth in receipts and international arrivals is shown in Figure 2.7.

Telecommunications and finance are also prominent. Trade in health-related services is less easy to document. Lautier estimates that it was 1.2

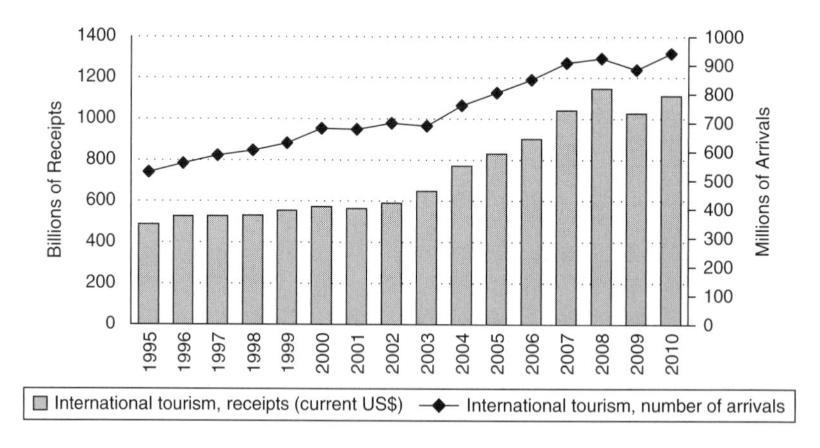

Source: World Bank (2013).

Figure 2.7 Global tourism: receipts and arrivals

per cent of total exports of travel services in 1997 and that it reached 1.5 per cent in 2010: 2.1 per cent for the United States, 0.7 for the non-USA developed countries, 1.6 per cent for the developing world which nonetheless had a market share of one-third (Lautier, 2013: 6). The rate of growth had been rapid: 'World exports of health services almost tripled from 1997 to 2010' (Lautier, 2013: 5).

World trade in health services, Lautier estimates, was worth US$11 766 million in 2010. Growth has averaged 8.1 per cent annually since 1997. The rate has been close to the average increase for all service trade. The reasons include the dissemination of information, the electronic revolution, the standardisation of treatment protocols, the enrichment of medical training, the liberalisation of exchange, the availability of drugs, the convergence in medical equipment. Exports from the South have increased more rapidly than those from the North. Lautier says that in 2010 the South commanded 54 per cent of the market, the North 46 per cent (Lautier, 2013: 6). The Tourism Research and Marketing Group anticipates that health-related travel will soon make up 4 per cent of total world tourism expenditures (TRAM, 2006).

Even within the GATS Mode 2 – consumption abroad – a selection must be made as to which candidates should be included and which should be dropped. A broad definition would include wellness treatments, acupuncture and rehabilitation. A narrow definition would concentrate on Western-type medicine alone. An intermediate definition would pick up indispensable collaterals such as airfares and accommodation as well as the doctors and the hospitals.

A broad definition is recuperation with a drink on the beach. A narrow definition is the trolley in the lift to the cyber-knife. An intermediate definition is onsite lodgings for worried relatives. Nor is Mode 2 the sum total of health travel. To Mode 2 must be added the outsourcing, the multinationals and the foreign talent. Consumers crossing frontiers are only one wing of a much larger mansion. Researchers will have to mark out their territory. Not all will home in on the same mix of treatments and complements.

Different researchers will select different services. Disaggregation makes a difference. The price elasticity for cosmetic surgery (a luxury demand) is likely to be higher than the price elasticity for a triple bypass (a life-and-death necessity). The price elasticity for stem cell therapy is likely to be indeterminate. It enhances the quality of life but it does not command the confidence of a sustained track record. A package made up of the high, the low and the indeterminate will be too big. Disaggregation would give a more meaningful result.

Disaggregation will also be appropriate if a country is seeking to spot fresh areas or identify comparative advantage. There is market segmentation. There is product differentiation. Singapore can separate Siamese twins. Thailand can reassign genders. Adding up the twins and the genders as if they were the same conceals the perceived heterogeneity that partitions off the package.

The same may be said of the patients. Foreigners who pass through the doors of the medical centres include holiday-makers, business travellers, emergency cases, students, expatriate employees paying local taxes, non-resident nationals going home to see their relatives, old-age pensioners who have retired abroad. Strictly speaking, a study of medical travel must confine itself to cases where the 'primary and explicit purpose' (Ehrbeck, Guevara and Mango, 2008: 2) of the trip is medical care. Intentionality is essential if medicine is to be seen as shopping. Reality is more complex. A tourist gets malaria: the visit to the hospital is unplanned. A businessman makes dentistry an incidental add-on: the journey abroad is multi-purpose. Just as all patients are not the same, so the degree of calculativeness is subject to considerable variation. Simple adding up is not enough. Catch-all does not fit all.

Adding up the appointments rather than the bodies inflates the figures through multiple counting. When the same patient returns for his follow-up he may go into the database as a second foreigner. Should he be readmitted for recurrence, he will be recorded as a third foreigner. By the time it is all over a single patient might have become a whole regiment of paper foreigners. No less misleading is the cost. Where all the treatments are delivered in a single episode the foreigner will go into the statistics as a single high-roller. Where some of the tests are scheduled for a second visit, the foreigner may end up as two customers, both cheap. Dr Jekyll consumes an appendectomy. Mr Hyde comes in for a blood test. The appointments are discrete. The body, however, is the same.

The data will often relate to treatments and tests. Patient census leaves the biggest stone unturned. It is medical outcomes and not medical inputs that in the last analysis determine whether an intervention is worthwhile. Proxies of quality like the doctor–patient and the bed–patient ratio, or the mix between locally educated and foreign-trained professionals, are not enough. The pudding must be tasted to see if it is good. For business, profit and sale are the normal success indicators. Medical outcomes, more ambitious, extend to restoration of function, complications, cross-infection in hospital, 12-month survival rates, delayed reactions that can only be identified through long-term follow-up. Not all cases of negligence will surface in the law courts. Since medical travellers return to their own country, and also because of the economic cost of a longitudinal study, full documentation is seldom available. It is not a satisfying meal.

Investigators want performance indicators and league tables so that they can make informed comparisons. They want audited data on hospital outpatients and walk-in clinics as well as on inpatient days. They want proof of evidence-based medicine and the rapid integration of new research. They want an explanation of practice variation which might be wasting scarce resources on over-medication and unneeded bed-nights. They also want information on the patient's own rating of the medical encounter. The consumer's perceived satisfaction is essential. Investigators need to find out what real-world people are thinking about their medical trip abroad.

2.2 THE SOURCES

Not enough is known. Everyone knows that. John Connell says of the industry that 'piecing together numerical data would have challenged decipherers of the Dead Sea scrolls': 'It is an industry that in some part has eluded detailed analysis since so much of it is both competitive and clandestine . . . No countries produce official data on medical tourism, since they have no means of collecting it, and no hospitals release data that has been verified by any independent body' (Connell, 2011: xi, 62). Lunt and his colleagues complain that no one even knows whether medical tourism is itself 'virus, symptom, or cure': 'There is a lack of systematic data concerning health services trade, both overall and at a disaggregated level . . . Mechanisms are needed that help us track the balance of trade' (Lunt, Smith, Exworthy, Green, Horsfall and Mannion, 2011: 2, 44).

Mechanisms are needed: 'There is a need to develop a comprehensive and systematic database on global transactions in the health sector' (Chanda, 2002: 162). It is important to tabulate and analyse new data. What must not be forgotten is the extent to which investigators can build on what they already know.

Thus macroeconomic data on the national product and the balance of payments are already available from the national accounts and the multilateral agencies. The requirement that 'the balance of payments always balances' restricts the statisticians' freedom to sweep imperfections under the carpet. Data on the current account shows what health-related goods and services are being traded. Data on the capital account identifies inflows for investment in subsidiaries and outflows such as dividends repatriated.

The International Monetary Fund produces standardised statistics in compliance with its *Balance of Payments Manual*. An example would be its *Balance of Payments Statistics Yearbook (BOPS)* which provides a seven-year run of data for 187 reporting countries. Under 'Travel', there is an item in the *Yearbook* on health-related travel. It provides information on GATS Mode 2 and on the residence, where this is known, of the principal trading partners.

In addition, the World Trade Organization (WTO) collects data on the 12 service sectors identified under GATS. It hosts a website on 'Services – Sector by Sector'. Health is picked up not just by 'health-related and social services' but by finance (health insurance, investment in overseas hospitals), education (the training of health professionals) and distribution (the retailing, for example, of pharmaceuticals). The World Bank has the World Bank Database. The United Nations has Comtrade and UNdata. The WTO, in collaboration with the World Bank, the International Monetary Fund (IMF), the Asian Development Bank (ADB), the United Nations Conference on Trade and Development (UNCTAD), the World Health Organization (WHO) (together with its subordinate National Macroeconomic Commissions on Health), Eurostat, the Organisation for Economic Co-operation and Development (OECD) and the World Tourism Organization (UNWTO) all have an input into the *Statistics on International Trade in Services*. Health-related and social services warrant a separate entry; and there is also information on travel and intellectual property (United Nations Department of Economic and Social Affairs, 2002: 12, 18, 75).

A coordinated effort like this is the harbinger of the international database that is to come. The World Health Organization already publishes *World Health Statistics* (WHOSIS). The World Tourism Organization already produces *Tourism Market Trends*. The next step must be *World Health Tourism Market Trends* which winnows out the patients from the holiday-making crowd.

On the manpower side there is the WHO's *Global Atlas of the Health Workforce*. Here as usual the data-set is incomplete. Outflow countries seldom keep data on professionals who go abroad. Inflow countries will know about the work permits issued and the registrations with professional associations but not about subsequent leakage into downskilling (the doctor who works as a nurse) or into non-medical lines of activity (the doctor who opens a shop).

Globalisation means that the accounts, like trade itself, can no longer be nation-specific. The dispersion in the statistics reflects the dispersion in the variables that some countries select and other countries do not. Carrera and Bridges rightly observe that there is 'conceptual ambiguity' surrounding the definition and a general lack of 'reliable and comparable data': 'Clarity in terminology is crucial' (Carrera and Bridges, 2006: 447, 450). Gaps in the statistics are only part of the problem. First and foremost, statisticians must agree on what to measure and how to measure it.

Categories must be standardised and definitions made consistent. A common rubric adopted, it will become possible to derive a world map of medical tourism that shows the flows of exports and imports.

The map would track the way in which electronic consultation feeds through into the international movement of patients, providers and professionals. It would trace the origins and destinations both of inputs and of outcomes. It would identify not just inward transnational investment but also the patients subsequently treated in an overseas facility. This could be a fully owned subsidiary of the hospital the patient would have visited at home. The map would distinguish between insured and non-insured patients. It would include dentistry, optometry, non-prescription pharmaceuticals, complementary therapies, unaccredited providers as well as inpatient care in inspected hospitals. It would reconstruct the networks of referral and appeal. It would draw inferences about quality and standards. It would single out particular countries which are performing very well or very poorly. It would include a healthcare Gini Coefficient that would permit an informed debate on the equity of allocations.

An international database is essential. Not least is this so since communicable diseases like AIDS are public bads that do not respect the national frontiers. Cross-border collaboration is necessary if all pieces of the puzzle are to be put in place. It is important to have a mechanism that tracks each patient through exit, entry and repatriation. Clinically interdependent but politically independent, however, the problem is that not all countries will have the skill or the technology to collect what is needed. Many countries lack resources to fund a national database or the willingness to assign a high priority to health-related information. Some governments resist transparency in the belief that known failures will undermine their credibility. Others practise need-to-know on the assumption that disclosure can only encourage an aggressor. Patchy submission defeats the point of the exercise. If one large player does not input its statistics, the entire matrix springs a leak.

Top-down depends on bottom-up. An international database cannot be developed without the full support of the discrete nation-states. It is easier said than done. Even within a single country, the individual ministries might not be willing to share their data with each other or with a central reporting agency. They must overcome their fears and their jealousies if a full picture of the nation's health is to be reconstructed.

The Ministry of Health will assemble figures on diseases, interventions, bedstock, throughput and professionals. In some countries it will demand even more. In Malaysia both state and private hospitals must report the number and mix of patients to the centre. That is why it is known that Malaysia provided medical treatment to 583000 foreigners in 2011; and that 49 per cent of them went to Penang. The figure is biased downward to the extent that it does not include outpatient visits. It is also biased upward in the sense that it does not make allowance for resident foreigners. The Ministry of Health estimates that 40 per cent of international patients are foreigners who have made Malaysia their home. That reduces the number of true incomers to something like 350000. The Association of Private Hospitals in Malaysia estimates that the country earned US$90.5 million from non-citizen patients in 2008 (Chee, 2010: 343). While only one-eighth to one-tenth of the equivalent earnings in Singapore, it is still a sizeable sum of money.

The Ministry of Immigration provides a double check on the Ministry of Health. It knows how many employment passes have been issued to the various grades of medical manpower; how many medical incomers have converted to permanent residence or secured citizenship; how many have entered only for a short spell in the framework of intra-organisational exchange or rotation schemes. It has data on the number of medical and long-stay visas that it has issued to foreign patients. Such visas are granted by India, South Korea and South Africa.

Where the point-of-entry card includes a question on primary purpose of visit, the Ministry of Immigration also knows how many foreign nationals have ticked the box for 'medical attention'. Not all countries use arrival cards in this way, and there is a natural human propensity to tick 'holiday' instead. A facelift or a bypass is not something one discusses with strangers. Besides that, some tourists do not actually plan elective treatments. They learn about the acne scars and the tooth-whitening treatments when they are already in the country. The Ministry of Immigration never finds out that they entered for the beach and later became medical tourists as well.

The Ministry of Immigration will not be able to pick up invisible health tourists. In the UK it does not hold data on UK citizens who are at home for less than 181 days in a year (if their second residence is in continental Europe) or for 90 days (if they live outside the European Union) and have therefore become foreign patients in the eyes of their National Health Service (NHS). Other countries such as New Zealand are more welcoming to returning citizens resident abroad. Be that as it may, a Briton living in Spain may not be identified as a health tourist by the Immigration officers at the airport or the Channel Tunnel. What happens then depends on whether he registered at a relative's address before he went abroad. Having a local surname may help as well. No one would suspect an obvious Geordie or a Scouse of bending the law.

In North America the Ministry of Immigration does not hold data on the Mexican-Americans who see a doctor in Mexico while staying with their extended family, or on the undocumented elderly who cross to Canada to buy their drugs. In Asia, it has little information on the illegals who trek through the jungle or the extra-legals who brave the Mekong because care in Thailand is all that they have. In Europe the Ministry of Immigration does not check identity within the Schengen borders. Once in Schengen, the traveller can be a health tourist or a recreational tourist or both or neither without having to fill in a form.

The Ministry of Tourism holds records on the total number of tourist entries. If it is interested in health tourism, it can fine-tune the figure through a face-to-face approach. Either directly or through a parastatal Tourist Board, the Ministry of Tourism can sample passengers at the ports and airports to find out their main reason for visiting the country. The sample is then scaled upward to estimate the total.

An example would be the exit surveys conducted in 2004 by the Singapore Tourist Board. On the basis of opportunistic interviewing at Changi Airport, the Board was able to work out that 410000 passengers (4 per cent of all passengers) had travelled to Singapore specifically for healthcare. A further 56000 had received healthcare incidentally while in Singapore for some other purpose. They were accompanied by approximately 89000 friends and relatives (Yap, 2007). Since the sample size was small, and sampling was done exclusively in the economy class lounge, there is bound to have been a significant margin for error.

The same methodology is employed in South Africa and, indeed, in the United Kingdom, where an International Passenger Survey is conducted at the principal exit and entry points. Even more data can be obtained if the investigators are willing to fish for it. Questions can be asked about residence, citizenship, gender, ethnicity, age, level of education, marital status, length of stay, the specific treatment the respondents have had, how much they have paid for it, their reason for choosing a particular destination, their household income, their insurance cover and its ceilings, their doctor visits within the previous year. Polling is done on the assumption, common to all self-reporting, that sick people will tell the truth. Truth-telling has a cost. Foreigners who reveal personal secrets risk being denied entry. At least the Ministry and the Board will have tried their best.

The Ministry of Commerce will have information on the business that was done. It will know about medicine-specific foreign direct investment that has been approved. It will keep records on tariff rebates and on hospital patients claiming the refund of goods and services tax in the departure lounge. An illustration would be the Department of Export Promotion in

Thailand's Ministry of Commerce. It collects data on stays and prepares an annual report.

The Central Bank will be able to quantify the foreign exchange. Its input will be especially valuable in countries with exchange control where the purpose as well as the amount of the transfers has to be cleared.

The Ministry of Social Security will know about national insurance being redirected abroad. Although the Canadian scheme is administered at the provincial level, the statistics on disbursements are tabulated centrally. From those submissions it is possible to establish that the province of Ontario saw a 450 per cent increase between 2001 and 2008 in the number of patients reimbursed for out-of-country procedures. The principal destination was the United States. The increase in spending shows how much the market has evolved (Hopkins, Labonté, Runnels and Packer, 2010: 188). Other single-payer systems will have a similar advantage in collecting accurate data. The UK National Health Service knows precisely how many home patients it is outsourcing and what they cost.

Private insurers, although not a one-stop shop, will also have their finger on the pulse. Not all medical travellers pay out-of-pocket. It is a reminder that valuable information is available in the commercial and not-for-profit sectors. The Ministries are not the only game in town. Insurance companies will know what they are paying and which destinations are being selected. The state, by making disclosure compulsory, could force them to put what they know in the public domain. Additional data-banks would be the medical tourism facilitators, the professional associations and, needless to say, the hospitals themselves.

Hospitals are notoriously uncooperative. They publish only what the law requires. Voluntary reporting is often no reporting at all. Telephone calls and emails are left unanswered. Interviews are punctuated with 'Why are you asking me these questions?' One reason for their compulsive retentiveness is that they regard medical records and itemised bills as ring-fenced by doctor–patient privilege. Another reason for confidentiality is that the information can be commercially sensitive. Many private hospitals are listed companies. They are at risk from competitors and takeover bids. Growth in non-resident numbers, in cost–profit mark-up and in aggregate income can be manipulated by speculators into a forecast of future performance. Medical failures are treated as a trade secret. Anecdotal evidence on operations that go wrong can easily mislead potential customers into a neighbouring oligopolist's shop.

Even public hospitals prefer to keep the facts under lock and key. Disclosure means exposure and exposure is a threat to a quiet life. Public hospitals seldom solicit commercial business or pay commission to agents.

They are, however, politically sensitive. Reputations can be dented if word gets out that they are shifting scarce beds from locals to foreigners.

There must not in any case be a presumption that hospitals actually possess the information that is required. They will record the foreigner's nationality but not the length of residence in the country, or whether the foreigner entered primarily for medical attention. No distinction is made between foreigners who live near the border and foreigners who fly great distances. Hospital statistics are not fully compatible with the information obtained from the frontier checkpoints. Most hospital files relate to patients in a treatment cluster. It will often be difficult to filter out the strangers in the beds. It will also be difficult to determine whether the procedure was simple or complex.

Where a hospital is accredited, facts collected by the Joint Commission International or a national agency can be used by investigators when they seek to build up their medical map. At least a common template will be employed. It makes comparisons possible. Further evidence may be obtained from private consultancies like Stackpole and Euromonitor International. Many researchers find their reports prohibitively expensive, the thrust of their investigations disproportionately commercial. Publication is intermittent and unpredictable. The fact remains that their insights and projections will often be the only port in a storm.

Investigators might be able to obtain data on inward travel from medical attachés at provider embassies. They might be able to proxy outward travel through the referral records of general practitioners. Hospital multinationals publish annual reports. They trumpet their investments abroad. Medical schools have an alumni base. Their circulation list documents the patterns of migration.

The researcher can draw upon trade and professional bodies like the Medical Tourism Association. There is in-depth journalism in high-end magazines like *The Economist* and the *New Yorker*. There are associations of private hospitals, non-governmental organisations, trade unions, members of Parliament. There is the British Medical Association and the Royal College of Nursing. There is also the personal approach. University academics use their research grants to approach the stakeholders directly. Much of the information that is required can only be obtained from the medical travellers themselves. Grassroots feedback is essential if intention and satisfaction are to be captured.

Proceeding as an anthropologist, the investigator can conduct fieldwork in a closed-off small community. An example would be Beth Kangas's study of Yemeni health tourists in Mumbai (Kangas, 2007, 2010). Structured interviews, telephone conversations, online questionnaires can establish the treatments and destinations that are selected, the source and nature of the information that is collected. Perceptions are subjective. Rational or contradictory, the investigator has no choice but to write them down.

Proceeding as a sociologist, *ex ante* the potential clients could be surveyed to determine the financial trigger that would be just sufficient to induce them to seek non-urgent medical care abroad (Milstein and Smith, 2007: 138). *Ex post* the returning subjects, contacted through their facilitator, can be asked to rank their experience overseas on a Likert scale of 1 to 10. They can be invited to separate out their score into anaesthetics, surgery, nursing, catering and surroundings.

In spite of that, there are lions the size of dragons in the path. *Ex ante* where the questionnaires are issued to a small convenience sample they might not mine at random a representative demographic. Undergraduates in a classroom may not be a good proxy for fellow citizens in the street or, still less, for the chronically ill.

Ex ante, and because the questions are by their very nature hypothetical, the respondents are being asked for possible reactions and not for cash on the line. Talk is cheap. What people say they might perhaps do is not the same as preferences revealed in a real-world situation. There is no guarantee that their actions will be in keeping with their words.

Ex post, the mindset that returns home is being taken to be the same as the mindset that went abroad. It may not be so. A patient accustomed to a functional ward in the NHS may experience a quantum upgrading of his expectations as a consequence of fee-for-service in the five-star luxury of the Bumrungrad or the Apollo hospitals. Because of the one-way ratchet of intransitivity he may come to regard the NHS as even more inadequate than he believed it to be at the time of his desertion. Alternatively, the sudden exposure to a private room and a deferential nurse who calls him Sir could make him into a Lord Muck, critical of his experience abroad because five-star should mean French wine and he was only given beer.

It is still not enough. Different observers will home in on different blind spots. Their needs will vary depending on whether their primary interest is business, economics, medicine, geography or sociology. No database can answer every question. Some, however, are capable of answering more questions than others.

2.3 THE FACTS

Sometimes the statistics do not exist. Just as frequently they do exist but they are wrong. Steering a middle course between the imprecise and the inconsistent, Keith Pollard is only one observer among many to have stated that the bulk of the published evidence cannot possibly be correct.

Pollard, who has personal experience of the medical travel industry, for-instances figures showing that there were 1 120 446 American medical travellers in 2009: 'These included dental travellers and cosmetic surgery patients but excluded spa and wellness travel. Let's assume that just one in five of these 1.1 million American medical travellers actually went for hospital treatment. And let's assume a five day length of stay in hospital' (Pollard, 2011). It is enough, he says, 'to fill over 3000 hospital beds every day for a year, enough to fill more than five Bumrungrad Hospitals to bursting 365 days per year. Does that sound likely to you?' (Pollard, 2011).

The published data is fragmentary, ambiguous, incomplete and unreliable. The facts, Pollard says, cannot be robust. Bumrungrad, based on published statistics, has only 538 beds but is filling them with 4000 international inpatients – 'An amazing achievement' (Pollard, 2011). The numbers do not add up. How can policy-makers do their job if they do not know the current state of play?

They do not add up but nor are they worthless. This section examines some results that have been suggested by the existing data. The results relate to the world as a whole, to the United States, to the United Kingdom and to Asia.

2.3.1 The Global Picture

The Tourism Research and Marketing Group (TRAM) estimates that 37 million health-related trips are undertaken each year by patients and their companions. These trips generate a cross-border flow of €33 billion (cited in Smith, Martinez Alvarez and Chanda, 2011: 278).

The United Nations calculated that the trade was worth an estimated US$40 billion in 2005 (United Nations Economic and Social Commission for Asia and the Pacific, 2007: 2). At approximately the same time the World Tourism Organization asserted that the industry was already worth US$513 billion. The UNWTO said that 617 million individuals were taking advantage of health travel. The trade was growing at a rate of 3.9 per cent per annum (cited in Carrera and Bridges, 2006: 450). US$513 billion is clearly not the same as US$40 billion. Nor is 3.9 per cent the same as 20 per cent. Macready insists that medical services provided to foreign residents worldwide grew annually by 20 per cent between 2000 and 2005 (MacReady, 2007: 1850).

Looking forward, calculations made by the Deloitte consultancy suggest that the likely annual growth in the near future will be not 3.9 per cent or even 20 per cent but at least 35 per cent (Deloitte, 2009: 2). Deloitte in 2008 worked out that the market for medical travel worldwide was probably worth about US$60 billion. They predicted that it would grow to US$100 billion within five years (Deloitte, 2008: 6). They put the number of medical travellers per annum at 6 to 7 million. Deloitte derived their total from two other estimates that they made, that about 600000 to 750000 Americans were going abroad annually for care and that Americans represented some 10 per cent of the worldwide patient pool. If the axioms fall, the deductions are unlikely to be worth very much.

2.3.2 The United States

Deloitte found that 878000 Americans went abroad in 2010. They predicted that the number would reach 6 million within five years (Deloitte, 2008: 3; Medical Tourism Association, 2011). Assuming that the base-point was correct and that the surveys were representative, the inference is that the US in 2008 was diverting money – perhaps US$600 million (Organisation for Economic Co-operation and Development, 2011: 159), perhaps US$15.9 billion (Deloitte, 2008: 14), perhaps US$20 billion (Ehrbeck, Guevara and Mango, 2008: 6) – that would otherwise have been committed to healthcare at home. The figure will increase exponentially as more Americans develop an interest in foreign care. Between 2004 and 2009 the amount spent by Americans on foreign care grew annually by 13 per cent in real terms (Organisation for Economic Co-operation and Development, 2011: 159). Numbers would increase even more if insurers became more willing to cover medical travel.

In aggregate terms, the impact of medical tourism is small. Healthcare imports were a mere 0.04 per cent of the US national expenditure in 2007. This is below the 0.05 recorded in the UK, well below the 9.49 per cent in Luxembourg. The import market overall is unlikely to account for more than 2 per cent of total US spending on non-cosmetic healthcare. Microeconomics paints a more sombre picture. In specific markets, the effect can be serious: 'The loss of even a small number of profitable insured patients could actually end up endangering the viability of many local programs and institutions that provide necessary services. Such a circumstance could eventually be devastating to us all' (Unti, 2009: 23).

American travellers are believed to constitute approximately 10 per cent to 12 per cent (Youngman, 2009) of the worldwide market. The figure is lower than the popular perception of an industry driven by unsatisfied American demand. Youngman makes clear that his figure excludes emergencies, expatriates, wellness tourism, check-ups and intra-country travel. His study is limited to planned travel specifically for medical purposes. A different definition would generate a different total.

The McKinsey organisation excludes dental travel: its figures do not pick up the 1 million Germans who travel annually to Hungary for their teeth. Youngman's totals include the teeth. Teeth make a difference: about 40 per cent of Americans who sought care abroad did so for dental procedures. Dental care is expensive and uninsured at home (Apton and Apton, 2010: 40). Youngman's totals would be higher still if he had included wellness spas, botox and therapeutic mud.

The Deloitte estimate is that 750000 Americans are currently going abroad for care. McKinsey arrives at the far more modest total of 60000 to 85000 (Ehrbeck, Guevara and Mango, 2008: 2). The reason for the much lower number is a less comprehensive definition. The study excludes American expatriates (25 to 30 per cent of all Americans seeking care outside the United States), American tourists who experience a medical emergency (a further 20 to 25 per cent of the total), Americans who seek outpatient rather than inpatient care, Americans who choose a non-accredited foreign hospital.

Patients with a primary or a holiday home abroad are, once again, a borderline group. They may see themselves not as medical tourists but as dual-locals, empowered by their multiple residence to select the treatment centre with the shortest queue or the highest subsidy. An American working in Taiwan joins the Taiwanese National Insurance scheme after three months. He may also be retaining the private insurance policy that he took out at home. If he is retired, he may be entitled to a company pension, social security or the continuation of his occupational health plan in the United States. He can use this to pay for medical treatment in the new nation where he hangs his hat.

Medical tourism is a mishmash of borderline choices like these. There is no correct definition and no central register. By the calculations in the McKinsey study, only 35 per cent to 45 per cent of all Americans treated abroad are genuine travellers in the strict sense of GATS Mode 2 (Ehrbeck, Guevara and Mango, 2008: 3). This is the logic behind the modest figure of 60000 to 85000.

Kher finds the 60000 to 85000 at variance with common sense. He reports that 55000 American citizens (nowadays far fewer as more Americans are choosing Latin America instead) were treated in 2005 at Bumrungrad Hospital alone; and that three-quarters of them had flown in from the United States expressly for the purpose (Kher, 2006). Johnson and Garman, admitting that 'little is known', also believe the McKinsey estimate to be too low. They collected data from the US Bureau of Economic Analysis and the US Office of Travel and Tourism Industries. They consulted the inter-agency *Manual of Statistics of International Trade in Services*. They also made use of the US Department of Commerce's

Survey of International Air Travellers. The sample is 65 000–95 000 passengers, inbound as well as outbound.

Johnson and Garman complemented this information with their own interviews. On that basis they calculated that the probable number of United States residents who had gone abroad for medical care in 2007 lay between 50 000 and 121 000. In the same year between 43 000 and 103 000 foreigners entered the United States for medical care (Johnson and Garman, 2010: 171). Cattaneo found the inbound figure in 2008 to be more like 400 000. He also said that residents of foreign countries were spending approximately US$5 billion on healthcare in the United States (Cattaneo, 2009: 2). His costings depend on his headcount. Clearly, 400 000 is rather more than 43 000.

Headcount is not the whole of the story. The balance of payments is more than the number of heads: 'The average amount spent per patient coming to the US was more than seven times greater than the amount spent per US patient abroad ($11 513 in the US versus $1722 abroad) . . . We estimate . . . a net gain of between $404 M and $1.0 B to the US economy' (Johnson and Garman, 2010: 176).

The USA is the world's largest single exporter of healthcare services by value. In 2010 its share in the export trade was 24.4 per cent. For Mexico the market share was 2.46 per cent, for Thailand 1.98 per cent, for Brazil 0.35 per cent (Lautier, 2013: 7). In spite of its lead the services only account for something like 0.02 per cent of the US gross national product (Lautier, 2008: 103). Healthcare exports were 11 per cent of total healthcare spending in the United States in 2009. The total value was US$2.3 billion (Organisation for Economic Co-operation and Development, 2011: 158).

2.3.3 The United Kingdom

Sample data from the International Passenger Survey suggests that about 63 000 UK citizens and permanent residents were paying for treatment abroad in 2010. Approximately 51 000 foreigners were travelling to the UK for medical care. As may be seen from Figure 2.8, the numbers have increased rapidly since 2002.

One-third of outbound medical tourists from the United Kingdom were cosmetic tourists. *Which?* magazine made the figure 28 per cent: 'This is likely to be a growing trend: 97% of people considering cosmetic surgery would consider travelling for it' (Hanefeld, Lunt, Horsfall and Smith, 2012: e7997).

Britons in 2010 spent about £62 million on foreign medical attention. Doing so, they freed up resources in the NHS. In the same year 52 000 overseas visitors (up from about 16 000 in 2000) came to the UK for care.

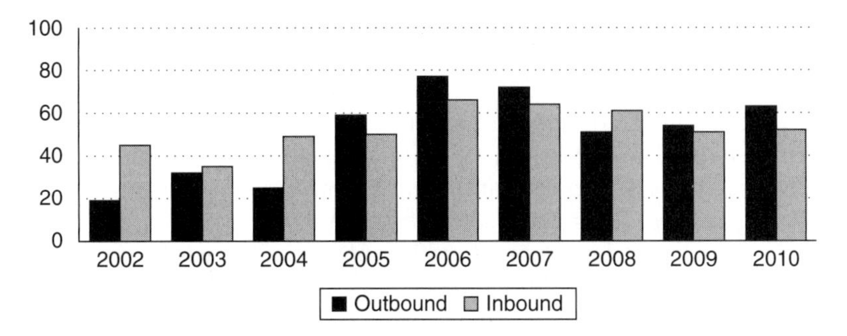

Source: Office for National Statistics (2010).

Figure 2.8 Medical tourists in the UK (thousands)

They spent about £132 million (Lunt, Mannion and Exworthy, 2013: 6). A sizeable amount of income was being earned, chiefly by the private sector. The figures were extrapolated from the International Passenger Survey. The sample is small and may not be a good cross-section. Lunt, Mannion and Exworthy conclude that the game may only just be worth the candle: 'There are no verifiable statistics published on the number of outward (or inward) bound UK medical tourists' (Lunt, Mannion and Exworthy, 2013: 6).

Of the UK patients, Pollard estimates that 73 per cent went abroad for cosmetic surgery or dentistry. These procedures are largely non-urgent and discretionary. The spend per patient is in the area of £3500 to £5000. Since overseas visitors tend to come for major procedures like heart surgery and cancer treatments, 'the value of inbound medical tourism is far greater than the value of outbound medical tourism' (Pollard, 2012). The numbers are not negligible. Pollard states that between 20 and 25 per cent of the revenues of London's private hospitals come from treating overseas patients. It is believed that foreigners account for approximately 130000 outpatient consultations in London and 7800 inpatient stays. They inject between £280 million and £330 million into London's treatment centres. The value to London's economy through hotels and restaurants may be as much again.

Europe is on the doorstep. The number of cycles of *in vitro* fertilisation (IVF) treatment for women travelling from one European country to another is 20000–25000 (Lunt and Carrera, 2010: 30). About 32 per cent of them came from Italy. The UK is a part of the broad regional market. In addition to patients covered by the NHS and its EU exchanges, there are at least 50000 UK patients who pay for private care in the European Union.

2.3.4 Asia

The main destination remains the North. The bulk of the movement is in the direction of the developed nations with the reputation and the head start. Yet the Third World is mounting a credible challenge. Africa is already receiving 4.8 per cent of the world's medical travellers, the Middle East 4.7 per cent. The great success story is Asia.

The Asian countries account for 19.5 per cent of the world's healthcare exports (Carrera and Bridges, 2006: 450). The Asian market is worth US$1.3 billion. It is predicted that it will be worth at least US$4.4 billion within a decade (United Nations Economic and Social Commission for Asia and the Pacific, 2007: 9; Aniza, Aidalina, Nirmalini, Inggit and Ajeng, 2009: 8). About 90 per cent of healthcare exports from Asia come from three countries: India, Thailand and Singapore (NaRanong and NaRanong, 2011: 226).

It is believed that India alone earned between US$310 million and US$480 million from medical travel in 2005–2006. The market in India may be growing annually by as much as 20 to 30 per cent (Aniza, Aidalina, Nirmalini, Inggit and Ajeng, 2009: 8). Jose and Sachdeva calculate that tourism as a whole already contributes 5.9 per cent to the Indian GDP. Export earnings of US$11.7 billion were recorded in 2008. Survey data suggests that 2.2 per cent of all foreign travellers and 10 per cent of non-resident Indians who visited India in that year had the intention of receiving some form of medical attention (Jose and Sachdeva, 2010: 376). India may have received something like 700 000 health tourists in 2010.

The regional market (notably Bangladesh, Sri Lanka, Nepal, the Maldives) is large. It is estimated that 50 000 Bangladeshis are seeking care each year in India. Yet a surprisingly large number of patients are coming from further afield. In the study of foreign patients conducted by Alsharif, Labonté and Lu, US citizens (many of them with roots in the subcontinent) were found to make up 43.8 per cent of the sample surveyed. In China, US citizens were 30 per cent of the sample. In Jordan they were 15.1 per cent (Alsharif, Labonté and Lu, 2010: 319).

Thailand, like India, has a high profile in the market. Between 730 000 and 1.3 million foreign patients are seen each year in Thai private hospitals. The Tourism Authority of Thailand and the Department of Export Promotion have produced figures which track the rapid growth in the numbers (see Figure 2.9).

Although about 20 private hospitals in Thailand are active in the industry (12 of them accredited by the Joint Commission International, the JCI), over half of all foreign clients go to Bumrungrad International

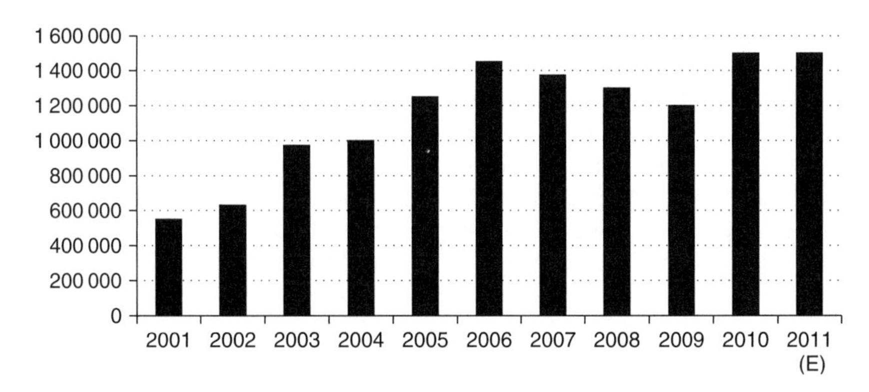

Source: *International Medical Travel Journal* (2013a).

Figure 2.9 Number of foreigners seeking treatment in Thailand

Hospital, Bangkok Hospital or Samitivej Hospital. The Bangkok Dusit Medical Group controls six brands (5000 beds) in 29 locations. It owns outright not just the flagship Bangkok Hospital (18 sites) but its prestigious rivals Samitivej (3 sites) and Phyathai (4 sites). Its hospitals compete as actively with one another as they do with Bumrungrad (the principal outside competitor), in which Bangkok Dusit nonetheless holds 20.28 per cent of existing shares in order to hedge its bets.

Between 35 and 50 per cent of the income received by the market leaders is derived from foreign patients. At Yan Hee in Bangkok 10 per cent of the patients are fly-ins. They account for 35 per cent of the revenues. At Bumrungrad Thais make up 53 per cent of the patient load but bring in only 40 per cent of the revenues. Fly-ins tend to come for more serious conditions. They require more (and more expensive) procedures.

Tourism accounts for 6 per cent to 7 per cent of Thailand's gross domestic product, health tourism about 0.4 per cent (Eden, 2012). The floods and the civil strife do not put the visitors off. Medical tourism to Thailand is growing at a rate of 16 per cent a year. The value of health tourism to the Thai economy is probably between US$400 million and US$433 million (NaRanong and NaRanong, 2011: 336).

The statistics are not easy to interpret. Most foreigners can stay 30 days without a visa that would oblige them to divulge their intentions. In Thailand, hospital reporting is voluntary. Data is broken down into Thais and foreigners but does not identify the subset of foreigners who come to Thailand exclusively for medical treatment. It is estimated that about 60 per cent of international patients are expatriates (resident either in Thailand or in its immediate region) and 10 per cent are tourists who require unplanned attention. Only 30 per cent are direct fly-ins in the strict sense of Mode 2 (United Nations Economic and Social Commission for Asia and the Pacific, 2007: 16; NaRanong and NaRanong, 2011: 337). Applying 30 per cent to the figures cited above, there were presumably 500 000 and not 1.5 million genuine medical tourists in Thailand in 2011.

Of the foreigners who came to Thailand expressly for medical treatment, many are from the Middle East (40 per cent from the Gulf) and a significant number from Japan. About 11 per cent come from the USA and 8 per cent from the UK (United Nations Economic and Social Commission for Asia and the Pacific, 2007: 16; Frost & Sullivan, 2012: 18). As for the treatments, about 83 per cent of health tourists in Thailand demand some form of cosmetic surgery.

Singapore is also a major healthcare destination. The government's target in 2003 had been to attract 1 million medical tourists by 2012. Precise numbers are not available but the Ministry of Health estimates that there were 850 000 foreign patients in 2012 and that there had been only 210 000 in 2003. The number for 2012 would have represented an increase of 15 per cent over 2011. It may be read as return to trend from the trough of a recession year.

Singapore's 850 000 is fuzzy. As well as international patients, the statistic includes business travellers, expatriates and tourists on holiday. It includes friends and family (about 40 per cent of the recorded total) who accompany the patient but do not themselves receive any treatment. No distinction is made between inpatients and outpatients. Outpatients are 90 per cent of all international patients in Singapore. Only 36 000 non-resident foreigners were actually hospitalised or offered day-case surgery in 2011 (*Straits Times*, 2013: 1).

As more than a third of the Singapore labour force is foreign and as Singapore is a popular leisure and recreational destination, the number of true medical tourists in 2012 might have been as low as 170 000: 'It seems likely that the real number of medical tourists for 2012 is nearer to 200 000 rather than 850 000' (*International Medical Travel Journal*, 2013b). Medical tourism might have been generating revenues of almost S$1 billion in 2012 (*Straits Times*, 2013: 1). An outlier estimate goes as high as S$4.31 billion (Ramchandani, 2012).

Singapore is a centre of excellence in high-end specialist care such as cardiovascular surgery and organ transplants. Its niche is high quality rather than low price: Bangkok is typically 25 per cent cheaper. Medical tourists are coming to Singapore because they know they can put their faith in world-class names like Parkway Pantai and Raffles Medical or in the public sector hospitals where one-third of health travellers are treated. Yap, studying the Singapore experience in 2004, estimates that medical tourists, including accompanying relatives, had been worth S$863 million to the Singapore economy. Since total receipts from all kinds of tourism in that year had been S$9.8 billion, international patients may have contributed as much as 8.8 per cent to total tourist revenues. As Yap says, 'that is not too shabby' (Yap, 2006: 20).

3. The preconditions for trade

Medical travel evolves historically through a sequence of stages. The first stage is minority and privilege. It is Harley Street and the Marienbad spa. The second stage is moderate participation. It extends the option of dentistry, optometry, cosmetic surgery and major surgery to the nouveaux riches who float upward on the tide of economics. The third stage is democratic inclusion. Whether seen as a luxury or treated as a necessity, care abroad becomes available, affordable and accessible even to a mass market. Ordinary consumers need no longer be on the outside looking in.

The modern era is the third stage. This chapter describes the preconditions for medical travel in an era that is both socially and geographically global. Section 3.1, 'Prosperity and payment', says that rising incomes make possible more choices. Sections 3.2, 'Private insurance' and 3.3, 'State insurance', argue that prepayment, itself made affordable by growth, is empowering ordinary people to demand better care. Section 3.4, 'The ins and the outs', assesses the patients who pay out-of-pocket and sometimes do not pay at all. Section 3.5, 'Region and alliance: the European Union', explains the implications of multinational communities for cross-border health. Section 3.6, 'Institutions and attitudes', argues that the built infrastructure is essential for medical travel but so is an open mind that does not regard every foreigner as a problem to be solved.

3.1 PROSPERITY AND PAYMENT

Economic growth is all around. Developing countries like India, China, Indonesia and Brazil are crossing the threshold. Modern, urban, industrial and affluent, their rising middle classes are increasingly in a position to spend on precautionary and comfort care.

In the short run there are fluctuations around the trend. In the long run the trend is a rise in healthcare spending as a percentage of the world gross domestic product (GDP). This is illustrated in Figure 3.1.

An unprecedented rise in per capita disposable incomes has released a latent demand for medical services. This is shown in Figure 3.2.

Whether a heart bypass that saves a life or a nose job that enhances

Source: World Bank (2013).

Figure 3.1 Health expenditure as a percentage of world GDP

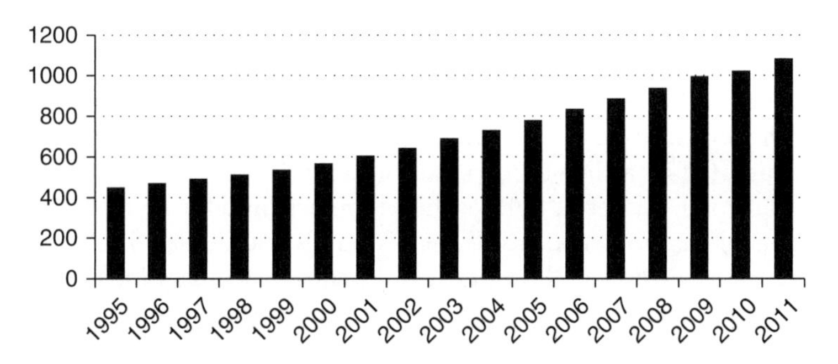

Source: World Health Organization (2013).

Figure 3.2 Per capita expenditure on healthcare (US$ adjusted for purchasing power parity)

the image, people can put teeth into choice because, South or North, they have more money to spend. Health tourism may be compared not just to an investment good but also to a luxury consumer durable. It benefits at once from rising earnings across the board and from a high income elasticity of demand.

3.1.1 Earning and Spending

The world is evolving from survival subsistence to something more. Society as well as economy is on the escalator going up. Healthcare – and health travel – may be expected to benefit from the dual dynamic of *embourgeoisement* and prosperity.

Homi Kharas defines the global middle class to be those households with daily expenditures of between US$10 and US$100 (purchasing power parity adjusted) (Kharas, 2010: 12). A relative definition would focus on the middle three income deciles or on per capita incomes lying between 0.75 and 1.25 times the median. Kharas finds the absolute definition more relevant to the topic of demand-led growth. Globally, Kharas predicts, the size of the middle class could increase from 1.8 billion people in 2009 to 4.9 billion people by 2030. Most of the growth (85 per cent) will come not from North America but from Asia. Asia's emerging middle class will be one of the main drivers of the world economy. Emerging economies like India will increasingly become the vanguard in both mobility and demand.

Globally, demand from the middle-class market is expected to grow from US$21 trillion in 2009 to US$56 trillion in 2030. The evolution in middle-class consumption is shown in Figure 3.3.

India well illustrates what is to come. India used to be textbook Third World. Parts still are, but parts are Silicon Valley. The middle class in India was 5 per cent to 10 per cent of the population in 2009. It is on course to be 90 per cent of the population in 2050. The population, given the fertility rate of 2.6, will itself be larger. The demand for private healthcare, fed by affluence, expectations and the demonstration effect of quality abroad, is a result both of the willingness and the ability to pay for best possible service: 'The recent rise of India's middle class has meant the emergence of several million new health care consumers looking to opt out of India's free public hospitals and instead pay for private health care

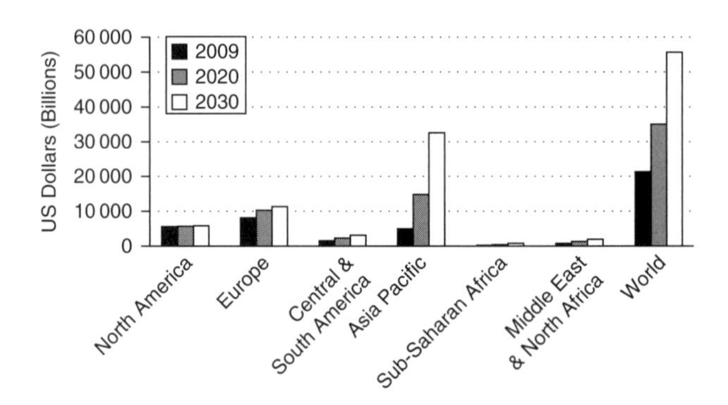

Source: calculated using data from Kharas (2010: 28).

Figure 3.3 Middle-class consumption (purchasing power parity adjusted)

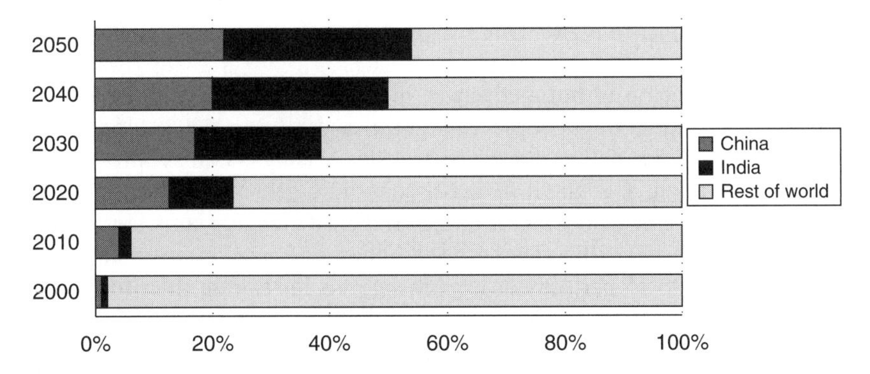

Source: calculated using data from Kharas (2010: 29).

Figure 3.4 Growth in the share of middle-class consumption: India, China, Rest of World, 2000–2050

services' (Richman, Udayakumar, Mitchell and Schulman, 2008: 1260). The rise in the share of middle-class consumption in India (contrasted with parallel developments in China and in the rest of the world) is shown in Figure 3.4.

There are already between 250 and 300 million households in India (more than the entire population of the United States) that have an annual income of at least US$25 000. They own appreciating assets such as property in Mumbai which can be monetised for capital gains or remortgaged for a loan. Adding wealth to income, the bottom line is a formidable wall of money. Some of the demand will go into health insurance. Some of it will go into tax – a part of which will go into public hospitals. Some of it will go into private treatment in India. Some of it will go into private treatment abroad.

Private treatment in India accounts for at least 75 per cent of total healthcare expenditures (Frost & Sullivan, 2012: 54). The private sector fields about 75 per cent of the dispensaries, employs 80 per cent of the (university-qualified) doctors and supplies 64 per cent of the hospital beds. The public hospitals deliver 90 per cent of the immunisations and 60 per cent of antenatal care. They are a ceaseless struggle. Patients complain that the buildings are dirty, hot and overcrowded; that the waits are long; that medicines and tests are not always affordable even if the consultation is free. A third of the patients in one study were asked for bribes to see a senior specialist or to secure a bed. Some had to put up coffee money to sleep in clean sheets or to receive subsidised drugs (Peters and Muraleedharan, 2008: 2136). Doctors may see 100 patients in a single session. Absenteeism is rife. One reason is that doctors have gone to their private practices.

The state sector is not delivering high-standard care: 'The medical system is failing its own people' (Sengupta and Nundy, 2005: 1158). The middle classes are better placed to translate rising incomes into good-quality attention. For them at least, economic growth is breeding economic growth. The healthcare sector in India already accounts for 5.2 per cent of GDP. It is worth at least US$68 billion and employs over 4 million people. At 13 to 15 per cent, it is growing at a faster rate than the GDP itself. So is the high-end private sector. Indians at the margin prefer to go to high-end private hospitals. It is precisely the failings of the state sector that give the private sector its critical mass.

3.1.2 Substitutes and Complements

Hospitals in the Third World normally leverage on the domestic consumer base. Medical travel reaps the unintended spillover. The Third World and the First World are not two worlds apart. The sequence builds on what went before.

Volume provides the fulcrum for economies of scale, specialised technicians and good-quality equipment. New capital can be worked intensively as a hedge against obsolescence and technological breakthroughs. Telemedicine can be offered to international patients because distance scans are already being performed for nationals. Domestic demand reduces the average cost. Lower cost in turn makes possible the international take-off. Competitive pricing in the private sector is drawing foreign patients to Delhi, Chennai, Hyderabad, Bangalore and Mumbai. They are following in the footsteps of the middle-class Indians for whom the public sector is no choice at all.

Even the hospitals that are synonymous with medical travel do at least half their business with the market at hand. The Hospital Punta Pacifica in Panama City is American-owned. It is affiliated with Johns Hopkins International in the United States. Yet, even at Punta Pacifica, only 25 per cent of the clients are foreigners, mainly from the USA and Canada (Paffhausen, Peguero and Roche-Villareal, 2010: 22). At Bangkok Hospital the percentage is even less: Thais account for 75 per cent of the business, resident expatriates a further 8 per cent. In Singapore, foreigners make up only 35 per cent to 40 per cent of the case-load at Parkway. They are only 30 per cent of the patients seen at Raffles.

Bumrungrad receives 400 000 foreign patients a year. They come from 190 different countries. In spite of its United Nations image, foreign patients make up only 39 per cent of Bumrungrad's million-plus cases.

Inpatients or outpatients, about 53 per cent of its patients are Thai and the balance expatriates. Most of the locals are from Bangkok.

The expansion of the domestic market normally complements the opening up to the world. It is not always so. In some cases the foreigners and the locals are in a position to confer an externality upon each other. Singapore is a good illustration of what it means in health policy to say that one hand washes the other.

Singapore has loanable funds. Its average national propensity to save, at 50 per cent, is higher even than that of Thailand (30 per cent), Taiwan (31 per cent) and other East Asian cultures. What Singapore lacks is the home market necessary to spread the overheads. The public hospitals have all the patients they can accommodate. There foreigners constitute less than 3 per cent of the patient load (Chee, 2010: 344, 347). The private sector, on the other hand, is undersubscribed. Foreigners in the Singapore private sector make up the numbers. Foreigners and Singaporeans give each other the chance to enjoy less expensive care.

A small country cannot sustain less-common interventions such as liver transplants without the supplementation of outsiders. Volume reduces the cost per case. The economies spill over and spill out. As Yap puts it: 'Singapore seeks foreign patients in order to serve local patients' (Yap, 2007).

In national economics as well as cost curves, foreigners and locals may be seen as collaborators who contribute to a common cause. Macroeconomic cycles are similar but not convergent. Symbiosis damps down the amplitude. International patients stabilise revenues in a downturn when domestic patients return to the state. At the same time, domestic patients cushion the hospital against the risk of not being able to pay interest on its loans. The elective services of international patients are more income-sensitive than are the basic necessities of the locals. The stability of the domestic patient base is an anchor.

The stabilising effect may also be observed where the international mix is drawn from a variety of regions. The overexpanded Thai hospitals in 1997 were able to replace their Thai business lost with foreign clients brought in from markets largely unaffected by the Asian crisis. There are two cases where this strategy will not succeed. The first is where there is a country-specific disturbance such as an earthquake, a revolution or an epidemic. SARS diverts a receiving country's exports to competing countries' airports. They might not return. The second case is where the world as a whole catches a cold. The globalisation of the interdependent national products may mean that if one is down, all are down. A recession brought on by an across-the-board eventuality such as an oil price shock or a contraction in the US hegemon will affect luxury services such as cosmetic surgery first. Medical travel trades in the margin. It is vulnerable to anything that makes the margin dry up.

3.1.3 Demography

Demography influences demand. Some countries have a high birth rate. Others are experiencing net immigration. All are benefiting from a lower infant mortality rate, improvements in prevention and nutrition, the diffusion of health-related education. Population is rising. The sheer numbers generate a growing demand for medical attention.

At the same time there is worldwide a rising proportion of the over-60s. The increase in old-age life expectancy is driving both the median age and the dependency ratio up. The services the elderly require, often reflecting chronic complaints, are increasingly complex and costly. Pensioners who used to be swept away by cheap influenza are having time to develop expensive conditions such as hypertension and joint attrition. The pressure on limited services is reflected in higher prices and longer waits. The advantage of India is that, with a relatively youthful population, its healthcare sector has not yet become bed-blocked with an ageing clientele. India is the mirror image of Europe. Demography suggests that there may be untapped synergies from trade.

Conveniently, the health status of older people has improved over time. More robust, alert and mobile, the over-60s are able, physically and mentally, to go abroad. Current income and lifetime savings are necessary conditions but they are not sufficient. Medical travellers must also be in a fit state to travel.

New technologies and drugs are expensive at home. Prices and insurance premiums are going up. Slow growth limits public spending. Exporting the surplus makes the pensions go further. In a four-nation study conducted by Alsharif, Labonté and Lu, most health travellers were 46 and above. In the Indian sample, it was 67 per cent, in China 78 per cent (Alsharif, Labonté and Lu, 2010: 319). Older patients might not welcome the option of travelling abroad. Where, however, demand is growing and supply is capped, pensioners may have no choice.

Higher incomes and occupational pensions mean that growing numbers are retiring abroad. The trend points to an untapped market for retirement villages with good medical facilities. Still more pensioners would go abroad if their entitlements were freely transferable. In Britain not only is the state pension frozen in a number of overseas destinations but a British subject 'not ordinarily resident' is obliged to pay the market rate for all but emergency care in the National Health Service (NHS).

Northern Europeans are retiring in Greece or Spain for the sun: they benefit from European Union (EU)-wide accords. Some Americans claim for global medical care through an occupational pension plan: an example would be the California Public Employees' Retirement Scheme (CalPERS). Some Americans resident in Mexico have enrolled in the Mexican social security system: it pays for medical attention. Americans retired abroad resume their Medicare entitlement once they return to US soil, broadly defined to include Guam. Medicare is an incentive for the ailing elderly to practise medical travel in reverse. In some cases there are reciprocal arrangements for retired persons who have made healthcare contributions in more than one country. Greece and Australia have such a system. If continuation of treatment and medication were ensured, they would have the freedom to choose at will between their country of origin, the country where they made their career, and a third country where they feel at home.

3.1.4 Discretionary Demand

The numbers can only grow. No one wants to live with the discomfort of a hernia or to do without better sight through LASIK. Looking good is becoming a lifestyle norm. Patients are less patient. Rising expectations are pulling up the cost.

Patients will be better able to benefit from medical travel if their condition is non-acute, if post-operative complications are not anticipated, if minimal follow-up will be required, if monitoring of recovery does not demand specialist attention, if it is possible to return home soon after surgery. Not all the patients will tick all the boxes. A chronic patient tied to hospital dialysis cannot easily be moved. A psychotic patient dependent on continuous care will be kept back for observation. An emergency case requiring urgent attention will only be put on a plane if there is no specialist unit nearby. A patient whose treatment proceeds in discrete stages will only be deemed suitable if he is prepared for a lengthy stay.

Medical travel is not the pill for every ill. It is, however, a feasible option for a growing proportion of conditions. An auspicious development would be day-case surgery which dispenses with an overnight stay. Outpatient procedures now comprise almost 75 per cent of all medical tourism surgeries (Deloitte, 2009: 11). Since so much of medical travel is funded out-of-pocket, any development that speeds up the turnaround and keeps down the bill will be attractive to the patient.

Youngman is clear that the bulk of the demand will be for second-tier interventions:

> Medical tourism must stop the foolish concentration on major surgery. Most major surgery is and will continue to be dealt with in a home country and paid for either by the state or insurance. Minor surgery, where people go overseas not for cost reasons but to avoid lengthy waits, is a potential market . . . The surgery aspect that still dominates much medical tourism advertising is only ever going to have a finite global demand. (Youngman, 2011)

The real market for medical travel is dental implants, orthodontic dentistry, bariatric surgery, aesthetic surgery, skin lightening, rhinoplasty, botox, liposuction, experimental drugs, treatments under trial, *in vitro* fertilisation (IVF). It is not the big things but the little things that constitute the bulk of the business.

Patients who travel for the add-ons and the top-ups are necessarily high cost and high maintenance: 'People paying out of their own pocket for non-essential treatment want to be nurtured, cosseted and treated as if they were in a top hotel' (Youngman, 2012). They expect to be pampered. Their core needs are often catered for by private or social insurance at home. They travel for the little extras. They are willing to pay.

State health budgets, overstretched at the best of times, are under pressure from recessions, deficits and fiscal austerity. Cancers and hearts will be given a high priority. Check-ups and fertility treatments will have to yield. Medical tourism can take over from the state system in areas such as these: 'People service their cars regularly and pay for repairs and improvements, leaving insurance only to pay for accidental damage; so the logic is that state healthcare should pay for the unexpected, but not for the annual service' (Youngman, 2011). Where there is a self-inflicted element, the state might adopt a judgmental posture that is closer to social values than it is to the Hippocratic Oath. If the state dispatches the obese, the nicotine-stained and the alcoholic to the end of the queue, private treatment abroad might for them be the only option.

3.2 PRIVATE INSURANCE

Initially private insurers were sceptical about medical travel. Some never reimbursed for out-of-country procedures. Some only provided cover for proven emergencies. Others only offered reimbursement after the patient had settled all the bills, however large, upfront. Their objection to treatment abroad was as visceral as corporate inertia, knee-jerk loyalty and fear of the unknown. It was also as calculative as the realisation that standards abroad are difficult to monitor and that, unpoliced, moral hazard may escalate into wasteful overconsumption.

Yet insurers in competition could not ignore the lower-cost option forever. At first they experimented with a higher co-insurance rate (Mattoo and Rathindran, 2006: 364). Later, reversing the burden, they offered lower deductibles and lower premiums to insured patients who agreed to take themselves offshore. Some paid for extra sick-leave and aeroplane tickets. Some paid the hotel bill for a relative or significant other. The result has been a slow transition towards global portability. Freely fungible protection is conducive to a single world market in medical services.

Blue Cross Blue Shield of South Carolina offers Bumrungrad and the Heart Institute, Bangalore (Meghani, 2011: 19). United Group Programs offers Bumrungrad. Bupa promises Wockhardt, Anthem Blue Cross Apollo and Bumrungrad. Health Net and Blue Shield of California ('Access Baja') offer a 40 per cent discount on their premiums for patients who agree to treatment in Mexico. It is good economics for the insurers to do this. Surgery for a hernia costs US$3900 in Costa Rica, US$14 000 in the United States (Butler, 2009: 51). Even if the insurer waives the excess it still makes a gain.

Provincial and state governments with a group plan will be better placed to withstand budgetary cuts if the policy they fund includes a foreign wing. Competing businesses sponsoring insurance as a fringe benefit will have an incentive to choose two-tier policies because they keep the price of final output down. Hannaford Brothers Supermarkets in the United States illustrates what happens when rational profit-seekers recognise that travel abroad can be value for money.

Hannaford Brothers Supermarkets has 27 000 employees. Where they require hip or knee replacements, the company absorbs their costs and co-payments if they agree to select one of the Joint Commission International (JCI)-accredited hospitals in Singapore. This saves the employee up to US$3000 in deductibles and the company 5 per cent to 20 per cent of the reimbursable cost (*The Economist*, 2008). Hannaford is Belgian-owned. Possibly footloose multinationals are more receptive to international options. Interestingly, a US hospital, hearing of Hannaford's initiative, subsequently offered to match Singapore's price. The company's director of health and welfare was in no doubt that a mould was being broken: '"Offering the Singapore option has changed the dialogue"' (cited in Einhorn, 2008).

Not all insurance companies are equally generous. Some have downsized their packages in response to economic stringency. Many have exclusion clauses for non-essentials such as massage and acupuncture. Often these are the very electives that have the greatest appeal. Even patients with insurance are obliged to self-pay when they go beyond the core. The fringe benefit is not a comprehensive umbrella. It is only a part.

Global medical insurance will greatly enhance the ill person's freedom to choose. Youngman warns, however, that the suppliers are dragging their heels:

> Insurers are not really interested . . . With the exception of a few small schemes, cross-border cover in Mexico and Europe or US domestic tourism, major health insurers are not prepared to pay for medical tourism. The downsides seem too many and their buying power means they are paying between a third and a half of the retail price for healthcare in the USA and Europe, so they cannot make the huge savings claimed by some. (Youngman, 2012)

It is an important point. The retail price listed on the website is not the wholesale price that the insurer must reimburse. Money off is common for purchases in bulk. Comparisons based on the full price exaggerate the true economic distance between home and abroad.

Even uninsured patients do not necessarily pay the rack rent. Sometimes they are quoted the Medicare price: 'The fact that overseas charges are reasonably close to Medicare rates suggests that there may be significant opportunity for US providers to compete with offshore facilities, in some situations, by offering highly discounted prices to uninsured American patients' (Alleman, Luger, Reisinger, Martin, Horowitz and Cramm, 2010: 496). A heart bypass carries a mean price of US$18 600 outside the US. The US Medicare rate is US$21 000. It is more but not much more; and the patient does not have to bear the cost of travel abroad.

3.3 STATE INSURANCE

Where the state is the insuring agency, it can make a considerable saving by reimbursing the out-of-country cost. Treatment in Mexico is cheaper but Medicare and Medicaid cannot be used for foreign care. Perhaps the government believes that the drain on foreign exchange would be intolerable. There are a large number of retired Americans living abroad. Perhaps it has come under the influence of the doctors' lobby. Competition in border states such as Texas may be seen as a threat to vested interest.

Singapore, in contrast, has since 2010 allowed its citizens and residents to draw down their medical savings accounts (their 'Medisave') for treatment abroad. The conditions are restrictive. The money can only be used in Malaysia, and then only in 14 private hospitals with a presence in Singapore. There must have been a Singapore referral. The accounts cannot be used for services like Ayurveda that are not eligible under Medisave at home. The take-up has been low. Only 30 per cent of Singaporeans in a 2013 survey even knew that the facility existed (Chioy, Lee and Teo, 2013: 48). Far more spend personal, non-hypothecated funds. The release of Medisave is, however, a very small foot in the door. Later on, presumably, additional countries will be included in the scheme. It would confer an unintended benefit on less developed countries with good, cheap medical services.

Singapore's Medisave, being mandatory savings, is not national insurance. The accounts belong to the discrete households which have built them up. The social insurance scheme (to which the state does not contribute) is Medishield. There are no proposals in Singapore to release pooled funds for treatment abroad. There are, however, precedents in foreign countries. The German Krankenkassen make use of rehabilitation centres in the Czech Republic: 'With foreign curative spas being renowned and tariffs up to 30–40% cheaper than in Germany, both the insurer and its members take advantage' (Glinos, Baeten and Maarse, 2010: 105). Norway goes further than simple reimbursement. It treats Norwegian patients in Spain in facilities directly owned by the Norwegian government itself.

Britain wraps both health insurance and the delivery of service in a single national system. Like the medical ethic, it is committed to all necessary care despite the budgetary constraints which result in long waits and occasionally something worse. Searching for economies and solutions, the NHS has made bilateral contracts for orthopaedic surgery in France, Germany and Belgium. It has also explored the outsourcing of medical interventions to India. This is an alternative to the insourcing of Indian doctors into the NHS.

Some patients, including some first- and second-generation new nationals, may prefer this option. One study, concentrating on a subset of common surgeries, found that the NHS could save between £120 million and £200 million annually if it sent its patients (together with a companion) to India. The waiting times would also fall (Lunt, Smith, Exworthy, Green, Horsfall and Mannion, 2011: 31). The NHS already exports state-funded patients to the domestic private sector. The international portability of entitlements would not be a new departure so much as a globalisation of a work in progress.

There is considerable scope for cost containment through state-sector shopping around: 'A hip replacement costs €1290 in Hungary but €8739 in the Netherlands' (Glinos, Baeten and Maarse, 2010: 110). It is an income effect which releases purchasing power into other markets. In the case of the NHS, it makes a limited state budget go further. Possibly the embarrassing disparity would force the NHS to raise its own productivity. Yet there is more to the national health than value for money. Even if quality standards are guaranteed, some people will argue that the NHS ought to be doing its own job rather than buying its way out of its duty.

In the EU-27 public spending constitutes about 77 per cent of total spending on health. In some countries it is 90 per cent (Lautier, 2013: 10). In the British NHS both outpatient and inpatient care are fully covered. Medical travel is to no small extent a topic in public sector economics. Chanda, pointing to 'the pre-dominance of public healthcare delivery in the EU and sensitivities associated with commercializing healthcare' (Chanda, 2011: 1), proposes that any significant change be made gradually. The first step would be for the European public sector to conduct small-scale pilots to confirm that outcomes abroad were satisfactory. Public opinion would have to be surveyed to establish if it was politically acceptable for taxpayers' money to be diverted to aliens and profit-seekers. Experiments with discretionary top-ups might be a good place for the NHS to begin.

To pay other countries for the hips and the hernias would verge on the separation of the purchaser and the provider functions. It could be the first step in an ideological sea-change. If the NHS were prepared to hold the bank but to let the Indians deliver the services, there might then be an argument for returning all British hospitals to the private sector. The state would administer the insurance system. It would reimburse the fees. It would not replace the joints.

The system in Germany is reimbursement according to a preannounced schedule. The system in the NHS is pure communism at the point of consumption. The difference is important. Because payment in Britain is married to provision, and because healthcare is provided without a user fee, it is not possible to reimburse the price that would have been charged. Such a price in an NHS setting does not and cannot exist. The NHS delivers in kind. All that can be proposed is that the NHS should reimburse the price that was paid abroad without regard to the pecuniary value of the patient's entitlement at home. Marginal cost is forever bygone. Average cost is water under the bridge. What remains behind is bargaining. We negotiate contracts. We try not to spend too much.

One solution, adopting the preannounced schedule, would be for the foreign supplier to contract with the NHS at an agreed value per diagnostic-related group. A second solution would be for the NHS and a foreign country to arrange for a payment-free swap. Britain and Malta had such a reciprocal agreement. Patients originating in either country were entitled to free care in the partner country as if they were resident locals. Later the scheme was found to be one-sided. It was replaced by reimbursement according to a predetermined schedule.

In the limit the patients could be given a sum of money and left to make their bargains for themselves. The NHS could distribute vouchers for use in the public, private or foreign sectors. This would be an acknowledgement that, even in a public system funded out of general taxation, what is evolving is 'a new role for patients as "consumers" of health care rather than "citizens" with rights . . . This will, of course, bring a range of attendant risks and opportunities for patients' (Smith, Legido-Quigley, Lunt and Horsfall, 2012: 39). The NHS would become only one shop among many. The consumer would make a choice.

3.4 THE INS AND THE OUTS

Some sick people have private insurance and some come under the state. Worldwide, even more have no third-party at all. It is an untapped source of demand. Rising incomes might fill the void. So, however, might social democracy which uses welfare transfers to package in the excluded. Either way, the healthcare industry is bound to benefit. Medical travel will benefit as well. Lower cost is attractive to the uninsured who must pay for themselves.

Health travel has an image which belies the reality. Often it is not the prosperous but the less advantaged who are the more likely to travel: 'Of those living at the lowest level of poverty, 3.9 percent of individuals had been treated overseas, compared to <1 percent of those in the highest income category . . . In the US, the percentage of people seeking care abroad declines as income rises' (Laugesen and Vargas-Bustamante, 2010: 227). The public safety net in many countries is minimal. The vulnerable use exit. Voice will not get them very far.

Kangas has documented the plight of the Yemeni sick. Between 40000 and 60000 of them self-pay each year for healthcare abroad. It is a sizeable proportion of the Yemeni population, currently 17 million. Richer Yemenis go to Germany, the US and the UK. Impoverished Yemenis go to Mumbai. The median Yemeni does not go for cosmetic surgery. He goes because a life-saving specialism is not available at home.

The Yemenis pay with money from family members, a grant from a charity, a gift from an employer or a contribution from the government. They borrow at exorbitant interest from a money-lender. They sell off their jewellery, home, land and livestock. There is the opportunity cost of lost earnings when a sick person has to be accompanied to India. Kangas reported that Yemeni medical travellers were spending on average US$3000 a year at a time when the average household income in the Yemen was only US$300.

Even that might not be enough. Having exhausted their wealth on diagnosis they might not be able to pay still more for a cure. A lifetime on expensive medication might be a lifetime cut short. Meanwhile, the central bank is losing much-needed reserves. Kangas calculates that the

Yemen, a poor country, is experiencing an annual loss of foreign exchange of between US$120 million and US$600 million (Kangas, 2010: 348). The capital and the dollars are lost forever. The drain is a brake on the rate of growth.

In India the position is similar. Between 75 and 90 per cent of outlays are out-of-pocket: 'Since this private expenditure is not significantly augmented by government expenditures, any prolonged illness can wipe out savings and push families into major debt' (Vijaya, 2010: 60). The average spell in hospital costs 58 per cent of the average annual household expenditure (Peters and Muraleedharan, 2008: 2136). It can make paupers of the poor: 'More than 40 per cent of all patients admitted to hospital have to borrow money or sell assets, including inherited property and farmland, to cover expenses, and 25 per cent of farmers are driven below the poverty line by the costs of their medical care' (Sengupta and Nundy, 2005: 1158).

It is not just in the Third World that large sections of the population lack insurance. The Senate Special Committee on Ageing in 2006 estimated that about 47 million to 50 million Americans (about 16 per cent of the population and 25 per cent of the labour force) were uninsured. The reasons were financial difficulties, denial of cover or a personal decision to bury their head in the sand. At least as many were underinsured. More than 120 million Americans had no dental cover. Pre-existing conditions and aesthetic treatments were automatically excluded.

Care cost inflation in the United States, above 5 per cent throughout the two decades from 1990 to 2010, has been more rapid than the rise in the retail price index. As costs rise, insurers protect themselves. They curtail the size of the package, put up the premiums and insist on high deductibles. The retired, the unemployed and the sick lose all or most of their occupational entitlement. Half of all employers in the US cancel cover within a year if an employee develops a chronic illness. Small employers discontinue benefits as an alternative to a slimmed-down workforce or lower take-home profits. Employees are forced to fend for themselves. It is not easy. Since 2006 the average insurance policy for an employed family of four has exceeded the entire annual earnings of a worker on the minimum wage (Milstein and Smith, 2007: 137). Public spending on Medicaid alone exceeded public spending on education (United States Senate, 2006: 11).

About 2 million Americans each year are driven into medical bankruptcy (Wolff, 2007). Medical bankruptcies make up 60 per cent of all bankruptcies in the United States. More than 75 per cent of bankrupts had health insurance of some kind. They could not absorb out-of-pocket the hospital bills and the cost of prescription drugs. Uninsured patients owed an average of US$26971 when they declared bankruptcy. Those with private insurance owed US$27 749. Low-income Americans on Medicaid owed US$14 633 (Himmelstein, Thorne, Warren and Woolhandler, 2007). Treatment abroad may be what stands between them and selling their home for whatever they can get.

Postponement makes their health status worse. It is estimated that as many as 18 000 uninsured Americans die each year from conditions that could have been treated if they were caught in time. Too rich for Medicaid but too poor for the cost-shares, many have no choice but medical travel. Their decision reflects the gaping holes in US insurance at least as much as it reflects the price, quality and differentiation of the outside market. Americans are going abroad for a 'costectomy' (*The Economist*, 2008). It is the only procedure that many of them can still afford.

High prices and inflated quantities keep the individual patient awake at night. No less are they a challenge to the government which must pacify a disgruntled electorate while putting a cap on the fiscal deficit. The United States now accounts for half of all healthcare spending in the world. At 17.6 per cent of the GDP, the share of health in the USA is almost twice the Organisation for Economic Co-operation and Development (OECD) average of 9.5 per cent, the world average of 10 per cent (Mortensen, 2008: 5n). Extrapolating, it is heading towards 20 per cent. The system costs more per capita than it does in any other developed country. It is not money well spent. Slippage, waste and transactions costs absorb 40 per cent of what an American spends on health (United States Senate, 2006: 12). As for the success rate, the United States is ranked only 37th in the world by its outcome indicators.

Whether at the individual or the national level, there is clearly an argument for trade that holds back the flood. Mattoo and Rathindran estimate that the United States could save US$1.4 billion annually if only 10 per cent of patients in need of one of 15 named medical procedures travelled abroad (Mattoo and Rathindran, 2006: 358). If coronary artery bypass surgery were added to the list, the cost savings would be in excess of US$2 billion. Cost saved by the nation is US$2 billion. Revenue lost by the domestic suppliers is the same US$2 billion. It is not possible to please everyone.

Ehrbeck, Guevara and Mango multiply the US$2 billion by ten. Making their own assumptions about numbers and prices, they calculate that the United States would spend US$20 billion less on health if elective surgery could be sent abroad (Ehrbeck, Guevara and Mango, 2008: 6). Milstein and Smith are not as bullish. They caution that medical tourism will provide only moderate relief. Their assessment is that 'offshore surgery is unlikely to reduce near-term total US health spending by more than 1–2 per cent' (Milstein and Smith, 2007: 141). While 1–2 per cent is a gain worth having, health travel, they say, can only be regarded as a short-run stop-gap. Sooner or later the Americans will have to grasp the nettle and do the right thing: 'Financially stressed Americans require a domestic health care system that perpetually reengineers its processes to deliver an internationally distinguished level of quality at a much lower cost' (Milstein and Smith, 2007: 141).

Medical travel provides a safety valve when the domestic system is unable to meet the demand. The Chairman of the Senate Special Committee on Ageing describes how it is seen by anxious Americans in the following words: 'The ease of international travel and the growth in quality health-care facilities in developing countries certainly plays a part. But I believe frustration with rising health-care costs in the US is also a contributing factor. American medicine is less and less competitive' (United States Senate, 2006: 3). He also says that 'Americans should not have to travel overseas to obtain affordable health care' (United States Senate, 2006: 3). They should have the choice to go abroad if they wish. They should not, however, be obliged to do so because the market and the state have failed them at home.

The system had to be reformed. The Patient Protection and Affordable Care Act of 2010 was the response. The intention was that it should extend to all Americans the mandatory cover that is the norm in Europe. Insurers would no longer be allowed to reject applicants even if the hearts and the cancers were proven bad risks. Policies were to be community rated even if known beneficiaries could be expected to impose a disproportionate burden. Caps on lifetime reimbursement and co-payments for essential services were to be ended. All individuals not covered by an employer-sponsored policy, Medicaid, Medicare or another public insurance plan were obliged by law to insure privately. Low-income families would receive a federal subsidy to absorb a part of the cost.

'Obamacare' sought to universalise the power to pay. It could prove a threat to medical travel. Americans who can afford a doctor in the USA might not see the need for a doctor in India. On the other hand, because the Act mandates no more than 'minimum essential coverage', services such as hair transplants and dental check-ups will remain ineligible for reimbursement. Americans who must pay out-of-pocket will continue to seek care in the cheapest market.

An additional 47 to 50 million Americans will flood the market. Widening the relativities, new demand undammed by the Act is likely to chase up the prices and put pressure on the clinics. Care-cost inflation will perpetuate the practice of buying foreign because foreign costs less. There is also the question-mark of portability. If a future amendment were to give Americans the right to claim treatment abroad, there is no limit to the wave of medical travel that might be unleashed.

3.5 REGION AND ALLIANCE: THE EUROPEAN UNION

Portability is conducive to mobility. An economic bloc can have the same effect. Insurance arrangements are coordinated and even pooled. Medical standards are made more uniform and more evidence-based. Patients have unimpeded access to a multinational marketplace. Entrepreneurs and professionals freely transfer their capital and labour in response to incentives. Multilateral arrangements like the World Trade Organization (WTO) and the General Agreement on Trade in Services (GATS) make it easier for medicine to become a transnational tradeable. A regional grouping like the European Union makes it easier still.

The European Union recognises the right of the member states to administer their own healthcare arrangements. The Council and Parliament of the EU express the commitment to subsidiarity in the following words: 'Decisions about the basket of healthcare to which citizens are entitled and the mechanisms used to finance and deliver that healthcare, such as the extent to which it is appropriate to rely on market mechanisms and competitive pressures to manage health systems, must be taken in the national context' (European Union, 2011: 3). The nation-state is the ultimate arbiter on both ethics and economics.

The Directive on the Application of Patients' Rights in Cross-Border Healthcare (adopted in 2011) warns member free-riders against the obvious temptation to dump their obligations on their more Samaritan team-mates: 'Notwithstanding the possibility for patients to receive cross-border healthcare under this Directive, Member States retain responsibility for providing safe, high quality, efficient and quantitatively adequate healthcare to citizens on their territory' (European Union, 2011: 3). The Directive is being frank. National resources are not infinite. Influx increases the pressure. Efflux leads to excess capacity. Member states have different systems of insurance and delivery. There is not a single health services market in the EU. There is not a single Ministry of Health. The Commission finds it difficult to negotiate externally for the whole so long as the independent members are making private pacts of their own. Until the loose threads are tied up, patient flows will of necessity remain limited.

The EU is cautious but at the same time it is libertarian. Committed to comparative advantage and the gains from trade, the free movement of goods and services is enshrined in Articles 49 and 50 of the mould-making Treaty of Rome and in Article 294 of the Treaty of Lisbon that augmented it. Medical travel is one beneficiary among many from the freedom of exchange.

Short-term displacements for leisure or business are covered under the terms of the European Health Insurance Card (EHIC) (formerly called the E111). In a tourist destination like Venice, accidents and unexpected emergencies can account for two-thirds or more of foreign admissions. EU citizens under the retirement age who go abroad for a longer period have the right to join the state health insurance scheme in their country of resettlement. They must inform the authorities at home so that their original entitlement can be cancelled.

The short-term tourists and the long-stay migrants fit fairly well into the system. EU nationals who go abroad exclusively for their health are more of a problem. Economically, they are the ones who will be the most sensitive to the costs and benefits. Yet they experience some difficulties in making the market work for them.

Normally, the transnational European will make payment first and claim reimbursement later. Because the two-stage process can be a burden to the low-paid, member states have the option of paying the purchaser directly. Pre-existent conditions are not covered. Travel, accommodation and a companion may or may not be reimbursed (European Union, 2011: 51). Treatments deemed unsafe or unethical at home may not be claimed. Since different countries underwrite different services, the entitlements are not the same for all EU nationals. A bed is not guaranteed. A loophole allows a country to turn away a fellow European if it can show that it is unable to provide adequate care for its existing residents.

Repayment cannot exceed the standard rate applied for the same or an equivalent procedure in the patient's country of residence. Some countries exercise discretion since the money paid out is clearly not the same. Taken literally, the insistence on a standard rate would not be fully compatible with frictionless competition, a level playing field and an EU-wide common market.

Home states can insist on a referral from a general practitioner. Prior authorisation is the triage and the filter. A local gatekeeper is asked to certify that the intervention is required on medical grounds. Prior authorisation imposes a cap on what otherwise could become an open-ended commitment. It is normally required where at least a one-night stay in hospital is involved. It is less frequently required for outpatient care.

The legal position has been clarified by the European Court of Justice in a series of judgments dating back to the Kohll and Decker cases in 1998. The Court has ruled (most clearly so in the Yvonne Watts case of 2006) that an EU patient should be allowed to seek treatment in any EU state if there has been an 'undue delay', medically unjustifiable (European Union, 2011: 57), in the patient's country of residence. 'Undue delay' does not mean the same as a non-standard wait. Different waiting times are not grounds in themselves for pass-through. EU foreigners coming to the British National Health Service take their turn in the queue. 'Undue delay' in their own country does not mean that they are exempted from additional delay when they go abroad.

When they do cross the borders EU patients will not necessarily experience a warm welcome. There may be discrimination against 'healthcare immigrants' who are accused of pushing locals out of beds and pulling up the price. This will especially be the case where incomers have access to public facilities without having to pay the local tax: 'With capital costs being subsidised in Belgium, hospital bills are ca. 10% cheaper than in neighbouring Netherlands' (Glinos, Baeten and Maarse, 2010: 110). It gets worse. If a foreign state reimburses above the odds, cash-strapped hospitals may divert resources away from the very taxpayers who made care locally so cost-effective. Such objections are less often raised if the medical travellers are seeking treatment in the private sector.

Judicial interpretations are one step ahead of cross-border statutes. Political guidance is handicapped by the lack of single-valued consensus and the bounded mandate of both Commission and Parliament. Even the Court is held back by the intricacies of the human condition. 'Reasonable' waits and 'appropriate' treatment are not easy to define, especially since the definitions will vary from one country to another. Besides that, 'objective medical assessment' and the 'probable course' of the patient's illness must also be taken into account. There is no end to the disagreements that can result.

The WTO countries could not reach unanimity in the abandoned Doha negotiations. Bilateral agreements were the second-best that took their place. A parallel may be found in the European Union, where some states are better prepared to cooperate and co-fund than are others. An example would be the Euregio Meuse-Rhine healthcare area that creates a single centre of excellence in adjacent regions of the Netherlands, Belgium and Germany. Some Europeans live in one country but work in another. The guns of August have come and gone.

Small regions like the Saar, in common with small countries like Luxembourg, do not have the catchment necessary for an economic balance of medical specialisms. Medical care must be sought just down the road where the border post used to be. Regions are becoming larger due to bullet trains, budget flights and the harmonisation of regulations. In the absence of a pan-European lead, regional planning to encourage optimal usage of facilities has the advantage that it is, like a bilateral agreement, a second-best step towards continent-wide co-determination.

Even so, the EU-28 are debating each other's experience and learning from it. Talk is the first step towards levelling and coordination. The EU countries are collaborating in public health, communicable disease and scientific research. They are not only putting health records online but are also arranging for the platforms to be made interoperable (European Union, 2011: 31). Transfer of records is an investment in continuity of care even where the treatment episodes are scheduled in different jurisdictions.

Cross-border medical services in the EU are probably less than 1 per cent of total healthcare spending in the community (Smith, Legido-Quigley, Lunt and Horsfall, 2012: 40). A common market is not essential to reap the benefits of coordination. Like a common currency, however, a common code can greatly reduce the transactions costs of getting health-care business done.

3.6 INSTITUTIONS AND ATTITUDES

Structure builds on infrastructure. Without the appropriate foundations, the edifice will collapse. Transportation is the *sine qua non*. Patients must be able to reach the treatment centre. This means an international airport linked up to the hospitals by a network of motorways and high-speed trains. Poor connectivity is a deterrent if a sick person is obliged to change planes several times. A direct flight to a hub destination makes medical tourism less stressful.

Long-haul travel can be painful. There is a chance of cramp, pulmonary embolism or deep-vein thrombosis. Airlines protect themselves: patients sometimes have to wait in a Yemeni bed until the carrier deems them sufficiently stable for the flight to Mumbai (Kangas, 2007: 303). In the limit the hospital can be situated in the airport itself. This minimises the travelling times and the stay. Munich Airport has a hospital with two operating theatres. While this does not do much for spillover tourism, it does make Munich more attractive to world travellers in a rush.

Travel can be expensive. Larger planes spread the sunk overhead of expensive fuel. Quick turnaround makes flights more affordable. Facilitators and hospitals sometimes have an ongoing relationship which allows them to negotiate discounted fares. They can also bargain rates with hotels or provide rooms of their own. Some allow relatives to sleep in the patient's ward. It reduces the cost of going abroad.

Accommodation is a background complement. Patients often pass through a sequence of tests, interventions, check-ups and follow-ups. Foreigners cannot return home immediately even after a day-case procedure. They, together with accompanying relatives, require somewhere to stay. Hotels should be conveniently situated because of road congestion and delay. They should offer appropriate amenities in case post-operatives cannot leave the room. Such amenities would include video recorders, satellite television, meals in bed, internet access and qualified first-aiders on the staff. Hotels collaborating with hospitals will sometimes have emergency buttons and oxygen tanks.

A further part of the care infrastructure is language. Communication with doctors and nurses is essential, not only where psychological support is needed and difficult choices must be made but also where the patient cannot reach his glass of water or would like some soap for the shower. More and more people are learning English. It is the language of the medical textbooks and the journals. It is to some extent the new lingua franca that Esperanto was designed to become. Fluency in other languages remains, however, an important asset in medical tourism. One study of German patients in Eastern Europe found that 87 per cent of them communicated with their doctors in German, only 5 per cent in English (Wagner, Dobrick and Verheyen, 2011: 15). Mandarin as well as close proximity is an important reason why mainland Chinese opt for hospitals in Taiwan.

The Japanese select the Japanese section in Bangkok Hospital. Myanmar patients are received by fellow nationals under a picture of the Schwedagon Pagoda. Arabs if they wish can sit on divans in tents pitched in the day room. Bangkok Hospital has interpreters fluent in 23 languages, including Ethiopian. At one time it employed half (two out of four) of all the Ethiopians resident in Thailand. Translators are not free. Even multilingual volunteers are not always around. It is not the same but it can be enough.

Education is clearly a part of the infrastructure. Languages aside, health travel presupposes skilled and semi-skilled manpower in the destination country. Making a success of cross-border travel requires not just surgeons, anaesthetists and pharmacists but also receptionists, filing clerks and ambulance staff. Some will have been trained abroad. Most will have been educated at home. Training must be aligned with jobs. Even taxi drivers must be able to read a map or understand simple instructions in a second language.

Education is a public good. Many public goods are supplied in the public sector. They are the responsibility of a government with a manpower plan. Needless to say, that government must also have the public finance to train up the various grades upon which health tourism depends. The alternative to educating its own people is to liberalise work permits and bring in professional staff from abroad.

The law too is a precondition. Locals and foreigners will not invest if contract, property and patent are not upheld by an independent judiciary; while guaranteed confidentiality is necessary for outsourcing and technology transfer. Personal security is important. Military coups, terrorism, crime, revolutions and the closure of the airport are a disincentive to go. Patients also expect a bedrock of state regulation. JCI visits are spaced at discrete intervals. Patients will want the quality in the treatment centres to be monitored continuously.

Patients, again, are more likely to come to a country if it issues multiple-entry one-year medical visas and simplifies the arrangements for retirement stays. Rapid turnaround may be essential if the patient urgently requires treatment. Within the EU the citizens of the member countries can enter and stay without restriction. In Thailand the hospitals help to procure visas. They can be extended if the episode lasts longer than expected.

The assumption is that medical travellers can get a passport and that there are no burdensome restrictions on leaving their country. Fortunately for health tourism, administrative formalities such as exit visas or exchange control are becoming less common. They are less likely to be used as non-tariff barriers than in the quasi-mercantilist 1930s when liberalisation was regarded as a threat.

There are also the non-tariff barriers of the mind. Patients themselves must be willing to go abroad. Cultural acceptance is necessary if customers are to go beyond their comfort zone. General tourism helps to correct the stereotypes of poor hygiene and inadequate drains that frighten would-be travellers into in-country care. Television, films, information technology and the media make people aware of the health-related services that are on offer in the vanguard nations. Awareness is the mechanism through which supply creates its own demand. As Yap puts it: 'The Internet and broadcast media show the best healthcare to the world, and people are no longer content to settle for the average and the merely proximate. This global mindset both increases dissatisfaction with one's own healthcare and presents options to respond to that dissatisfaction' (Yap, 2006: 18).

On the side of supply as well as demand, the electronic revolution has upgraded the infrastructure. It has made possible the outsourcing of call centres, e-payment by credit card and teleconferencing before and after the treatment episode. Cable, satellite and video links ensure the real-time transfer of scans. Surgery can be performed at a distance with a robotic arm. Hospital websites can publicise success rates, unique technology and doctor–patient ratios. Electronics allows hospitals to answer queries, forward testimonials and take bookings. The very name of one facilitator – Tour2india4health – demonstrates that even language is tweeting in time with the funk.

Facilitators as well as treatment centres cry their wares in cyberspace. Travel agents take over the logistics. They book tickets and hotels. They arrange airport transfers. They identify tours and cookery classes for accompanying relatives. Medical travel is a joint product. All the pieces of the puzzle must fall into place. The check-ups and the surgeries are a part. What the traveller needs is the whole.

It is a seamless web, and somewhere in the web is the state. Medical travel presupposes a reliable power supply and water from the mains. If the private sector fails, the public sector must step in. It is seed-corn that leads to growth and jobs. Whether through direct tax, indirect tax, responsible borrowing or foreign aid, the government must be able to pay. Growth is therefore on the side of the state. A rising gross domestic product provides governments with the natural dividend that they require to increase public spending without going into the red.

Infrastructure is a mix, but so is government itself. Visas, roads, exchange rates are the responsibility of more than a single ministry. Apart from public–private coordination, public–public cooperation is essential. Medical tourism depends on the elimination of bureaucratic red tape and of corruption at the centre that prices in a confusing surcharge. Not least, however, does medical tourism presuppose a government that talks to itself.

4. Price and quality

There are many contributory factors. Most are the periphery. Chapter 4 and Chapter 5 are concerned not with the fringe but with the centre. It is not enough for the facilities to be there. Foreign patients must be willing to travel to them. Price, quality and differentiation are the three variables that most influence them when they make up their mind to go.

Differentiation is the subject of Chapter 5. Section 4.2 of the present chapter considers price and section 4.3 considers quality. Before that, section 4.1 examines the evidence. It tries to establish what is known about the relative impact of the three causal variables, together with the very human fear of the unknown that tempts potential travellers to stay at home.

The relative impact will not always be the same. Over time the prices in a single marketplace will tend to converge. Transparency, information, supply and demand will act to enforce the law of one service, one price. It could have a dampening effect on medical tourism. If prices cluster around a single equilibrium, there is then less of an incentive for the money-minded to go abroad. The medical tourism industry will have to rethink its role. Competition based on quality and differentiation is likely to be the new distinction that divides.

4.1 WILLINGNESS TO TRAVEL

Quantity and price are inversely related. The familiar gradient is the staple of the economics class. In the real world the relationship is not so simple. Milstein confirmed that price is the tipping point but that it operates with a threshold effect.

Milstein found that few consumers would opt for surgery abroad if the expected savings were less than US$1000. Habit, convenience and familiar surroundings introduce a non-price wedge. Above US$1000, however, the foreign option could no longer be ignored: 'Among people who have sick family members, about 45% of the underinsured or uninsured declare they would get on the plane; even 19% of those who have insurance say they're game. Above $5000, the percentage of takers climbs to 61% and

40%, respectively' (quoted in Kher, 2006). There is no demand curve below US$1000. Above US$1000 the demand curve becomes a sequence of steps.

Price matters but other things matter too. The McKinsey team surveyed 49980 medical travellers. Of that sample, 32 per cent said they were going for better quality and a further 40 per cent for the most advanced technology. About 15 per cent put quick access first. Only 13 per cent said that the primary reason was price (Ehrbeck, Guevara and Mango, 2008: 4). This time there was a threshold of US$10000. Unless they could shave at least US$10000 off their bill the patients would opt for the higher price and stay within their comfort zone. Comparing the responses across the nations, however, something interesting emerges. Although only 13 per cent of United States respondents said that the price was the deal-maker, almost 99 per cent of the respondents who did put price first were American. Underinsurance, fee-for-service and care-cost inflation were making them rational and cost-aware.

Singapore is rich and business-conscious. In spite of that, a survey of 103 working adults found that 60 of them ranked quality first. Only 23 made price their primary consideration. Interestingly, a parallel sample of 104 students came up with 61 and 9 respectively. Students, it would appear, were even less price-sensitive than their seniors. Political stability in the destination country was ranked first by eight of the students although by only five of the working adults (Chioy, Lee and Teo, 2013: 38). The younger generation has grown accustomed to strong government.

The Deloitte report also disaggregated the respondents. It showed that only 37 per cent of late-middle-aged and retired Americans would go overseas at all. The figure for the under-35s, at 51 per cent, was higher but still surprisingly low. Hispanics and Asian-Americans were more willing to travel than Caucasians and African-Americans. The reason is likely to be family contacts abroad. It was not in the first instance price.

In the Deloitte study, the majority of respondents reiterated that medical travel was not for them. As for the minority, 31 per cent said they would consider an elective procedure in a foreign country but only if it cost half as much or less and the quality were just as good. The percentage rose to 33 per cent for a necessary procedure. It is all conjecture. Only 1 per cent of the respondents said they had actually used an offshore care provider in the previous two years (Deloitte, 2008: 3, 5).

Khoury, canvassing 5050 Americans in 2009, found the same antipathy and the same 'yes but'. Of Khoury's sample, only 29 per cent said they would be willing to travel abroad for medical procedures such as bypass or cosmetic surgery that were routinely performed in the US. The hidden text is that perhaps they would be willing to travel if the service were known to be radically different. The 29 per cent rose to 40 per cent once the respondents were told to assume that quality abroad was the same but that the cost was significantly less. A figure of 29 per cent or even 40 per cent is hardly a strong endorsement of the price incentive to go abroad.

Health insurance made foreign travel less likely. About 44 per cent of all respondents without but only 26 per cent of all respondents with health insurance were prepared to go abroad. In the case of cancer patients, the figures were 37 per cent and 22 per cent respectively. Khoury's figures, different from those of Deloitte, suggest that Americans may be less likely to travel for necessities than for luxuries (Khoury, 2009). In the more traditional parts of the United States (the South, the Midwest) affirmative responses were below the average. In the West they were above. Possibly this is because the West fields a disproportionate number of residents who have already uprooted themselves at least once. For them, tradition, anxiety and minimax may not have as powerful a deterrent effect.

Reddy, York and Brannon canvassed the opinions of 336 American undergraduates who had not previously considered the possibility of Third World care. Initially they were ambivalent or slightly negative (Reddy, York and Brannon, 2010: 517). Nonetheless, they were consistently positive when the questions homed in on quality, speed, sightseeing and price. The authors predict that the overall score would have been higher if the respondents had had a greater familiarity with the facts. Information counts: 'Educational intervention may be exactly what is needed to promote acceptance of medical tourism' (Reddy, York and Brannon, 2010: 519). Preferences were not fixed but malleable. Attitudes would change once the initial bias had been overcome.

Gallup in 2007 conducted a poll in the European Union. As in the other surveys, price is relevant but it is in no way primary. About 91 per cent of respondents said they would travel for a treatment not available at home, 78 per cent for a higher quality of care, 69 per cent to see a renowned specialist, 64 per cent (rising to 88 per cent in the United Kingdom) to circumvent the waiting lists and have an earlier consultation. Overall, only 48 per cent cited price (Gallup Organization, 2007: 11).

Better quality is especially salient in less-developed European Union (EU) states such as Slovakia and Bulgaria where medical standards are often said to lag behind. The German case is different. Quality is high. Up to 20 per cent of Germans may, however, have travelled within the EU for medical care. Holiday emergencies were frequently the cause but lower cost was also a factor. Interventions were planned and the reason was price. As for the outcomes, up to 94 per cent were 'highly satisfied' or 'rather satisfied' with their medical practitioner and 97 per cent with the outcome. Only 4 per cent said they would not have treatment in another EU country again (Wagner, Dobrick and Verheyen, 2011: 9, 15).

In Tartu, Estonia (the only city in Estonia with a university medical school), 60 per cent of the respondents in a study said that they preferred medical care in their own country (Jesse and Kruuda, 2006: 29). The remaining 40 per cent were prepared to go abroad. Quality was the main reason. Respondents mentioned better equipment and surgical techniques not locally available. Favoured destinations were mainly Finland (18 minutes away by helicopter) and nearby Sweden. Proximity was a major consideration. Price was not. Nor was waiting time. The Irish and the Danes would travel for a shorter wait. The Estonians and the Germans were less likely to do so. The waiting times in their countries were not perceived as excessive.

About 4 per cent of the Europeans sampled by Gallup reported that they had already seen a doctor abroad. Many had done so as tourists. About 54 per cent said that they were open to the prospect. The positive responses varied from 88 per cent of Cypriots to 26 per cent of Finns. The main obstacles were language skills, limited income, lack of information, geographical distance, mistrust of foreigners, cost of travel, the possibility of failure. In the UK, 40 per cent of respondents in a nationwide poll said they would be willing to travel outside the UK for medical treatment. Approximately 26 per cent said they would be willing to go anywhere in the world (Beecham, 2002: 10). Prices for cosmetic surgery, waits for hip replacements, played an important but a non-quantified role in their calculus.

Unskilled workers in Europe are less likely to travel. The willingness to travel, Gallup found, rises with educational qualifications. The younger demographic is more adventurous. Two-thirds (66 per cent) of Europeans aged between 15 and 24 said they would travel: the figure is 43 per cent for those over 55. As for gender, there is not a great difference: 55 per cent of the men and 53 per cent of the women told Gallup that it was by and large all right (Gallup Organization, 2007: 8).

Learning by doing had a positive impact. About 82 per cent of Hungarians who had gone abroad for medical treatment in the previous 12 months said they were prepared to go abroad again. Only 46 per cent of Hungarians who had not done so said that they were willing to try (Gallup Organization, 2007: 9). One inference might be that the world upsurge in recreational tourism will have beneficial spillovers for health. By 2012, 1 billion persons – one-seventh of the world's population – were crossing the international borders each year. It is the highest number in human history.

In all, 72 per cent of EU citizens travelled in 2011 (Youngman, 2012). They were seeing the world. If they liked what they saw, perhaps they would want to return. It is already happening. One study in Germany of patients enrolled with an insurance fund found that in 2003 only 7 cent had obtained non-emergency treatment in another European country. In 2008 the 7 per cent had become 40 per cent (Wagner, Dobrick and Verheyen, 2011: 5)

Where EU citizens were reluctant to seek care abroad, the main reasons reported to Gallup were that the service at home was perceived to be satisfactory (83 per cent) and that travel when one is sick is troublesome and inconvenient (86 per cent). There are the transactions costs of identifying the best bargain. There are the psychological costs of trusting to strangers whom one will never see again. Other reasons cited were inadequate information about alternatives abroad (61 per cent), the language barrier (49 per cent) and the expense (47 per cent). The majority of Europeans had insurance at home. Lack of portability was a deterrent. So, no doubt, was the deterrent as a taxpayer of paying twice (Gallup Organization, 2007: 11, 18). The numbers add up to more than 100 per cent. Respondents were allowed more than one choice.

As with Europe, so with Canada. Approximately 8 per cent of Canadians have travelled within Canada for medical attention but only 2 per cent have gone abroad. In a national poll conducted by Deloitte, 69 per cent said they would be willing to go out-of-province provided that their insurance could come too. Only 31 per cent said they would travel within Canada if they had to pay. Interestingly, the figures for transnational care, at 60 per cent and 20 per cent, were lower but not dramatically so (Deloitte, 2010: 9).

Better quality was frequently cited by the Canadian respondents. No doubt the pain and anxiety of waits mattered to them as well: 'In Britain and Canada . . . the waiting period for a hip replacement can be a year or more, while in Bangkok or Bangalore, a patient can be in the operating room the morning after getting off a plane' (Aniza, Aidalina, Nirmalini, Inggit and Ajeng, 2009: 8). The wait for coronary bypass surgery in the UK can be six months. The wait for bariatric surgery in Canada is over five years. It is not primarily a question of price.

Bumrungrad claims to see 3000 patients a day. They spend on average 17 minutes in the waiting room. Walk-ins are seen without an appointment. Most patients make an appointment. Their case history will have been taken in their own country and there will have been virtual consultation. The beds are there. An average of 14 per cent of operational beds at Bumrungrad are unoccupied on any one day. The buffer means that a patient can be admitted without delay.

The Department of Health Systems Management in the USA estimates that between 47000 and 103000 foreigners came to the US for treatment in 2007. The main draw was quality of equipment and doctoring, often proxied by a famous name like Mayo. The principal sources of international patients were Mexico (21.18 per cent), the Middle East (14.07 per cent), South and Central America (excluding Mexico) (23.58 per cent) and Europe (11.23 per cent). The flow is disproportionately from the South to the North, and mainly driven by the search for top-end expertise. About 31.69 per cent were going for oncology, 14.17 per cent for cardiology and 11.75 per cent for neurology (Stackpole & Associates, 2010: 3, 4). These are not luxury interventions. For the big things, medical travellers were willing to pay whatever it costs to secure a superior service.

One does not cut corners with one's heart. Quality and differentiation are irreducible. Price matters. Other things matter more. One consequence is that the top-end American suppliers may have chosen to charge whatever the traffic will bear. The rate of return from foreign patients in the US was estimated in one investigation to be double the rate of return from American patients (Lee and Davis, 2004: 43).

Most studies have been hypothetical and *ex ante*. Completing the feedback loop have been the studies that were time remembered and *ex post*. In 2009 the Medical Tourism Association conducted a survey of international patients: 70 per cent said the service was 'excellent', 27 per cent said it was 'very good', 3 per cent ranked it 'average' and no one ranked it any lower (Medical Tourism Association, 2009: 35). In 2010, focusing on Bumrungrad alone, 68 per cent of its respondents said the treatment was 'excellent', an additional 25 per cent 'good'. Only 2 per cent ranked it 'below average' or 'poor'. About 88 per cent said they would be prepared to travel again for medical care, 82 per cent that they would encourage a friend to do so.

Comparing home and abroad, 62 per cent said their medical experience was better than it would have been in the USA, 32 per cent that it was about the same. Only 6 per cent felt it was inferior (Medical Tourism Association/Bumrungrad International, 2010: 23, 24, 25). The 2009 survey had produced figures that were slightly more encouraging: 63 per cent better, 37 per cent about the same, 0 per cent worse (Medical Tourism Association, 2009: 36).

The results of Treatment Abroad's Medical Tourism Survey 2012 reaffirm the verdict. Perceived quality was ranked above price as the main reason for travel. Even so, 71 per cent of UK patients said that they had saved more than £2000 by going abroad: 12.7 per cent had saved more than £10000. The average trip was 16 days. Since the average inpatient stay was only three days, patients were clearly spending money outside the hospital setting. The price of care must be discounted to allow for the other options to which treatment abroad had opened the door.

About 42 per cent of Britons sampled went abroad for cosmetic surgery and 32 per cent for dentistry. Belgium and Hungary, respectively, were the main destinations. Of respondents in 2012, 90 per cent said they would go abroad for treatment again, 84 per cent that they would return to the same doctor or clinic, 51 per cent that they had travelled to a country they had never previously visited, 65 per cent that they were 'very satisfied', 20 per cent that they were 'quite satisfied' (Treatment Abroad, 2012). That left 15 per cent who said they were not satisfied at all. Their reasons included standard of care, level of customer service and quality of communication. Their dissatisfaction is disseminated and multiplied. Bad news sells newspapers. Good news is no news at all.

In the survey, 83 per cent of UK respondents said that cost was the main reason for seeking treatment abroad. Waiting lists were cited by a minority of patients. Curiously, less than 10 per cent had taken out special insurance for medical travel abroad. Ordinary holiday insurance would not have covered them. They seemed not to know. On the one hand they were cost-conscious. On the other hand they were not. Market economists assume rationality, transitivity and consistency. Ordinary people muddle through.

4.2 PRICE

Table 4.1 gives an indication of the dollar costs and the dollar savings of surgery in selected countries. No two patients are alike and the prices are no more than representative. Prices do not tell the whole story. Total costs include travel, accommodation, accompanying caregivers, unfamiliar surroundings, complications that lead to a longer stay abroad, loss of income from days off work. Even so, the figures speak for themselves.

4.2.1 The Dispersion in Price

Colonoscopy costs US$2260 in the US, US$602 in Thailand (Butler, 2009: 51). Hip resurfacing costs US$47000 in the US, US$12500 in Malaysia, US$7905 in Poland (Lunt, Smith, Exworthy, Green, Horsfall and Mannion, 2011:12). Hysterectomy costs US$32000 in the US, US$5000 in Costa Rica, US$4000 in Thailand (www.healthbase.com). A general medical check-up costs US$5000, kidney transplantation US$150000 in the United States. The figures for the Philippines are, respectively, US$500 and US$25000 (United Nations Economic and Social Commission for Asia and the Pacific, 2007: 14).

A cycle of *in vitro* fertilisation (IVF) in Israel costs US$3000–US$3500; in the US it costs US$16000 to US$20000. The figures for bypass surgery

Table 4.1 Relative costs (US $) in selected countries

	Hip implant	Knee replacement	Cataract surgery	Rhinoplasty	Breast reduction
United States	43 000	40 000	1500–2500	6000	5000
United Kingdom	14 000	16 000–17 000	4500	6000	8500
France	8000–10 000	7500–9000	2300–3300	3000–5000	4000–6000
Hungary	–	–	–	1600–2200	–
Tunisia	3000	3500–4000	900–1000	2300–3000	3000–3500
Turkey	7000	7500	1500	3500	4000
Thailand	12 000	10 000	–	1200	2900
India	8000–10 000	8000–9000	1000–1500	1500–2500	2000–3000

Source: Lautier (2013: 6).

are, respectively, US$35000 and US$120000 (Steiner, 2009: 127). In India, where hospitals like Fortis offer comparable quality, bypass surgery costs only US$6000 (Richman, Udayakumar, Mitchell and Schulman, 2008: 1261). In another estimate a bypass costs US$6700 in India but US$200000 in the United States (United States Senate Special Committee on Ageing, 2006: 7). If the quality is good, then the claim is justified: First World treatment at Third World prices.

Residents in one medical tourism hub sometimes choose to have their own medical intervention in another. Bypass surgery in a Singapore public hospital costs US$20000 in a moderately priced ward. It costs US$9000 in a private hospital in Malaysia. No doubt the cross-border element in Singapore healthcare will increase with the development of the Iskandar Malaysia economic zone and its multiple healthcare facilities. It will be situated just across the Causeway from Singapore. Some of the clinics will be Singapore-owned.

In general, the cost saving varies from 28 per cent to 88 per cent when the patient goes from a developed to a less-developed country (Deloitte, 2008: 13). For complex surgeries such as coronary artery bypass graft or bone marrow transplant the disparity can be 4:1 or even more. Even within the developed world there are economies to be made. Singapore is more expensive than Thailand but less expensive than the United States. An American does not need to go to Thailand to save.

High quality, low-cost medical care in Europe is 40 per cent to 80 per cent cheaper than in the United States (Gerl, Boscher, Mainil and Kunhardt, 2009: 66). In Germany overall prices are about 65 per cent below their American equivalent. Some are even less. Mitral valve repair costs US$45000 in Germany, US$120000 in the United States (Boscher, 2009: 88). In Hungary dentistry costs one-third of what it does in the UK.

As many as 25000 Britons in 2007 travelled from the UK for dentistry (Haslam, 2007: 4). About 40 per cent of Americans who travelled abroad for medical care went for dental work (Apton and Apton, 2010). In Europe the figure is 43 per cent. Medicare in the US does not cover dental care. Patients who are paying for themselves have an incentive to shop around.

It is only stating the obvious to say that price comparisons are based on the rate of exchange. Singapore uses the appreciation of its currency as a macroeconomic tool to contain the rate of inflation. An alternative use of the parity would be to devalue in order to boost its export-led growth. The world is not on the Gold Standard. Exchange rates are political economy. Fixed, floating and managed rates are a topic in foreigners' perceptions of what healthcare will cost on the day when they settle the bill.

4.2.2 The Reasons for the Dispersion

Labour costs make up 18 per cent of total costs at Bumrungrad. They are 55 per cent (*The Economist*, 2008) or even 71 per cent (Mattoo and Rathindran, 2005: 2) at an equivalent hospital in the United States. Medical, nursing, technical and laboratory staff cost less. Even US-trained specialists cost less.

A general practitioner in the UK earns 13 times as much as a general practitioner in Ghana (Connell, 2010: 98–99). A nurse earns US$2000 in the Philippines, US$45 780 in the United States. A cardiac surgeon earns US$300 000 at Apollo, US$417 000 in the United States. The yearly annual income of a radiologist in India is US$20 000. In the United States it is US$300 000 (Smith, Chanda and Tangcharoensathien, 2009: 594). A hospital stay in the United States costs 25 times more than an equivalent bed-night in Thailand. This is largely due to the lower cost of the human input (Arunanondchai and Fink, 2007: 12).

Doctors in Thailand are paid 40 to 50 per cent less, nurses 80 per cent less, than their counterparts in the USA. Living standards are, however, a different matter. Money goes further in Thailand, not least if medical professionals themselves take advantage of cheap labour to employ maids, gardeners and drivers. Besides that, there is the fringe benefit of psychic income. The food is familiar. The climate is good. There is a family network. There is a non-confrontational culture which shelters doctors from patients who in the West might show them inadequate respect or aggressively dispute their diagnosis. Some hospitals try to retain top professionals by setting up a clinic or research centre in their field. Others try to attract complementary professionals to a single site.

Psychic income aside, money is not always what it seems. Doctors in a hub such as Bangkok may have a second appointment in a medical school or a private practice outside. They may operate in more than one hospital. Even within a single hospital, they may receive extra income. Doctors in one Bangkok hospital earn a basic salary of US$3500 per month, nurses US$800. Unlike the nurses, however, the doctors are also entitled to a percentage of the fee. Assuming the patient pays US$2800 for breast augmentation and that the surgeon performs a sequence of augmentations in a single session, an assiduous doctor can take home US$60 000 per month while still charging each patient a relatively low fee per case. Throughput keeps the incomes high but the fees competitive. While not every doctor will be in a position to perform a series of specialised interventions in a day, many doctors will be able to make additional income through additional procedures such as noses and chins. An income of US$720 000 in Thailand or anywhere else cannot be described as low.

Psychic income or money income, skilled professionals in short supply are fully aware of their opportunity cost. They price themselves not by Bangalore but by Los Angeles. Allowance made for the lower cost of living, they expect their reservation wage to be internationally competitive. They can without difficulty go abroad if it is not. Non-medical staff are in a weaker position. Low-skilled grades like cooks and auxiliaries are locked in to the Third World and not the global market. Limited education and surplus labour tie their pay to the minimum wage. Workplace regulations are less stringent. Unions are less strident. Multitasking is not demarcated. Low-skilled and unskilled grades are cheap. It keeps down the cost of care.

Land too can be less expensive. The advantage, as is illustrated by inner-city Bangkok or Singapore, is not universal. Often, however, a green field with easy access to an international airport will not be hard to purchase or rent. The Chang Bin Show Chan Memorial Hospital in Taiwan is located in a price-competitive industrial park two hours from Taipei. Unlike town-centre hospitals, it has room to expand. Construction costs as well as land are cheaper. The sheer newness of the buildings means there will be less obsolescence to repair or replace. Lower maintenance keeps down the price per bed.

Capital is purchased at world prices, shipped in at a cost, sometimes surcharged with a tariff. New institutions learn to turn disabilities into advantages. Because a scanner or a cyber-knife is so expensive, it is worked to capacity – 'Equipment utilization in India is twice as high as in the United States' – and is made to last: 'The expected economic life of the equipment is twice as long' (Oberholzer-Gee, Khanna and Knoop, 2005: 14). Some hospitals lease their equipment to keep down the upfront cost. Leasing allows them the freedom to upgrade quickly in case of obsolescence.

It all adds up. Investigators found that the capital cost per cardiac surgery in the United States was US$2400. In India it was US$600. In terms of the total cost per surgery, the respective numbers were US$4080 and US$680 (Oberholzer-Gee, Khanna and Knoop, 2005: 4, 14). Quick turnaround and critical mass make possible the sub-specialisation of skills and the synergies from interdependence. High patient throughput spreads the fixed overheads.

Competition too has a tendency to keep the prices down. Intra-nationally or internationally, patients who must travel long distances study the selling points. Knee-jerk repeat business to a local monopolist does not satisfy them. There is more than one domestic supplier in a big country like India, China or Nigeria. In Canada a patient in the Yukon or the Northern Territories has no choice but to execute a *tâtonnement* for himself.

Lowe's, the US's second-largest home improvement retailer, now sends employees in need of heart surgery not to India but to the Cleveland Clinic (Firhat and Abratt, 2011: 9). The Cleveland Clinic has agreed to match the foreign price. It is not the only US institution to react in this way to the bracing cold shower:

> Some hospitals in the US are offering discounted bundled care for particular procedures in order to compete with overseas medical providers. Galichia Heart Hospital in Wichita, Kansas, for example . . . decided to challenge itself to see if it could offer comparable prices . . . By cutting prices, the hospital found it was attracting an additional two medical tourism cases a week, or approximately 100 a year, which generates $1 million in incremental revenue per year. (Hudson, 2011: 43)

The American patient gains. The American hospital gains. The Indian hospital does not gain. Competition is not a win–win game.

Competition has a tendency to keep medical costs down. A tendency is not a prediction. If there is excessive entry into the industry, surplus bedstock and underutilised equipment can raise the average cost. One consequence is that private hospitals may expand into medical travel. Their intention is to tap into a new patient pool that they see as 'distinct, profitable and growing' (Lee and Davis, 2004: 42). In some countries they may have to do this because the public sector, subsidised and not profit-seeking, is more attractive to the domestic market.

Medical facilities in newer settings are less inhibited by professional conventions, existing networks, price leadership, reimbursement caps and Medicare regulations. This freedom to act contributes to competitive pricing. Hospitals as entrepreneurs experiment with cost-cutting new techniques and modes of organisation. They use generics to circumvent the patents. They manufacture their own catheters and stents to save on brand-name imports. They downskill technical functions to the lowest feasible grade. They buy in bulk to obtain a quantity discount. They employ business graduates in the belief that medical doctors lack the background, the aptitude and the time to run a bottom line. They rely heavily on rapid turnaround. Bumrungrad has 538 beds. It sees 1.1 million patients annually. Of that 1.1 million, only 30 000 are inpatients. The rest are seen on an outpatient basis.

The business model will extend to computerised scheduling that leaves no hour unused: 'An example is continuous use of radiology equipment at Care, with outpatient studies done by appointment during the day and inpatient radiology studies done overnight, avoiding periods of downtime for capital equipment' (Richman, Udayakumar, Mitchell and Schulman, 2008: 1264). Care in India buys heart valves in bulk. Computers track the depletion of buffer stocks. Precautionary over-ordering is kept to the minimum. Electronic communication ensures speedy access to notes and records. Bumrungrad is becoming a paper-free hospital. No time is wasted in sending down for the files. Computerisation of notes reduces the slippage of time into routine paperwork. Going against the trend is Yan Hee in Bangkok (motto: 'Youth and Beauty') which is recorded in Ripley's *Believe It or Not* as employing a fleet of young women on roller skates to transport up to 2000 files a day.

The will to succeed keeps the prices down. Payment patterns have the same effect. Interfering insurers can insist on unnecessary tests and time-consuming paperwork. There can be a delay in processing the claim. Patients who pay for themselves are not caught in the reimbursement maze. A deposit equal to the estimated cost is handed over in advance. Patients settle the balance on check-out by cash or credit card. Spot payment is cost-effective. There is little bad debt. Waste would in the long run have to be passed on in price.

Where payment is out-of-pocket the patient has an incentive to make a rational choice. The absence and not the presence of a third party may keep down the cost of care. Suppliers may be less inclined to pile on marginal tests, more willing to settle for day-case surgery, if they know this is all the patient can afford. Yet there is another side to the coin. Some hospitals report that self-pay patients demand longer inpatient stays than an insurer would be prepared to reimburse. Hospitals are by no means enthusiastic. While a convalescent might be paying for an idle bed, where the bedstock is nearing full capacity the hospital would make more money by concentrating its beds on the surgical stage.

There is a final reason for lower prices in newer markets. In entrant nations there is no tradition of early litigation and punitive damages. There is no history of defensive medicine and malpractice insurance that in more settled markets can raise the premiums and frighten off the surgeons. Section 4.3.9 below asks if the law courts in up-and-coming destinations are doing enough to keep medical standards high. The present section is about price. It says that lower premiums are a reason why care in newer markets will often cost the patient less.

In Singapore in 2012 insurance for a general practitioner cost only S$1600. It is not a great deal of money. Singaporeans should not be too complacent. For gynaecology the premium was S$21 020. For cosmetic surgery it was S$33 520. Cosmetic surgery is cheaper in Bangkok. One reason is that, in Singapore, a cosmetic surgeon has to price in cover that exceeds the Singapore median income by one-third and that is rising by 20 per cent a year.

Malpractice cover for a general surgeon in Long Island, New York, costs US$134 867. His counterpart in New Delhi pays only US$4000 (www.indushealth.com; Unti, 2009: 20). The cost is less because a lawsuit in India is less likely to be successful and a judge less likely to award realistic compensation. One consequence is that care costs less than if US$134 867 had to be factored in to the price.

The threat of legal action is a reason to eschew cost-cutting innovation. In older countries it can happen that a novel deviation from 'community standards' will be stigmatised by the profession as irresponsible and dangerous. Even if the status quo standard is believed, medically and economically, to be unnecessarily high, the regulators may still insist on protracted trials and cost-effectiveness studies: 'Thus, tort law can lock in expensive and conventional practices and expose potential disruptive innovators to liability' (Richman, Udayakumar, Mitchell and Schulman, 2008: 1268). Ossification in older countries is a form of insurance. It perpetuates practices that have stood the test of time. New countries can afford to be more daring. Prices are lower because new entrants are not afraid to break the mould.

An example would be the Narayana Hrudayalaya chain of hospitals in India. Its cut-price clinic provides no-frills surgery in prefabricated buildings. The wards have overhead fans. Nursing is minimal. Relatives are taught to change the dressings. More importantly, perhaps, the poor can afford to pay. Narayana Hrudayalaya says that, using the budget airlines as its model, it can perform heart surgery for US$800. It could not introduce a radical departure such as this if the climate of opinion were less receptive to new ideas.

4.2.3 Prices and Problems

Prices are lower abroad. Yet which price is the relevant price when profit-conscious facilities are tempted into price discrimination? Providers print multiple menus in order to maximise the revenue they capture from the differentiated submarkets of a stratified client base. The lowest price is an attractive price. It may not, however, be the price that the medical tourist is asked to pay.

Healthcare, because it is tailored to a single body, does not lend itself to arbitrage and resale. This gives hospitals the freedom to shade their prices in line with the perceived ability to pay. An example would be Care in India which 'provide[s] services either with minimal margins or below full cost (but above variable cost) to approximately 75 per cent of its patients' (Richman, Udayakumar, Mitchell and Schulman, 2008: 1263). The 75 per cent pay less. The 25 per cent pay over the odds. The hospital performs an *ad hominem* means test through the use of proxies such as place of residence or standard of ward. It is a test which few foreign patients are likely to pass.

Some international patients are charged at super-scale rates. Even Singapore is not safe from free markets that discredit themselves. A bill for S$26 million that was submitted in Singapore in 2007 to a member of the Brunei Royal Family led to a senior surgeon being fined and suspended for three years. One procedure alone, billed at S$211 000, was found to have been performed by a subcontractor for S$400. The Singapore Medical Council (SMC) ruled that doctors were bound by their internalised ethic not to overcharge for a service even if a mutually acceptable price had been agreed upon in advance. The SMC was confident that professional misconduct had occurred. What it could not do was to say precisely where the ethical limits lay.

Also in Singapore, a medical tourist from Indonesia was charged S$100 000 for a procedure that usually cost S$10 000: 'There have been enough cases of shameless profiteering to earn some hospitals here a bad reputation . . . The government hopes to promote medical tourism. But news of overcharging spreads very quickly abroad. Unless action is taken soon, greed will kill the golden goose' (Lee, 2008: A23). Historically, there once were Guidelines on Fees (GOF) in the Singapore private sector. They were promulgated by the doctors themselves through the Singapore Medical Association. In 2007 these Guidelines were swept away by the Competition Commission. The Commission maintained that, although never binding, floors and ceilings were leading to bunching. A wider spread of prices would better serve the consumer's interest.

In any case, the liberals reasoned, the Ministry of Health will continue to post the charges for a range of procedures in the Singapore state sector. Published benchmarks stabilise the variance in market prices. They give some indication of what an 'excessive' charge would be. Where there is transparency and the internet, patients and facilitators can avoid crass exploitation by researching the prices in the hospitals over which the Ministry has some influence.

The comparison is not entirely valid. Medical travellers in the public sector are not entitled to subsidised beds. Posted ward charges must be scaled up since they are the charges for the resident locals. Government-owned hospitals have operational independence. They set their own prices. Most foreign patients in any case are seen in the private sector where a comparison with public services may not be very useful. A famous specialist will normally charge more than the going rate because he is one-of-a-kind. Quantities too can confuse the estimates. Even if the doctors conform to a guideline price, their pursuit of a targeted income may induce them to supply more tests and more procedures than are clinically indicated.

Hospitals in Singapore, Thailand and Taiwan do not have a consistent policy of charging foreigners a discriminatory rate. Equity aside, they reason that more foreigners will come to their country if the aliens are quoted the local (private) price. In Korea, however, two-tier pricing is the norm. The result is a significant disparity between the rate posted by the hospitals on their website and the rate actually billed to non-Korean patients. Hospitals are required to publish the local rate but claim that foreigners are not covered by the law. There are no government guidelines on fair prices for medical tourists. The mark-up is 1.5–2 times in one survey, 2.5–3 times in another (Lee, 2010).

Local hospitals say that foreign patients cost them more. Foreign patients object that translators, food and airport transfers do not justify a multiplier that can approach 300 per cent. Exploitation or not, the average cost of medical care in Korea is 20 to 30 per cent less than in the United States. The Koreans should not expect that the Americans will necessarily come. The average charge in Thailand is 74 per cent less than the charge in Korea. Even in Singapore it is 20 per cent less. The Koreans must know that foreign patients do not like to be treated badly. Thailand and Singapore are always there.

Discrimination is not the only way in which pricing can be a problem. Lower prices can mean lower standards. An example would be pharmaceutical generics. They are less expensive than the drugs in top-end hospitals but they might not be as good. Some are genuinely marginal. Forgione and Smith warn that 'developing countries are flooded with counterfeit medications' (Forgione and Smith, 2006: 30), often ineffective, sometimes harmful, sometimes fatal. Drugs that normally require a doctor's prescription might be sold over the counter. The upside is that they are cheap. Presumably hospitals under scrutiny from regulators will use information technology (IT) to document and date-stamp their inventories in order to keep the quality up.

There is not much the JCI can do about malaria or dysentery in the surrounding environment. That is a risk to which even the most prestigious hospitals are exposed. The danger is that the lower-priced hospitals will cut corners on blood and sputum. Employees will be expected to take their own temperature before they report for work. If they are suffering from AIDS, they will be expected to reveal the truth even if it costs them their job.

4.2.4 State and Prices

Prices may be lower in a newer market because a hands-on government is providing financial support to create a new competitive advantage. Medical travel is a sunrise sector. The government may be funding seed-corn in the hope that an infant industry will develop into a major source of social spillovers. Whether the support is a *sine qua non* or a functionless rent is a question that can only be answered case by case. All that can be said with certainty is that governments are often in the business of artificial insemination. Support to medical travel is no more extreme a mode of trade distortion than support to electronics or aviation because that is what our nation needs. Public finance forgone or public subsidies paid out, measures such as these have the great advantage to the health tourist that they keep the price down.

Yet exemptions and subsidies can do harm as well as good. In terms of equity, lower prices confer a disproportionate benefit on rich locals and on foreign carpet-baggers who have not contributed to tax. Also, where foreigners are charged the marginal rather than the average cost, they are *de facto* passing their share in the fixed cost on to the government which will have to make up the shortfall. There is no reason to think that the locals will regard this transfer as fair.

In terms, moreover, of efficiency, proactive policies will function as non-tariff barriers. They can diminish trade even as they seek to divert it. The World Trade Organization (WTO) is opposed to discrimination. Developing countries argue that protection is essential for economic growth fed through import substitution and embryonic exports. Sometimes they are allowed to postpone the liberalisation of their international arrangements. Where this is granted, the exemptions and the subsidies may keep the price of healthcare down.

The state can further subsidise the price of care through general infrastructure such as education and roads. It can hand-pick a subset of hospitals for endorsement overseas. It can represent the medical exporters through international conferences and trade missions. It can also sponsor marketing strategies through bodies such as, in Cuba, Servimed: 'The success of the Cuban medical tourism model is due to the strategy of coordination and collaboration of the Ministry of Health with other institutions in tourism, commerce and industry' (Paffhausen, Peguero and Roche-Villareal, 2010: 26). Servimed markets hospitals, all of which are state-owned. It has a presence in territories as far-flung as Mongolia, Sudan, Kuwait and Angola. Servimed is a subsidiary of Cubanacan S.A., which operates a large chain of hotels in Cuba.

In Singapore there is SingaporeMedicine. In association with the Ministry of Health and the Ministry of Trade and Industry, it is a joint initiative of the Economic Development Board (which brings in new talents and investments), the Singapore Tourism Board (which markets Singapore as a recreational and business destination) and International Enterprise Singapore (which assists Singapore companies to penetrate new markets). The consortium has a stand at trade exhibitions. It publicises niche treatments. It promotes Singapore as a short-break destination.

In Korea there are the Council for Korea Medicine Overseas Promotion (CKMP), the Korea Health Industry Development Institute (KHIDI) and the Korea Tourism Organization (KTO). In Taiwan there is the Taiwan External Trade Development Council (TAITRA). In Costa Rica there is the Council for International Promotion of Costa Rica Medicine (PROMED). In Japan there is the Medical Tourism Promotion Office (MTPO). It is embedded in the Ministry of Land, Infrastructure, Transport and Tourism (MTILIT).

In Malaysia there is the National Committee for the Promotion of Medical and Health Tourism (NCPMHT), the Malaysia External Trade Development Association (MATRADE) and the Malaysian Healthcare Travel Council (MHTC). The Council has selected 72 out of the 253 private hospitals in Malaysia as the best suited to handle international patients. It operates a dedicated call centre for international patients and a reception counter at the airport. It has offices in Bangladesh, Indonesia and (for the North Asian market) Hong Kong. The private sector also markets the country directly through through the Association of Private Hospitals Malaysia (APHM).

Whether MHTC or APHM, the system is industrial self-regulation. If the Malaysian government is hands-on, it is hands-on at one remove. Hands-on or hands-off, at least the hospitals are not obliged to internalise the whole cost themselves. It keeps the prices down.

4.3 QUALITY

Cortez rightly says that ‘quality is the great unknown in medical tourism’ (Cortez, 2008: 107). Home or abroad, things can go wrong. The Australian Society of Plastic Surgeons, surveying its members in 2007, found that the risks abroad were especially great. Of 68 respondents, 40 said they had had to do repair work on patients returning from cosmetic surgeries such as breast augmentation in Malaysia and Thailand. It said: ‘Beware of slick advertising that promises the earth. Remember you get what you pay for’ (Australian Society of Plastic Surgeons, 2007).

4.3.1 A Low Standard

There is no denying that preventable cross-infection, avoidable complications, permanent scarring, simple mistakes, underinformed consent, mislabelled sperm, infected blood and unrefrigerated drugs can be a threat to the patient's health. Impure water may be used to cleanse medical apparatus. MRSA and NDM-1 can come in through the air-conditioning. Hospital staff, careless about hand hygiene, may carry germs from *favela* slums. The profit motive can lead to supply-side gambles. The patient might have to pay a second time to have the damage put right at home. Sometimes a home doctor will not want to patch up a foreign doctor's mistake. Sometimes even insured patients will not be in a position to claim for corrective procedures. Sometimes a botch will result in death.

Harling and his colleagues cite the case of hepatitis B, where the prevalence rate in India is 2 to 8 per cent. There is a growing tendency for South Asians in the UK to travel to India for care. Some have kidney transplants because of the shortage of donated organs in the UK. It is a mixed blessing: 'There is a thriving black market for human kidneys, screening of donors is inadequate, and renal transplants and haemodialysis are often carried out in small private clinics where standards of infection control are poor' (Harling, Turbitt, Millar, Ushiro-Lumb, Lacey, Xavier, Pope, Ijaz and Teo, 2007: 738–739). Doctors and nurses may be carriers. Equipment and clothing may be contaminated. Disease is passed on when the patients return to the UK. At the very least they should be counselled before departure, screened on their return: 'In fact there may be a case for offering free hepatitis B vaccination to all travellers to high-prevalence countries' (Harling, Turbitt, Millar, Ushiro-Lumb, Lacey, Xavier, Pope, Ijaz and Teo, 2007: 739).

Birch, Caulfield and Ramakrishnan found that 60 per cent of plastic surgeons in their UK sample had had to treat complications from cosmetic procedures performed abroad. They are by no means uncritical of patients who are lured by a cheap price in the East and then expect the NHS to pick up the pieces: 'They are an avoidable pressure on already overstretched plastic surgery, accident and emergency and general surgical units' (Birch, Caulfield and Ramakrishnan, 2007: 1077). Some investigators have put a price tag on the hidden costs. Miyagi in the UK studied 19 cases of cosmetic tourism that had subsequently to be put right. They found that the mean cost to the National Health Service was £6360 (Miyagi, Auberson, Patel and Malata, 2012: 22). Approximately equal to the full state pension for a year, it was not a negligible sum. The full cost of health tourism must include the cost of bending back the bent rod. It is a pollutant that must be corrected through the further commitment of scarce healthcare resources.

You get what you pay for. Surgeons may lack experience. Anaesthetics may be ineffective. Capital may be vintage. Auxiliaries may lack training. Medical expertise may be inappropriate. Medical certificates may be forged. The electricity supply may fail. Some countries may be so keen to establish themselves as epicentres in cutting-edge procedures that they overlook the extent to which the stem cells are bogus, the interventions untrialled, the accounts unaudited. MacReady speaks of 'unscrupulous charlatans' and 'questionable therapies' (MacReady, 2009: 318). Shetty draws attention to the lack of proper follow-up: 'Duty of care and accountability are particularly murky issues in cross-border health care' (Shetty, 2010: 671).

Things can go wrong. In spite of that, surveys of returning patients find that medical travellers are broadly speaking satisfied with their experience. A recent figure would be 90 per cent for orthopaedic patients, 88 per cent for dental patients, 80 per cent for cosmetic surgery patients (Treatment Abroad, 2012). Patients undergoing cosmetic surgery are notoriously difficult to please; and opinions on bestness are bound to differ. The 20 per cent who said they were 'not satisfied' may simply have been voicing the regrets and the disappointments that always accompany a free consumer choice. Or maybe not. Only 10 per cent of patients receiving cosmetic surgery in their own country reported that they were 'not satisfied'.

A kidney can be rejected. Liposuction can leave lumps and dents. Post-operative complications can set in. That is the risk the patient takes. The real question is not whether the dangers can be eliminated but whether they are greater in poor countries than rich. Turner, studying reported deaths, found no evidence that they were. Comparing good hospitals with good hospitals, he concluded that the correlation with national income was tenuous (Turner, 2012: 27).

Quality can slip. Yet it can also slip at home. Something like 98 000 Americans die each year because of medical error. Hodges and Kimball report that 'health care-associated infections continue to affect roughly 1 in 20 patients hospitalized in the United States. In Europe, healthcare-associated infections cause an estimated 37 000 deaths annually and add €7 billion (US$9.4 billion) in direct costs' (Hodges and Kimball, 2012: 122). In Europe the chance of error is 20 per cent. It is rather a lot of error.

National data in truth is misleading. A top-tier clinic in a Third World country will often have better-quality capital and manpower than a second-tier hospital in the USA or the UK. Medical travellers typically go to the high-standard hospitals. They are seen by an English-speaking specialist and not a houseman. They benefit from a high ratio of doctors and nurses to beds. They are treated with state-of-the-art equipment by local staff just returned from a refresher course. Outside it may be heat and dust. Inside it may be the best that money can buy.

4.3.2 Medical Outcomes

The proof of the pudding is in the eating. Good outcomes proxy the quality of the care: 'For example, the Apollo hospital chain has reportedly maintained a success rate of 99 percent in more than 50000 cardiac surgeries performed, which is on par with the surgical success rates of the best US cardiac surgery centers (such as the Cleveland Clinic)' (Mattoo and Rathindran, 2006: 360). The exact figure, at 99.6, is almost a perfect score (Meghani, 2011: 18). Of 138 bone marrow transplants, 87 per cent were successful. The figure for 6000 kidney transplants was 95 per cent. Only Cleveland Clinic and the Mayo Clinic surpassed Apollo's record (Oberholzer-Gee, Khanna and Knoop, 2005: 1). In Singapore the incidence of ventilator-associated pneumonias in 2005 was 2.53 per 1000 patient days. In the US it was 4.4 (Yap, 2007).

In Korea, the five-year survival rate for all surgeries is 96 per cent that of the USA (Ho, 2009: 34). The mortality rate for coronary bypass surgery at Fortis Escorts Heart Institute in India was 0.8 per cent at a time when the equivalent rate at New York Presbyterian Hospital was 2.35 per cent and few good hospitals in the United States could do better than 1.5 per cent (Cortez, 2008: 103n). The message is clear. The average quality of care in India is lower than in the West. Yet the real comparison is not with the average but with the top. The medical tourist having treatment at the top has good reason to expect at least the same chance of full recovery that he would have had at home.

Going abroad, there will be new risks. There are germs in the air against which the incomer will not have built up an immunity. It is common knowledge that poor countries play host to disease:

> One review found that 22 to 64 percent of people who travel to the developing world report some health problems, and that each day abroad increases the risk of illness 3 to 4 per cent. Two of the most common medical travel destinations, India and Thailand, are countries where infectious diseases of global concern such as TB and malaria are endemic. Asia accounted for 55 percent of all new TB cases in 2009. (Hodges and Kimball, 2012: 120)

There are the sun, water, food, reptiles, bugs and insects. There is the cultural and linguistic divide. There is the certainty of discomfort and the possibility of deep-vein thrombosis when a sick person takes a long-haul flight. There is the painful void when a support network of family and friends must remain behind.

The hospital may dispense with procedures which are non-chargeable and therefore a waste of time. The patient may find it hard to discover how many chargeable procedures can safely be packed into a single trip. It may be difficult to buttonhole an adviser who can spare the time to explain. Informed consent may be demanded after only a brief consultation.

There are costs as well as benefits. That is why track records and outcome indicators are essential if the patient is to make a rational choice. Needed is information on documented misdiagnosis, documented cross-infection, the ratio of complaints to procedures, the medium-term survival rate, the incidence of deaths on the operating table. The patient has the right to know the velocity of throughput as an indicator of focused expertise: 'Surgical complications and mortality rates are inversely related to the volume of procedures' (Mattoo and Rathindran, 2006: 366). Doctors specialise on an intervention. Because they perform it repeatedly, their expertise does not atrophy through lack of use.

4.3.3 Professional Qualifications

Education is not the same as competence. Even a certificate from a leading medical school is no guarantee that a doctor or nurse will be above-average in the field. That said, data on outcomes is usefully complemented by information on training. A top university in the United Kingdom, Australia or the United States is widely assumed to pass on state-of-the-art knowledge. A graduate from a top university is generally taken to be a professional who knows how to deliver a good quality of care.

Medical schools in the Third World benchmark curricula and practice on the First World brands. Many teach in English. Many adopt the textbooks that are the market leaders in the West. Some bring in foreign teachers who can reproduce and replicate. It makes the trust and the trustworthiness transitive. A must be good. He studied with B who studied with C.

Some medical schools in newer countries are peer-reviewed for best practice by transnational bodies like the World Federation for Medical Education and the Institute for International Medical Education. Some have established links with recognised foreign schools and world-class hospitals. Harvard Medical International is an associate of the Tokyo Medical and Dental University and of the University Hospital in Dubai. Johns Hopkins Medicine International has tie-ins with Apollo in India and Punta Pacifica in Panama; the Royal College of Surgeons of Ireland with the Medical University of Bahrain; Duke University with the National University of Singapore Medical School; the Mayo Clinic with Médica Sur in Mexico. Apart from the international transfer of expertise, these partnerships are a useful conduit for referrals upward where a case turns out to be too complicated for an up-and-coming country.

A Stackpole survey found that 67 per cent of responding US hospitals doing an international business had referral relationships (4 or 5 being the median) with hospitals outside the United States (Stackpole & Associates, 2010: 3).

Education signals quality. Certificates signal quality. Diplomas and credentials are easy to authenticate through the internet. Degrees will be complemented by professional awards such as the United States Medical Licensing Exam (USMLE) and the National Council Licensure Examination for Registered Nurses (NCLEX-RN). Medical personnel will be able to produce records of relicensing tests. They will hold appropriate memberships in international professional bodies. They will typically have done specialist courses overseas and served there as interns. About 220 of the 1200 doctors at Bumrungrad are board-certified in the United States (Cortez, 2008: 83).

4.3.4 Accreditation

The quality of the hospitals is assured through accreditation (repeated at regular intervals) by independent assessors. The boards are both national and international.

At the national level, there is the Health Care Accreditation Council of Jordan (HCAC), the Institute of Hospital Quality Improvement and Accreditation in Thailand (IHQIA), the Philippine Health Insurance Corporation (PHIC), the Malaysian Society for Quality in Health (MSQH). In India there is the National Accreditation Board for Hospitals and Healthcare Providers (NABH) (advised by the Australian Council on Healthcare Standards and the Confederation of Indian Industry) and the National Accreditation Board for Testing and Calibration Laboratories (NABL) (a part of the Board of Quality Control of India).

National boards, parastatal or private, are not always a success. The benchmarks can be imprecise, the follow-up intermittent, the enforcement imperfect. The norms can be too close to the American heuristic, too far removed from the local culture. Interpreted too strictly, they can perpetuate restrictive practices by making the market non-contestable. Interpreted too loosely, they can satisfy a popular preference for affordable medicine at the expense of the high-cost gold standard that the doctors believe to be best.

National boards are national. They describe what is more often than they recommend what ought to be. One-country certification inhibits meaningful comparisons. It also limits the mobility of labour and capital. Devolved to the state or province, it can mean separate registration even within a single citizenship. Multinational boards are the more reliable tool. They are the more likely to open doors and to promote medical travel.

At the international level the certifying function is performed by organisations such as Accreditation Canada International (ACI), the College of American Pathologists (CAP), the National Committee for Quality Assurance (NCQA), the European Society for Quality in Healthcare (ESQH), the Australian Council for Accreditation of Health Standards International (ACHSI). Three have a particularly high profile. They are the Joint Commission International (JCI) in the United States, the Trent International Accreditation Scheme (TAS) in the UK and the International Organization for Standardization (ISO) in Switzerland.

JCI was originally established (as the Joint Commission on Accreditation of Healthcare Organizations) to vet domestic facilities for Medicaid and Medicare. It is under the supervision of leading professional bodies such as the American Medical and the American Hospital Association. It expanded abroad in 1999. TAS came into being as a quality-control panel within the UK's National Health Service. The globalisation of its competence built outwards from its national base. The ISO, made up of representatives from 162 member states, was given the mandate in 1947 to monitor technological specifications. Its interest in hospitals and healthcare was an add-on to its core interest in capital.

Accreditors like the JCI, TAS and ISO are themselves accredited by the International Society for Quality in Health Care (ISQua). ISQua seeks to standardise the measures and the proficiencies while respecting the national differences. Acting as the regulator of the regulators, its stamp of approval is a signal that a body such as JCI will do its job.

Accreditation is a hallmark. It is an indicator – but not a guarantee – that world best practice may be expected. It is an indispensable marketing tool. In a study at Bumrungrad 62 per cent of patients said that accreditation played some role in their decision to seek treatment abroad: 19 per cent said it was the 'most important' factor, 36 per cent said that it was 'important' (Medical Tourism Association/Bumrungrad International, 2010: 25). The equivalent figures worldwide were 81 per cent, 59 per cent and 22 per cent (Medical Tourism Association, 2009: 36). Insurance companies and group plans share the patients' confidence in the piece of paper. They cannot afford to take a gamble with their shareholders' and their policyholders' money.

Accreditation has an upgrading effect. The improvement in quality benefits local as well as international patients. Where only 71 to 75 per cent of medical records in Jordan pre-accreditation were completed without a slip, post-accreditation the number rose to 88 to 98 per cent. The performance of 89 per cent of nurses was observed to have improved as a result of adopting the JCI benchmark (Abu Sneineh, 2011: 72). Ordinary Jordanians as well as foreign incomers were able to share in the spillover.

The boards are the impartial judge but their decisions do not come cheap. The JCI is paid by the facilities it inspects. The cost can be a burden and a deterrent, not least for smaller hospitals in less-developed countries. The JCI charges in the region of US$50 000 (plus expenses) for an accreditation that must be renewed every three years. The TAS is paid approximately US$80 000 for a non-European Union (EU) hospital with more than 600 beds. To that must be added the time spent in preparing the submission and interacting with the delegation.

There is also an element of risk. Applications do fail. Wishing to avoid the loss of face, candidates sometimes pay the validators to coach them in advance on what the panel will expect. Validators, receiving one fee for the test and a separate fee for the counselling, have been accused of pursuing a corporate, commercial agenda. The defence, and it is a good one, is that sick people will receive better treatment as a result.

Different agencies apply different standards. The result is a cacophony of unexplained hurdles policed by a multiplicity of shadow governments. A single accreditator, cross-border and non-profit, would ensure that inspection and audit are made consistent. A world government could issue a single certificate. There is no world government. There are, however, transnational bodies such as the World Health Organization (WHO).

4.3.5 National Regulation

Much depends on what the other players are doing. Crooks and Snyder rightly recognise the spectre of competitive devaluation and beggar-thy-neighbour market share where the regulations are not both comprehensive and cross-national: 'If these guidelines are developed piecemeal they risk being less effective or not implemented owing to worries that less regulated countries will develop pricing advantages' (Crooks and Snyder, 2010: 1466). It is not just hospitals but nations that are in the race for foreign business. Cohen draws attention to the possibility of 'regulatory races to the bottom' where each nation in order to compete must relax its prohibitions and controls (Cohen, 2012: 10). It is an arms race, a prisoners' dilemma, a chicken game. The first player to stand up for his principles will lose.

Nice guys finish last. One inference is that national regulation will be driven into the margins and the footnotes by the natural laws of privatisation and countervailing profit. A different inference would be that social democracy still has a chance against the libertarians and the economisers but only if it comes to terms with the new global order.

Nationally, the nation-state still has the power to mandate a clinical floor. It also has the carrots and the sticks that go with moral suasion. It can restrict social insurance to foreign hospitals that make a full disclosure of outcomes and readmission rates. It can exert informal pressure on destination states to provide adequate care for their poor and their hard-to-reach. It can direct its marketing boards not to represent local facilities which it knows to overcharge. The state can rely on affiliates and subsidiaries to apply home-country standards in order to attract home-country patients. An example of extra-territorial compliance would be the Centro Médico Internacional in Matamoros, Mexico. The Centro has chosen to adhere to all United States regulations on safety and medical care in order to safeguard its American business. It is situated 3.2 miles from the US border.

Regionally, the nation-state can enter into bilateral and geographical agreements that can coordinate policies and stave off the lose–lose dystopia. Blocs have reached consensus on core medical training, the recognition of licences, the portability of insurance. Countries have negotiated face-to-face to create a seamless protocol for follow-up treatment and a common platform for malpractice suits (Smith, Martinez Alvarez and Chanda, 2011: 278, 280). In some cases they have extended local subsidies and fees to patients from signatory states. The world is a big place. The region is a smaller place. It is more manageable. Most medical travel is within the region.

Worldwide, the nation-state has entered into multi-country pacts to universalise a common template. This is especially urgent where it is not just sick people but epidemic diseases that travel across the national frontiers. H7N9, like the Marxian proletariat, has no country. Nor does TB have much of a parliament. The Declaration of Istanbul on Organ Trafficking and Transplant Tourism in 2008 was a declaration of the nephrologists and not their governments. Multilateralism is lagging behind.

That, of course, is one of the attractions of going abroad. Regulation may be more permissive and less hands-on. Price and differentiation may compensate for the shortfall. Quality is a range and not an absolute. Who is to say when quality standards are too high, too low or just right?

4.3.6 Referrals and Monitors

Primary care contributes in its own right to quality. As always in the referral process, the family doctor learns from personal experience which specialist can be trusted to produce good results. Foreign doctors and hospitals know that they must please their customers if they are to enjoy continuing referrals.

The home-country doctor will examine the patient. He will make a first assessment of what has to be done. He will liaise with the foreign supplier to ensure that the referral is clear. Videoconferencing makes possible open-ended discussion. Later on, the home-country doctor will monitor the patient to ensure that the treatment was good.

There will be no interruption in the notes. There will be continuity of care. Outcomes will be tracked, often for years. A doctor's office is a talking shop. Patients share their experiences. Feedback gets the information out. It must have an impact on the future referrals that the first-call doctors make. The overseas surgeon will live in a house of glass.

With all of this, the economic relationships can be complex and ambiguous. The general practitioner agrees to take back the foreign doctor's mistake: can he insist on a waiver of liability or is he obliged to share the blame? The local doctor is a member of a professional association: what is the status of his watching brief when he invites a foreign doctor to perform a procedure deemed unethical in the patient's country of residence?

There is also the matter of fee-splitting. Bribery is illegal. Otherwise, it is said, a hospital would be endorsed not for its track-record but for its side-payments. An alternative view would be that the practice should be actively encouraged. A doctor known to be receiving a consideration for a referral becomes in that instant a party to the contract. If general practitioners were made financially liable for the treatment centres they select, they would have an incentive to screen foreign providers with especial attention.

4.3.7 Networks: The Internet and Social Capital

One survey found that 49 per cent of patients first discovered medical tourism through the internet. Only 17 per cent did so through a friend or relative (Medical Tourism Association, 2009: 34). Another study made the figures 44 per cent and 23 per cent (Medical Tourism Association/Bumrungrad International, 2010: 22). Another survey said 35 per cent through the internet and 45 per cent through personal contacts (Alsharif, Labonté and Lu, 2010: 320). Another study said 15 per cent through online search and 44 per cent through friends and relatives (Wagner, Dobrick and Verheyen, 2011: 13). The proportion of the population that goes online to research conditions and identify providers might be as high as 66.9 to 84 per cent (Wangberg, Andreassen, Kummervold, Wynn and Sørensen, 2009: 693). It might be 73 per cent (Medical Tourism Association, 2009: 34).

There is dispersion in the results but not necessarily inconsistency. Much depends on where the survey was carried out. Some cultures are more computer literate than others. Much also depends on the nature of the intervention. A study in the UK found that most patients who travelled for cosmetic surgery chose foreign providers through the internet. They were 'unlikely to consult their general practitioner out of fear of being judged' (Hanefeld, Lunt, Horsfall and Smith, 2012: e7997).

The samples are not friendly to the family doctor. Only 10 per cent (Wagner, Dobrick and Verheyen, 2011: 13) or 13 per cent (Alsharif, Labonté and Lu, 2010: 321) acted on the recommendation of a medical practitioner. Only 5 to 7 per cent used the services of a travel agent. Perhaps surprisingly, only 1 per cent sought information on the potential risks of medical treatment (Wagner, Dobrick and Verheyen, 2011: 13). Even the health-seeking, it would appear, like to bury their heads in the sand.

The internet allows low-cost, border-free, real-time transmission of files. A hospital with its own website can list its specialists and publicise its services. It can catalogue its accreditations, its success rates, the number of times a named doctor has performed a named intervention, the capital backup. It can provide testimonials from satisfied customers and pass on their telephone numbers. It can provide a link to related services in the country. It can showcase its hotel ('hospitel') wing that is there for long-stay patients and concerned companions. After that it can reel in its catch through an immediate 'Contact Us, 24/7'.

Schwartz reports that 'web sites actually influence the health-related decisions of 70 per cent of the people who consult them' (Schwartz, 2004: 56). The disadvantage is that there is no quality control in cyberspace. Ranking the sites, the posts and the blogs, Schwartz concludes that they omit and commit as they see fit: 'With rare exceptions, they're all doing an equally poor job' (Schwartz, 2004: 55). It is not expensive to publicise online. Since the primary purpose is to sell, information can be inaccurate, redecorated, exaggerated or massaged. Shoddy services and dangerous products can be touted as panaceas. Flagrant 'infomercials' can mislead and occasionally frighten. An unfounded slur can be posted by an over-critical patient or a Machiavellian competitor. There is no way of verifying if the complaint is justified. Reputation and income may be inexcusably harmed.

Lack of regulation traps online search between the unreliable and the non-comparable. Poor-quality surgery might be made to seem good. Before-and-after photographs might owe much to the airbrush. Patients are not doctors. They do not know a good gamma knife from a 64-slice scan. The sheer number of medical websites imposes search and transaction costs of its own. Steering gingerly between information overload and information asymmetry, Lunt and Carrera conclude that it can all end in tears: 'The information highway is no foolproof source of credible information' (Lunt and Carrera, 2011: 64).

Lunt and Carrera concede that 'regulation of online information, as such, is difficult on both practical and political grounds', but that the internet nonetheless cannot be left to its own devices: 'Self-regulation based on accepted benchmark/criteria may be an option that various stakeholders may be amenable to' (Lunt and Carrera, 2011: 64). The model would be the printed media where litigation may result if false claims are made and where advertising of medical services is often confined to verifiable facts alone.

Guidebooks like *Patients Beyond Borders* (separate editions are available for the major destinations) give an independent perspective. The *US News and World Report* annually publishes a league table, ranking them by 16 adult specialities, of 'America's Best Hospitals'. Television programmes and Thomson Reuter make known what is available. Also important, they publicise the abuses and the failures. It is not always easy to spot a quack or a miracle if all that one knows comes from an inflight magazine.

The internet is one superhighway. Social capital is another: 'Word of mouth and human perspectives have become probably the most effective do-it-yourself forms of accreditation' (Connell, 2011: 111). Personal recommendations may be especially influential in closed communities or established networks in a foreign land. An example would be overseas Indians, Mexicans or Koreans returning home for care. They have acquaintances in the new country and family members in the old.

These people have local knowledge. Reputation acquires momentum. Second-movers have to struggle to break in. Sometimes they do this by piggy-backing on the established image of an American parent, a Bumrungrad management team or a joint venture with a well-known partner such as the government itself.

It is the informal route to high-quality care. Medical centres want repeat business from friends of friends who are passing on the message. Some hospitals estimate that as many as 80 per cent of new patients come to them because of word of mouth. It is a recognised safeguard against malpractice. A chain like Fortis that does international business cannot afford to lose its good name. Reputation tends to snowball but it must first be acquired: 'The competitive market-driven nature of the industry acts as an incentive for hospitals to ensure that patients are happy with their aftercare' (Shetty, 2010: 672). Competition raises standards because success pays off in the currency of personal recommendations. The professional ethic is not the only safeguard against abuse. Capitalism imposes its own checks and balances on supplier-induced demand and unsatisfactory workmanship. There is a temptation to improve quality even as there is a countervailing tendency to cut corners and costs.

4.3.8 Facilitators

More formally, there are travel consultants, known as facilitators, who specialise in medical travel. They know the right questions to ask. They can advise on prices, waits, amenities, translators, legal rights, legal systems, special diets, track records. Good facilitators will have visited the hospitals to form a first-hand impression. They will know if nearby beaches are polluted. In cases where there is no JCI accreditation (where, for example, the professional is a dentist in sole practice), the facilitator can give a personal assessment. The facilitator can advise the patients on alternative destinations and guide them through the confusing scenarios. Acting as travel agents, facilitators book flights, transfers, tours and hotels. Facilitators make hospital appointments. They arrange for the translation of notes. Some have an on-the-spot representative who befriends the patient from arrival to departure.

Facilitators make the market more rational and more transparent. Some are general: Planet Hospital, MedJourneys and Medretreat ('where smart medicine and exotic travel come together'). Others concentrate on a single medical condition or a single foreign country: IndUShealth for India, Plenitas for Argentina, Go Cuba and Choice Medical Services for Cuba. Some have long-standing partnerships with foreign hospitals that neither party would wish to jeopardise. Some cater to whole groups such as a small company that wants to reduce its medical overhead.

Some facilitators have had medical training. In Russia some doctors double as agents for extra income. Most have not. Lacking medical knowledge, they can only summarise the facts. Facilitators have no medical liability save where they examine the patient and make a clinical diagnosis. Even if they are in the wrong, it is not easy to serve a summons on a virtual entity that may be no more than a Blackberry in a basement. The turnover in the industry is high. Entry is easy and so is fly-by-night. One study, examining medical tourism companies based in Canada, found that half had gone out of business (Turner, 2011b). Another study, attempting a follow-up, found that 15.6 per cent of facilitators originally interviewed could no longer be contacted two years down the road (Alleman, Luger, Reisinger, Martin, Horowitz and Cram, 2010: 496). By that time they had changed their name and gone into something else.

Facilitators face a worrisome conflict of interest that was documented in one sample survey as follows: 'Almost one third of companies engaged in promoting medical travel received referral fees from the overseas providers to whom they were referring patients . . . The payments have the potential to influence the providers to whom companies choose to refer patients with potentially worrisome results' (Alleman, Luger, Reisinger, Martin, Horowitz and Cram, 2010: 496). Not only the providers but the procedures as well: 'Because medical tourism companies profit from arranging medical procedures, there is risk of a framing effect in which benefits of treatment are highlighted and risks of treatment are minimized' (Turner, 2011a: 4).

About half of the facilitators, commercial and gain-seeking, were found in a survey to be sending Americans abroad for unapproved therapies. They were doing this 'even in the absence of rigorous clinical data about safety and treatment efficacy' (Alleman, Luger, Reisinger, Martin, Horowitz and Cram, 2010: 496). It seems to be a clear case of supplier-induced demand. In medical travel, however, nothing is ever clear. The evidence does not reveal whether the patients first approached the facilitators for the stem cells or whether the facilitators first pushed the therapies because money is the root of all evil.

Forgione and Smith are not convinced that all facilitators are up to the mark. Some, they say, have little grammar and less common sense: 'Some offer free medical opinions by email without the doctor's ever having to examine the patient in person. Many offer commissions up to 20 per cent or more for patient referrals – a felony if accepted directly or indirectly by a doctor in the United States' (Forgione and Smith, 2006: 32). Some require waiver clauses. Some breach confidentiality. Some abscond with the money. Some, coming from the tourism industry, cover their ignorance by recommending only JCI-validated clinics. The best buttress is a test. This will promote the universalisation of best possible practice: 'Given their role in organizing health services for patients, medical tourism companies should be subject to external evaluation and accreditation' (Turner, 2011a: 2).

Cortez says that 'licensing would make the market more transparent' (Cortez, 2008: 125). Examining and registering would act as a clearing-house for quality. Certification is already being provided by non-profit trade associations such as the Medical Tourism Travel Association, the Medical Tourism Association and HealthCare Tourism International. They are supported by independent consultancy firms like Medical Insights International and Medical Tourism. Not only do these associations insist upon top-score standards and an annual report, but they also provide a complaints and appeal mechanism.

At some stage their activities could be amplified into a mandatory compensation fund. Patients who did not employ a licensed facilitator would not enjoy this protection. Patients who did would be covered against errors, complications, unexpected stays and emergency repatriation.

The question the international patient must answer is whether it is worthwhile to go abroad through an agency. At Bumrungrad (a hospital with name recognition and JCI status), a study found that 9 per cent of all patients were recommended to it by a facilitator. About 80 per cent of those patients reported that the agent had been 'extremely helpful'. In spite of that, only 27 per cent said they would advise a future patient to pay for a middleman (Medical Tourism Association/Bumrungrad International, 2010: 23, 24). Worldwide, the figures were significantly different: 51 per cent of respondents had used an intermediary and 59 per cent believed that future patients should do the same (Medical Tourism Association, 2009: 35). The figures vary from country to country and condition to condition. Patients with life-threatening conditions were more likely to take advice.

Some observers estimate that less than 20 per cent of Americans going abroad are using a facilitator. Most (especially prevalent among dental patients) are booking do-it-yourself (DIY). The marketplace is evolving. Hotel reservations and airline tickets are increasingly DIY. It is not just outsourcing that is going through an electronic revolution.

4.3.9 Malpractice

When all else fails, there is the suit. It is a counsel of desperation. Litigation in a foreign language is difficult to follow. The court protocol is not the same. Norms governing accountability, the rule of law and the sanctity of life may be different. The jurisdiction is that of the provider, not the consumer: the exception is where the foreign hospital maintains an office in a high-damages country or where it is the subsidiary of another country's chain. The foreign patient may need to return regularly to testify. The award may not warrant the expense of legal representation, accommodation, travel and translators. Judges may baulk at compensation for subjectivities like 'pain and suffering'. The sums awarded may be small: 'The average medical malpractice payout in the United States, through both court judgments and settlements, is around $312 000. In contrast, the average payout is only $2500 in Thailand and $4800 in Mexico' (Cortez, 2012: 193). There is also the delay. Anecdotes can be cited of lawsuits that took up to 25 years to resolve.

Hospitals often refuse to release notes and medical records. Doctors often decline to testify against one another. In some countries the doctor-defendant must admit to negligence. There is little case law or precedent. Contingency fees are not always permitted. The courts in Singapore have traditionally assumed that the doctor knows best: 'Judges are not permitted to determine the reasonableness of the medical opinion . . . even if it is shown that the medical practice is wrong' (Amirthalingam, 2003:137).

Loopholes such as medical history or a co-existent complaint may make legal redress difficult. Contributory negligence may be alleged where the patient had not seen a dentist for years or where the referring doctor had done insufficient tests. Cosmetic surgery is a legal minefield. Expectations are quintessentially idiosyncratic. There is also a question of distributional inequity. The poorest of the poor do not have the resources to sue. Mexican-American labourers travelling home for care will barely be able to pay for the bus. Presumably a cohort of patients with a common grievance could club together to lodge a class action abroad. A phalanx of litigants would spread the overheads. It would make the courts more accessible.

Even at home, guilt is not always easy to establish. In the US the 'blood shield laws' exempt blood, blood products, human tissues, organs and sometimes semen from product liability suits. A wronged consumer does not have a right of redress. Treatments that are not permitted in the United States cannot be taken before an American judge. American-owned hospitals abroad might avoid interventions that are forbidden or experimental at home. Good citizenship is a business asset. An out-of-court settlement, free corrective surgery, a full refund may be offered without admission of liability in order to avoid adverse publicity.

Corporate self-restraint need not work to the benefit of the consumer. Americans abroad might be driven into lower-quality hospitals which put them at greater risk. This grey area will often be the very reason why they choose medical travel. Transplants, euthanasia, stem cells and surrogacy are procedures for which the law, domestic or international, is not watertight. Legal action is a gamble.

A lawsuit involves a defendant. One of the greatest problems in a malpractice suit is to identify the locus of guilt.

The chain of contract begins at home, with the facilitators, the doctors and the insurers who dispatch the client to his doom. While brokers who do not actually supply medical treatments do not have vicarious liability for medical slippage, a claim may still be made that they were negligent in researching a hospital's standards or did not warn the patient against misleading publicity. A similar claim could be made against a referring doctor. The doctor could be accused of sketchy history-taking or a failure to pick up a major allergy. He could be sued for underestimating the risks in a service delivered abroad.

By the same token a domestic insurer such as an employer's group plan or the UK's National Health could be sued on the grounds that it cut corners on due diligence. The charge will be that they should have known that the outsourced supplier was manifestly inadequate. The defence will be that the foreign supplier was not responsible for cross-infection with AIDS since the foreign supplier effectively did his best. Informed consent never extends to all eventualities.

The defence will be that no one, domestic or foreign, can be expected to work wonders all the time. Prevention is better than care. Where domestic insurers are financially liable for repair surgery, they would have a strong incentive to weed out treatment centres likely to impose a downstream burden later on. They would also want to conduct pre- and post-operative physicals to ensure that the patient does not fabricate malpractice in the expectation of a settlement.

The chain of contract continues in the foreign country. A foreign hospital might be sued on the ethical principle of *primum non nocere*. The principle of non-maleficence means that avoidable harm must not be inflicted, especially such as would leave the patient worse off than before: 'A medically indicated elective procedure performed under substandard conditions could do more harm than good' (Weiss, Spataro, Kodner and Keune, 2010: 598). The illegal use of locally produced generics or the excessive use of non-prescription antibiotics might count as avoidable harm. So might infected blood.

A foreign doctor, again, might be sued for the recurrence of a complaint when it ought to have been under guarantee. The doctor's defence might be that delayed symptoms or post-operative complications only detected after the patient returned home can no longer be laid at the door of the treatment centre that was visited abroad. Too much water has passed under the bridge.

The malpractice suit is always problematic. To cover the risk some health travellers take out earmarked insurance. It may not be value for money due to the disclaimers, the escape clauses and the cost. Besides that, a policy in advance of an operation is an acknowledgment that something might go badly wrong. Patients want to get well. They do not want to think about damages if the wrong leg is amputated or they are dropped on the floor.

The fear of a mistake seems not in any case to be a widespread anxiety. A survey at Bumrungrad found that only 19 per cent of respondents were concerned about litigation overseas for medical malpractice: 56 said they were 'not concerned at all' while 25 per cent described it as a 'small concern' (Medical Tourism Association/Bumrungrad Hospital, 2010: 25). If we cannot trust our doctors, who then can we trust? It is best not to answer that question.

5. Difference

Western medicine has become general. New hospitals, like old hospitals, incorporate the lessons of biomedical research. Difference is more often marginal changes in the same universal drill than it is a revolutionary new departure that transforms monopolistic competition into a walled-in local monopoly. Yet difference it is nonetheless and it is a powerful selling point. Youngman, welcoming the many in the one, advises new suppliers that they should not make the mistake of assuming that one size fits all: 'If you want to fail, market to everyone the same way with every treatment and concentrate on price. If you want to succeed, select niches and specific markets within individual countries and find out what their buying triggers are' (Youngman, 2012).

This chapter is about the many in the one. Section 5.1, 'The right pond', is concerned with selecting the niche and capturing the triggers. Section 5.2, 'Location', says that sometimes the stock in trade will be no more than a convenient spot at a crossroads bottleneck. Section 5.3, 'Cultural community', argues that a shared lifestyle and a common world-view are themselves business assets that deliver a head-start advantage. Section 5.4, 'The trade in body parts' and section 5.5, 'The trade in births', say that sometimes the most lucrative pond will be out of bounds because morally it is taboo.

5.1 THE RIGHT POND

Going abroad gives the patient access to a range of services, some of them essential, that cannot be found at home. Such patients may be seen as health refugees or health exiles. What they need cannot be had without a trip.

There may be the opportunity to participate in the clinical trial of a wonder-drug or a new procedure. There may be the chance to benefit from alternative, fringe and experimental treatments. There are natural resources such as unpolluted salt mines, sulphur-rich swamps, invigorating mud, *onsen* hot springs and the Dead Sea float. There are cultural resources such as shamans, ashrams, gurus, herbalists, yoga, acupuncture, temple retreats, Ayurveda and traditional Chinese medicine (TCM). In the

Philippines there are kidney transplants, the Philippine Heart Center and, in Baguio, faith-healers who can remove an organ without a cut. In Cuba there are skin clinics for vertiligo and psoriasis, eye clinics for retinitis pigmentosa. The genuinely unique attracts.

Abroad can mean risky amniocentesis for a congenital anomaly. Abroad can mean prenatal screening for the gender of the foetus. Abroad can mean sex selection, human cloning, businesslike abortion, a kidney transplant from an anonymous cadaver, a kidney transplant from a living donor, designer babies mixed in a test tube, assisted conception for an unmarried or for an over-age woman, donor anonymity to prevent lifespan tracing. Abroad can also mean the opposite: well-documented sperm or egg with a photograph of the donor and proof of IQ. Race is relevant. Parents might prefer that their babies be ethnically appropriate. Travellers wanting white sperm and Caucasian eggs will go to Argentina and not to Zimbabwe. Sometimes they will order more cream in their coffee because a lighter-skinned child may be regarded as more prestigious.

Abroad can mean sex change without the embarrassment of counselling, the implantation of an inter-uterine device in an under-age girl, bariatric surgery for an obese teenager, a xenotransplant from an animal to a human. Abroad can mean the insemination of a woman with the frozen sperm of her late husband. Abroad can mean assisted suicide for patients in terminal pain. Euthanasia is permitted in Switzerland. It is prohibited in Germany. It is confined to residents in Holland, Belgium and Oregon.

Death tourism, like reproductive tourism, widens the freedom to choose. Stem cell tourism has the same effect where the patient is denied the untested service at home. Stem cell therapies are available to paying customers in over 700 clinics in countries such as Costa Rica, Russia, India and China. Patients, trapped between hype and hope, grasp at straws: 'If we remove alternative options for these individuals, there may be an argument that we rob them of hope, hope that itself could produce a net beneficial outcome . . . The power of hope can often trump the power of expertise' (Murdoch and Scott, 2010: 20, 21). No one wants to admit failure or give up. No one wants to suffer from muscular dystrophy or be condemned to a wheelchair if a cure can be found.

Fraud cannot be ruled out. The regulation of regenerative medicine is thin or non-existent. There may be a placebo effect which patients mistake for a permanent cure. Yet there might also be a real improvement. Lack of scientific knowledge can work both ways. Paternalism, erring on the side of caution, can deny to a whole cohort the benefit of new procedures while it protects itself through multiple trials. Hip resurfacing was available to Americans in Canada, Europe and Asia before, in 2006, it was ultimately licensed at home. Delay is not necessarily the right response.

Tolerance and discourse without endorsement or condemnation might be a more balanced reaction: 'Wholesale dismissal is not the proper scientific response to all stories of unknowns in science' (Murdoch and Scott, 2010: 21). Meanwhile the patients go abroad.

Differentiation exists because the cultures differ in their attitude to risk and their valuation of life. The nations do not see eye to eye on human rights, moral conventions and family values. Differences in history, economy, religion, politics and society have created an international marketplace for sterilisation, contraception and *in vitro* fertilisation precisely because different world-views legitimise different codes and statutes. When in Rome do as the Romans do. Yet there is something else. Consensus aside, countries differ in perceived proficiency. Even if the service is available at home, differences in quality may make the cost and the inconvenience of travel worthwhile.

Superior experience comes from and consolidates the head start. Routine procedures are cheaper in Thailand or Colombia. What the US is selling is the quantum leap: 'The treatment of less complex illnesses is easily within the capabilities of physicians in developing countries. The advantage of US hospitals lies in complex care and oncology [that] few hospitals in emerging countries can provide' (Lee and Davis, 2004: 43). The advantage of United States hospitals lies in complicated surgery for which top-notch training, uncontaminated blood, high-tech equipment and fault-free laboratories are believed to be *de rigeur*. Familiar names like the M.D. Anderson Cancer Centre, Mount Sinai Medical Centre and Johns Hopkins Hospital are synonymous with best possible care. They can safely leave the cosmetic surgery, the check-ups, the fillings, the detoxification and the tooth whitening to new entrants who have yet to refine their technique.

Travel abroad by itself differentiates the product. A famous surgeon or a brand-name clinic may be seen by the status-conscious as a conspicuous consumable. Alternatively, patients may seek out a foreign clinic because distance and isolation can buy them privacy and confidentiality. Anonymity and discretion are a plus in the case of bosom rejuvenation, drug addiction, alcoholism and abortion. Especially if they are well known, patients will want to escape publicity. Rehabilitation at the Crossroads Centre in Antigua, with internationally trained staff, is not only one-third cheaper than at the Betty Ford Center in Rancho Mirage, California, it is also more remote. There are no paparazzi in Antigua. When the patient returns home, the improvement in his health might simply be put down to the rest.

The rest itself is a differentiating factor. Countries differ in their recreational facilities. Thailand offers not just surgery but also tours, temples and convalescence on the beach. It has an established infrastructure of buses, restaurants and hotels. Its hospitals are conveniently situated in the capital, the main resort areas and the retirement centres. In the United States, Orlando boasts not just Disney World and Cape Canaveral but also a 650-acre medical complex, the Lake Nona Medical City, in partnership with the University of Central Florida Medical School. In South Africa there is the option of a safari. In Singapore there is the Asian Civilisations Museum and the casinos. In India some treatment centres offer holistic healing on the premises plus a trip to the textile workshops at Kanchipuram.

The US offers a medical holiday with a difference. It offers birthright tourism. Children born on the territory of the United States automatically acquire American citizenship. It is worth the outlay for a passport and a flight if a child will be born an American. Not all at once but later on the US-born child can take steps to bring in his aged parents as his filial dependents. In Hong Kong it is not full citizenship but at least it is permanent residence. Pregnancy tourism is seed corn. It is an investment in the parents' old age. Weight loss in Mexico or a firmer chin in Korea are seed corn as well. De-stressing and self-esteem can lead to a better-paying job.

The image of the country itself differentiates the product. Stereotyping attracts. Association of ideas repels. Slobovia is drug-fuelled murders and cross-infected blood. North Bodoh is slumdogs and flies on the food. Thailand is orchids and luxury hotels. Singapore is clean and green. The presentation of the treatment centres makes a contribution of its own. A piano in the lobby. A conference room for recovering chief executive officers (CEOs). A cinema showing recent releases. In promoting their amenities the hospitals contribute to the image of health tourism as a whole.

Perceived difference draws the business in. Rightly or wrongly, a consumer culture is a materialistic culture. The product must look like value for money. Cutting-edge technologies are marketed and publicised. The website is attractively designed, multilingual and welcoming. Electronic booking enables patients to make appointments without delay. Diagnostic tests are scheduled in the patient's home country and town. Emergency visas are arranged for collection at the airport. Interpreters are on hand. Front desk and concierge staff have a professional look.

Suites are luxurious. Décor is appropriate. Music is played in a darkened hall, temperature controlled. It relaxes the body and focuses the mind. Prayer rooms, prayer mats, halal, kosher and vegetarian food are on offer. They convey the unwritten message that the hospital is sensitive to cultural diversity.

Bumrungrad is in the tourist area. It has restaurants, several Starbucks, a McDonald's. It has a travel agency. It is located near the shopping malls. One patient commented: 'The hospital looks quite modern and even the faint hospital smell is masked by an overriding odor of capitalism' (Leenhouts, 2009: 23). Be that as it may, it differentiates its product and differentiates Thailand as well.

5.2 LOCATION

A geographical catchment is larger than a nation-state but smaller than the world. Much that is called global health is in fact intra-regional health. Comparative advantage is to a significant extent a neighbourhood thing. Long-haul is painful, disruptive and costly. Distance is a deterrent. Most medical travel, as Hamid states, is care close to home: 'It is time for the latitudes and longitudes in global healthcare to be defined. The sooner the regional context of globalisation is taken cognisance of, the better served will be patient mobility around the world' (Hamid, 2010).

Location draws lines between the pools. In Hungary the border town of Sopron has 200 dentists and 200 optometrists out of a total population of 20000 (Herrick, 2007: 5). In Sopron, 42 per cent of all practices report that at least 60 per cent of their revenue comes from foreigners. Many of the dentists speak German (Österle, Balázs and Delgado, 2009: 427). Travelling by land, 84 per cent of foreign dental patients in Western Hungary come from Austria. Travelling by air, about one-fifth of foreign dental patients in Budapest are from the United Kingdom. Budapest is cheap, it is near and most patients do not need a visa. Dentistry is well suited to medical travel. It is not normally an emergency procedure. Also, because patients are not seeing a dentist for the first time, they know what price and quality to expect.

Clinics, dental and medical, flourish in Matamoros, Nogales and Nuevo Progreso on the Mexican–US border. Some are owned by Mexicans and some by Americans. In Los Algodones dentistry costs 10 per cent to 30 per cent of the price in the USA. There are between 200 and 300 dentists in Los Algodones, where the resident population of 5474 plays host each day to 3000 day-trippers (Hyo-Mi, Leong, Heob, Gaitz and Anderson, 2009: 70). In some towns in northern Mexico approximately 80 per cent to 90 per cent of the dental patients are American. About two-thirds of them are aged 60 and above. At the same time there are ethnic Mexicans residing in neighbouring California, Arizona, New Mexico and Texas. They depend on Mexico for their eyeglasses, prescription drugs, check-ups and even surgery.

The numbers are there but their significance should not be exaggerated. There is not a single hospital in Mexico that sees more Americans than Mexicans. The hospital with the highest proportion of Americans is Christus Hospital at Reynosa. Reynosa is only ten minutes by car from the border. In spite of that, Americans make up only 30 per cent to 35 per cent of the inpatient census (Hyo-Mi, Leong, Heob, Gaitz and Anderson, 2009: 70). Location is not the only way in which the Mexican hospitals cover their rent.

Old friends are the devil we know. Medical tourists from Latin America spend US$6 billion a year on treatment overseas (Bookman and Bookman, 2007: 3). It is approximately the same amount as is spent on medical travel by the whole of the OECD (Organisation for Economic Co-operation and Development, 2011: 158). About 87 per cent make their way to the United States or Canada. The Latins are looking north. The numbers are very different for medical tourists from other regions. Only 58 per cent of all patients from the Middle East, 33 per cent from Europe and 6 per cent from Asia are treating North America as their main point of reference.

As for the Americans the bias is still regional but markedly less so. About 26 per cent of American medical travellers went to South America and a further 27 per cent to Mexico or Canada (Ehrbeck, Guevara and Mango, 2008: 5). This means that only 53 per cent of American medical travellers stayed within the region. Just under half were going outside.

In Europe, as was discussed in Chapter 3, Belgium, the Netherlands, France and Germany have economic regions that span the frontiers. It makes sense for them to integrate some or all of their facilities on a multinational basis. In Germany 88 per cent of healthcare service imports originate within the European Union (EU). Even in island Britain the figure is 61 (Lautier, 2013: 13).

In Scandinavia, one Swede in ten has seen a doctor in the Baltic states. In the Middle East, between 70 and 90 per cent of foreign patients in Jordan originate in the Arab world: 1800 Americans, 1200 British, 400 Canadians, but 45000 Iraqis, 20000 Yemenis and 10000 Libyans (Abu Sneineh, 2011: 72). Non-Jordanian Arabs occupy as many as a quarter of the hospital beds in Jordan. In Tunisia the pattern is similar. There 84 per cent of foreign patients come from neighbouring countries (Lautier, 2013: 13). The potential is great. Just as growing China lies within Bangkok's natural catchment, so sub-Saharan Africa is only a few hours by plane from the hospitals in Tunis.

As for Turkey, ideally placed between Europe, Central Asia and the Arab countries, it is trying to draw patients from the distant United States but obtains significantly more business from Syria, Iraq and Azerbaijan. Location sells, as South Africa has found out. As much as 85 per cent of South Africa's medical tourists are from other African countries, just as 80 per cent in Cuba are from Latin America or Canada. Only 4.3 per cent of foreign patients in South Africa come from the UK and 3.1 per cent from Germany (Crush, Chikanda and Maswikwa, forthcoming). Rather than pursuing the highly contested Western market, South Africa should learn from the example of Turkey that only a fool turns his back on a bird in the hand.

In Asia, short distances make a difference. About 70 per cent of medical incomers in Korea are from North Asia: 20 per cent from China, 20 per cent from Japan. In planning their Jeju Healthcare Town, the Koreans were aware that 18 Asian cities, each with a population of 5 to 10 million, are situated only a two-hour flight away. The list includes Tokyo, Beijing, Shanghai and Hong Kong.

Thailand recruits between 80 and 90 per cent of its foreign patients from South-East Asia and the Middle East. Most patients spend less than seven hours on the plane, and most of them much less. In 2012 at the Bangkok Hospital 20 per cent of patients were from the United Arab Emirates, 16 per cent from Myanmar, 13 per cent from Qatar and only 2 per cent from the United States. There are only about 220 of them per month, and mainly resident in Thailand. Only a small number of US-based Americans travel all the way to Thailand for care. Hospitals in Udon Thani and Chiang Mai see a number of patients from Laos and Cambodia for whom Thailand is the neighbourhood centre of excellence. The Franco-Vietnamese Hospital in Vietnam at one time saw so many patients from Cambodia that it operated its own shuttle.

About 10 per cent of foreign patients in Malaysia are from Singapore. About 14 per cent of foreign patients in Singapore are from Malaysia (Frost & Sullivan, 2012: 13). By far the largest single group of foreign patients in both countries are, however, the Indonesians. Approximately two-thirds to three-quarters of the foreign patients in Malaysia and almost one-half of the foreign patients in Singapore come from Indonesia. Medan is practically the suburbs of Penang. Pekanbaru is a ferry-ride from Malacca. Jakarta is just over an hour by plane from Singapore.

The proximity to Indonesia is a hostage to fortune. In Singapore 47 per cent of foreign patients come from Indonesia and 14 per cent from Malaysia. The next three concentrations of incomers to Singapore are all but insignificant: 5 per cent from Bangladesh, 4.1 per cent from Vietnam and 2.7 per cent from Myanmar. Americans and Britons are no longer in the top five nationalities. Other destinations are nearer and cheaper. Indonesia, currently one of the top suppliers of medical tourists in the world, will one day want to build its own medical cities. Apart from rising incomes at home, there are multinationals in Indonesia that are currently airlifting injured employees to Singapore or Dubai whenever there is an earthquake, a tidal wave, a terrorist bomb or a fire on an oil rig. They would not have to do this if Indonesia itself were to become a regional hub. A comparison may be drawn with Bermuda. In 2010 money spent out-of-country was 15 per cent of the nation's total expenditure on care. It was a leak that could be plugged. Bermuda is building hospitals of its own in order to reverse the flow.

In Oman there was a fall of 92 per cent in government-funded overseas travel for cancer care when a specialist oncology centre was opened locally. In Abu Dhabi the equivalent fall for cardiology was 55 per cent (Ehrbeck, Guevara and Mango, 2008: 8). The Dubai Healthcare City offers a range of services for patients from the Middle East but also from the Maldives, Sri Lanka, Nepal, Bhutan, Afghanistan, Bangladesh and Pakistan. In the past they would have travelled to India, Thailand or Singapore. Tradition was pushed aside by proximity. Nigeria deserves to be next. Its healthcare system was ranked 197th out of 200 nations in the world by the World Trade Organization (WTO). About 60 000 of its people go abroad each year for medical care. India earned over US$260 million from Nigerian patients alone in 2012. Things are changing. The Apollo group from India is already advising the Lagoon group in Nigeria how to proceed to Joint Commission International (JCI) accreditation (*International Medical Travel Journal*, 2013c).

Patients like what is near at hand if it is reliable, price-competitive and good. So do their social insurance agencies. Historically, over 80 per cent of patients going abroad from Kuwait have been funded by their government. The average cost to the social insurance budget has been US$200 000. The burden on public spending and foreign exchange is not sustainable.

5.3 CULTURAL COMMUNITY

Globalisation is mobility. People move from one country to another. Frequently they move more than once. Sometimes they change their citizenship as well as their residence. Their culture is less amenable to rapid transformation. One consequence is that some emigrants will want to return to their origins when they are ill. They will want to experience their medical encounter in a familiar cultural setting. The latent demand is there. Three per cent of the world's population (approximately 215 million people) already live outside the country of their birth (Warner, 2009: 3).

More migrants mean more exports. Migrants demand products that satisfy their traditional and remembered needs even as their consumption patterns reflect their education, income and peer-group abroad. Lennon has documented the feedback effect on the volume and structure of exports from the country left behind. She finds that it has a class bias: 'Doubling the number of highly qualified migrants increases services exports by 14.7 per cent, and goods exports by 9.3 per cent. When considering migrants with low level of education the effects are 4.3 per cent and 6.7 per cent respectively' (Lennon, 2009: 15).

In the case of better-educated emigrants it is services rather than goods that increase the more rapidly. In the case of less-educated emigrants the rankings are reversed. The core point is, however, the cultural community. Some Indian-Americans fly to India when they require elective surgery. Other Indian-Americans buy Indian saris because a sari is the look of home. Either way, services or goods, emigration always has a positive effect on the old country's trade.

Going home produces comfort as well as cure. Comfort in itself is therapeutic. Lee, Kearns and Friesen, studying first-generation Korean immigrants in New Zealand, explain that identity and 'emotional geography' should be seen as an independent cause of demand: 'Our investigation suggests that patients not only seek effective health care but also *affective* care in which notions of being "in-place", trust and familiarity are significant factors in promoting feelings of well-being' (Lee, Kearns and Friesen, 2010: 114).

Communication is non-verbal signals as well as linguistic codes. Word-tools are embedded in communities that travel with their own proscriptions and prescriptions. Cultures differ in their reactions to transfusions and transplants, in their dietary norms and their religious observances. To read the patient it is necessary to access the baggage. One solution is for patients living in the diaspora to return to the tribe of their birth when they are seriously unwell.

Home and homeland are two different concepts. First-generation emigrants will often have extended networks in the country that they left. They might have come back to the homeland of their birth primarily for a holiday and a family reunion. Local knowledge is a source of information about doctors and hospitals, while blood and kinship ensure companionship and support. Yet there is more to going back than simply the utilitarian means to a clinical end: 'Home is as much a "feeling" as a physical place where one experiences attachment and is able to gain a sense of security, belonging and identity' (Lee, Kearns and Friesen, 2010: 109). Community is a closed shop. Cultural competency makes medicine difficult if the doctor is not one of us.

Lee, Kearns and Friesen found that Koreans in New Zealand were used to Korean-style customs and mores. The Western system was not satisfying their acculturated expectations. In Korea the doctor is authoritative, assertive and confident. If the doctor hesitates, an admission of uncertainty undermines the patient's trust in his proficiency. The Koreans in New Zealand tended to describe such a doctor as 'stupid'.

In Korea the doctor speaks to the family unit as a whole. Koreans do not understand why the patient in New Zealand is told the diagnosis in private. Koreans say that the relatives are involved and have a need to know. Again, in Korea self-diagnosis is common. The first port of call is the specialist. Koreans in New Zealand see no reason to approach a general practitioner for a referral. A referral means a wait. Koreans do not appreciate a delay. Finally, in Korea there is a preference for name recognition and eminent surgeons. Koreans in New Zealand become anxious and insecure when told that the hospital and the doctor will be selected for them by the system.

Korean patients are not, in short, always at their ease in New Zealand. The problem is with the hidden messages more than with the surgery itself. They return to Korea for treatment because in Korea, culturally as well as linguistically, the doctors and the nurses all speak their mother tongue.

As with the Koreans in New Zealand, so with the Turks in Denmark. A nationwide sample survey in 2007 found that 26.6 per cent of first-generation and 19.4 per cent of later-generation Turks had made use of cross-border healthcare. Among ethnic Danes the figure was only 6.7 per cent. Since price in social Denmark is not a consideration, the inference is that the Danish healthcare system does not mesh with the immigrants' internalised expectations (Nielsen, Yazici, Petersen, Blaakilde and Krasnik, 2012). The fact that 39 per cent of foreign patients in Turkey come from Germany may reflect not just the excellence of the Turkish hospitals but the high concentration of ethnic Turks who went as *Gastarbeiter* and stayed on (Frost & Sullivan, 2012: 18).

Ethnic Chinese are at ease in the Sinitic world. Mainland Chinese come to Taiwan because the food is similar and the locals speak Mandarin. Taiwanese investors in new hospitals at Subic Bay ensure that the enclave is as Chinese as Xiamen or Guangzhou even though the treatment centre is situated in the low-cost Philippines. Overseas Filipinos might themselves want to see a doctor in the Philippines. There are 10 million cultural Filipinos living outside the country. About 4 million of them are in the United States alone.

There are 25 million cultural Indians living abroad. Some are non-resident Indians (NRIs) who retain their citizenship but live as expatriates. Others are persons of Indian origin (PIOs) who have an ancestral link but were born or naturalised outside. A proportion of them will want an Indian comfort zone when they are ill. It is a considerable pool for the better Indian hospitals to tap. Many of the patients recorded as coming from the Gulf are in fact overseas Indians. About 85 per cent of medical travellers to India are citizens of neighbouring states or are NRIs (Hamid, 2010).

Malaysia is a second home to Indonesians. Malays speak a similar *bahasa* and practise a similar *adat*. Apart from the language and the customs, there is also Islam. Muslims (not least Pakistanis) are reported to experience difficulties in entering countries like the United States. Before September 2001, 44 per cent of medical travellers from one (unnamed) country in the Middle East went to the United States. By 2003 only 6 per cent did so (Ehrbeck, Guevara and Mango, 2008: 8). Entry into Malaysia is much simpler. Malaysia offers visa-free entry to member states of the Organization of the Islamic Conference.

Mexicans in the USA too are returning to their roots for their health. About 46 per cent of a convenience sample reported that they, a friend or a relative had gone to Mexico for medical care (Bergmark, Barr and Garcia, 2008: 610). While Mexicans living within 100 kilometres of the border were the most likely to cross, they were not the only ones. Mexicans from as far afield as the Bay Area stated that they were in the habit of going south.

About 60 per cent of ethnic Mexicans in the United States are uninsured (Einhorn, 2008). Some, being undocumented, have difficulty in accessing the United States system. Some work for small firms that cannot afford insurance. Some gamble that they will reach the border without delay if worst comes to worst. Approximately one-third of total US residents without a health plan are concentrated in the four states closest to Mexico. Mexican outlets 'make border regions the best place to *not* have health insurance coverage' (Brown, Pagan and Bastida, 2009: 37). Brown, Pagan and Bastida calculate that the demand for private health insurance in the border states would rise by 16 per cent if it were no longer possible to obtain low-cost care in Mexico.

Yet money is not the only consideration. Cultural Mexicans also go south because, living abroad, still they feel that they are coming home. Medical practice in Mexico involves fewer injections and diagnostic tests. Mexicans living in the US prefer the no-nonsense approach of their childhood to the Americans' bells and whistles that they see as costly, painful and unnecessary. They know that quality is lower, negligence more likely. They believe that the difference is well worth the risk. In Mexico they can speak the language. They will not face discrimination. They have a family network that will assist them in their search. Prices matter to them and so does location. What must not be forgotten is that Mexicanness too explains their choice of a familiar destination. Diaspora tourism confirms the well-known proposition that sick people do not want to be confused.

The Koreans, the Turks, the Chinese, the Indians and the Mexicans are doing it. Globalisation, evidently, has not melded the cultures into one. Lee, Kearns and Friesen find it at variance with both good economics and good citizenship that new settlers should feel the need to go forward by going back: 'It seems unfortunate for hospital treatment to be the prompt for international travel in an era of escalating travel costs and consciousness of carbon emissions' (Lee, Kearns and Friesen, 2010: 114). They say that health tourism is not the only answer to the perception of medical embeddedness.

Over time new residents will absorb the local customs. They will become not Koreans but New Zealanders of Korean descent. They will become bicultural as well as bilingual. The model is the Indians returning from the US who can switch effortlessly from one realm of discourse to another. Besides that, a tolerant society has a duty to provide a variety of pathways to the sun. Westerners treated at Apollo will see a doctor who has lived abroad and who knows their assumptions. A Turk treated in Denmark has a right to the same degree of respect.

It is a village as well as a global village out there. A plurality of cultures are getting on the planes. One airline survey found that 46 per cent of health travellers exiting the United States for care (the study estimated the total number to be 500 000) were foreign-born US citizens and 36 per cent were non-citizens. Only 17 per cent were US-born US citizens (Warner, 2009: 3). Some foreigners will expect conversation. Some foreigners will expect a black box. Some will expect to be monitored. Others will expect to be drugged. Practice variation is cultural variance. Medical travel has no future if one culture tells another culture that it should mind its own business and do as it is told.

5.4 THE TRADE IN BODY PARTS

Milton Friedman, starting from autonomy, respect and dignity, says that nothing can be equitable that does not emanate from 'free discussion and voluntary co-operation' (Friedman, 1962: 22). Market exchange is legitimate first and foremost because it is grounded in consent: 'Both parties to an economic exchange benefit from it, *provided the exchange is bi-laterally voluntary and informed*' (Friedman, 1962: 13). Material well-being is the secondary selling point. Primary is the right of each individual to chart their own course. The market, Friedman says, 'gives people what they want instead of what a particular group thinks they ought to want. Underlying most arguments against the free market is a lack of belief in freedom itself' (Friedman, 1962: 15).

Ego has tastes and Alter has preferences. A pineapple is swapped for a green apple. A kidney is traded for a shop. The underprivileged get the money. The under-provided get the organ. Exchange makes both Alter and Ego better off in their own estimation – '*provided the exchange is bilaterally voluntary and informed*'. Libertarianism is win–win by consent. That is just the problem. What if it is not?

5.4.1 Coercion

The Nurnberg Code, the Belmont Report, the Declaration of Istanbul and other unquestioned standards of medical ethics all condemn the exercise of physical force. Psychological force and financial force dwell, however, in a no-man's-land. The marginalised and the vulnerable know what they are doing when they put their cross on the contract. They also know that their family is starving and that nothing else will pay the bills. It is a last-ditch deal which only in the most literal and legalistic sense can be reconciled with the non-negotiable absolutes of freedom, choice and respect for persons.

Scheper-Hughes speaks evocatively of 'the howl of the hungry wolf at the door' which leaves the kidney sellers at the mercy of 'the despicable greed of organs brokers' (Scheper-Hughes, 2011: 63). The context of the choice is relevant. Scheper-Hughes describes organ selling as 'a hidden "body tax" on the world's poor' (Scheper-Hughes, 2011: 85). The slums who cannot buy organs are under 'undue pressure' to auction themselves off. The suburbs who can buy in a new liver have no possible desire to sell on their own. Legally speaking, both parties have voluntarily given their assent to the trade. Morally speaking, the contract cannot be said to be equal and opposite. It is forced exchange. Economically and socially, it is not free.

Scheper-Hughes treats the 'human trafficking in spare body parts' (Scheper-Hughes, 2011: 57) as a structured dominance that she sees replicated in area after area of human life. She regards the organ industry as a pure case of injustice and stratification: 'A grotesque niche market for sold organs, tissues, and other body parts has exacerbated older divisions between North and South, haves and have-nots, organ donors and organ recipients. Indeed, a kind of medical apartheid has also emerged that has separated the world into two populations – organ givers and organ recipients' (Scheper-Hughes, 2002: 61). Organs are not the only way in which the population of the world is streamed into Posh and Steerage. They are, however, one visible and tangible abuse: 'Life-saving for the one demands self-mutilation on the part of the other' (Scheper-Hughes, 2003: 1645).

Scheper-Hughes is in no doubt that it is a deeply immoral imbalance of power. Describing the trade as 'neo-cannibalism', 'bio-terrorism', 'biopiracy', 'body theft', 'crimes against humanity', 'violence and inhumane behavior', she draws attention to 'the scars left not only on the ruined bodies of disillusioned kidney sellers but on the geopolitical landscapes where the illicit transplant trade has taken place' (Scheper-Hughes, 2011: 57, 58). It cannot do much for the moral fibre of a people that fellow human beings are chopping each other up for fuel. It cannot be called a victimless crime when a moral absolute is being trod underfoot.

Physical coercion is at odds with Friedman's condition that the exchange must be consensual. Horror stories abound of abduction, murder, organ theft from mental patients, the military dragooning of powerless orphans. These are clear cases of deception and abuse. Organs are taken from cadavers in police mortuaries because the dead are presumed to have given consent. Criminals threaten the wavering with guns because a deal has been struck and *caveat emptor* cannot wait. Body parts are harvested from executed prisoners because an offender who has violated the social contract is deemed to have lost both his citizenship and his personhood.

In the past (the practice was outlawed in 2006) something like 95 per cent of organs transplanted in China were obtained through seizure and not negotiation. Biggins and his colleagues conducted a survey of (predominantly American) professionals in the transplant field. Although as many as 87 per cent said that transplants per se were ethically sound, only 4 per cent believed that they were ethically sound in China (Biggins, Bambha, Terrault, Inadomi, Roberts and Bass, 2009: 834). Professionals were reluctant to recommend a transplant in China. Some refused to train postgraduates who might later be involved in procurement 'legitimated by default' (Mendoza, 2010: 264). Some would not provide follow-up to a patient whose donor had involuntarily been shot in the head. That, however, is physical coercion. It is possible that economic coercion is no less reprehensible. Where people are hungry and there is no work to be found, it is only true in the most literal sense that the exchange is '*bilaterally voluntary and informed*': 'The idea of consent is problematic when one has no other option but to sell an organ' (Scheper-Hughes, 2002: 78). The marginalised are poor, needy and in debt. The bartered kidney is 'the organ of last resort' (Scheper-Hughes, 2003: 1645).

5.4.2 Ignorance

Compulsion is compounded by ignorance. Information is always asymmetric. Urgency cuts short the search. Informed consent may degenerate into premature acquiescence when the buyer and the seller are both desperate to get the deal done. All potential risks, side-effects and complications can never be spelled out: there are not enough hours in the day. A selection based on relevance and probability must always be made. A glass half full is a better selling-point than a glass half empty.

Between 58 and 86 per cent of kidney donors are believed subsequently to experience a deterioration in their health (Shimazono, 2007: 960). They may have been blind-sided as to the risks. They may have been misled by an authority figure in a suit. They may lack the computer literacy to read up online. Even, moreover, if they are told the facts, uneducated people are not always fluent in the language of frequencies. They may not fully grasp what a 30 per cent probability of irreversible damage to the immune system actually means.

There is a lot to take in. The scar may be a stigma. The donor may be ostracised. Isolation and depression may result from social exclusion. Marriage may be out because of long-term debility, chronic pain or the probability of premature death. Agricultural or construction work may be too exhausting. The donor, unemployed, may experience a chronic loss of self-worth. Cross-infection with AIDS or hepatitis may lead to burdensome medical bills. If the remaining kidney fails, there will not be money for dialysis. It is hard to think of everything when the agent is pressing the donor for a decision.

Time-preference distorts the rational calculus. Money in the hand increases felt welfare in the here-and-now. Long-term regret may be left to look after itself. The middle classes discount over the whole of their expected life-span. People in the *bidonville* are more likely to live for today. Smoking, drinking and selling their blood, they know from observation that they are less likely to survive into extreme old age. Morally speaking, a middle-class life cannot be ranked above a working-class life merely because the time horizon is not the same. Revealed preference, however, rides roughshod over facile generalisation. Respect for persons means respect for real persons and not for classroom cut-outs. Real persons are, economically speaking, not all the same.

The condition is that the transaction must be '*bi-laterally voluntary and informed*'. The condition is not that the transaction must be risk-free. Workers go up scaffolds because the danger money compensates them for the actuarial falls. Smokers smoke and drivers speed because possible cancers and probable crashes do not deter them from more immediate and more salient gratification. A liberal society cannot stop people from acting in their own best interest, self-perceived. Where it has the right to turn paternalistic is when it believes that its citizens do not have the core knowledge that they require to give their informed consent. Still more does it have the right to become involved when vested interest is wholesaling incorrect probabilities and retailing downright lies.

An 'organs mafia' (Scheper-Hughes, 2011: 58) has no incentive to tell the truth. Brokers encourage blood-sellers to give too often; they advise their stable to conceal a history of drugs and shared needles. Middlemen promise lifetime follow-up; a pre-treatment screen is needed to satisfy the buyer but the donor is callously tricked out of his subsequent care (Mendoza, 2010: 258). Legal redress is not an option. Because the 'global kidney bazaar' is so often forced by well-intentioned prohibition into the criminal black market, there is not a lot the courts can do.

5.4.3 Thorns and Roses

Iran is the only country to have made selling legal. It has a central agency to distribute the organs and compensate the donors. Foreigners are excluded from its transplant market. Yet the *de jure* ban in other countries is easily avoided. *De facto* the market exists. The law is circumvented through 'reasonable reimbursement' of highly padded costs, the use of forged documents proving bogus consanguinity, the payment of bribes to corrupt officials, the conclusion pre-transplant of marriage or divorce arrangements. Many countries *de facto* have more buying and selling than they would wish to confess.

Lax enforcement is clandestine and it is sordid. Recipients live, however, who would otherwise have died. Thorns come with roses attached. Patients who go abroad shorten waiting lists at home. Domestic kidneys are freed up for the poor because the affluent buy from sterile middlemen abroad. Needed is not a blanket condemnation so much as the use of thorn-and-rose analysis. Differentiation of product can help medical travellers to regain their previous good health. Sometimes even crime can be in the public interest.

About 10 per cent of the world's transplants are believed to be economic transactions crossing the international exchange (Shimazono, 2007: 959). Shimazono estimates that 5 per cent of all kidney transplants are commercial in nature. Other estimates of underground kidneys go as high as 20 per cent. India, Pakistan and the Philippines are all said to be active in the trade. China in 2005 was charging US$70 000 for a kidney and US$140 000 for a liver. Pakistan was charging only US$14 000 for a liver. South Africa was expensive. It was flying in living non-related sellers from Brazil and Eastern Europe. They were paid US$6000 or less per kidney, plus an occasional safari. The kidney then travelled on until finally it was resold for US$180 000 (Scheper-Hughes, 2011: 72, 75).

In the Philippines, where 40 per cent of the population lives below the poverty line, the typical vendor is a low-income married male with a family. Approximately 60 per cent of the recipients are foreigners. High concentrations of them are from the Middle East, South Korea and Japan.

The median fee to the vendor in 2008 was US$2133. This was 15 to 30 times lower than the US resale value. Titmuss's 'blood proletariat' has moved into kidneys because the poor are running out of things to sell.

Many, contemplating what it means to be human, would argue that it is morally wrong for a human body to be made an instrument, its owner the occupant of a role. Even if the transaction truly is '*bi-laterally voluntary and informed*', still, they would say, the marketisation of biology offends against the common values that define the identity of the whole. Factoring down can be bad for our health: 'Focusing on the individual makes the concerns of others invisible' (Widdows, 2011: 87).

To focus on the buyer and the seller to the detriment of the community with a stake is, Widdows stresses, narrow and myopic: 'There are many ethically significant features that are structural, communal or relational and are relevant to the ethical status of any act or practice' (Widdows, 2011: 87). The knock-on effects and the hidden multipliers make social actors into strangers whose only mode of contact is cash on the line. As Scheper-Hughes says: 'The division of the world into organ buyers and organ sellers is a medical, social, and moral tragedy' (Scheper-Hughes, 2003: 1648).

Cross-jurisdictional trade in functioning pieces of our neighbours is just such an act or practice. The Istanbul Declaration contains a warning that exports can undermine a country's ability to meet the 'transplant needs of its residents' (Steering Committee of the Istanbul Summit, 2008). Charity begins at home. So, it would appear, does business. If a life is to be saved, it ought to be a domestic life. A domestic life has contributed to the overhead of citizenship. A foreign queue-jumper has not. If it is a foreign life, then it is a loss from trade.

It is all very confusing. Respect for persons means what it says. Even the rights of the rich white plutocrat deserve their day in court. It is a singular breach of the Kantian Imperative to sentence an equal human being to death merely because he is a foreign human being, a rich-country human being and not a card-holder in our inward-looking horde. It is, for that matter, extremely bad ethics to deny a retired person a life-saving kidney simply because he is no longer adding value to our nation's wealth. Xenophobia and exclusion on the one hand, cost-effectiveness and ageism on the other – what basic rights are superordinate and which can go by the board? A person cannot legally pay his doctor to terminate his existence. His fellow beings may nonetheless deny him the scarce transplant that would keep him alive.

A better solution would be to increase the supply of organs for all. A free market for biological materials would provide an incentive for the money-minded to come forward with body parts. Private vices, public benefits. The market saves lives. If patients remain too long on the waiting list there is a chance that they will die. A parallel may be drawn to the action taken in 2012 by the Human Fertilisation and Embryology Authority in the United Kingdom when, concerned about the number of UK patients seeking fertility treatment abroad, they increased the authorised payment to egg donors. It went up from a maximum of £250 (basically, the reimbursement of travel expenses and earnings lost up to £61 per day) to a maximum of £750 (attractive not just to the lower-income deciles but to university students and young graduates who enjoy above-average health). A greater reliance on purchase and sale can reverse the organ shortage that is driving desperate locals into medical travel.

Self-interest is one solution. Benevolence, however, is another. A gift relationship in bone marrow and blood would provide an incentive for the well integrated to do what they can to fill the gap. Good outcomes can result from good intentions. The roses need not come with thorns attached. No client of the UK National Health Service, donor or recipient, has any reason to lie for profit or to deny himself the supreme satisfaction of compassionate altruism. Benevolence makes him feel good about himself. As Bevan put it: 'What more pleasure can a millionaire have than to know that his taxes will help the sick?' (Bevan, 1958: Col. 1389).

5.5 THE TRADE IN BIRTHS

It is not immediately appealing to treat eggs and sperm, wombs and babies, as a free market stock in trade. Surrogacy is banned in countries like Germany and France because of an intuitive revulsion at the idea of conception as a paying proposition. Revulsion or not, the body is an economic asset and the freedom to rent it out may be seen as a human right: 'If individuals were allowed to procreate and to contract, then surely they should be able to procreate under contract' (Spar, 2005: 294). Surely it is the woman's labour that is being sold and not the woman herself.

Most people would want at least to be reassured that the substitute had not been coerced or bullied by her extended family, and perhaps also that the trade had been regulated and accredited. Low-status women are expected to earn their keep, even if doing their duty is emotionally and physically painful. A surrogate carrying another woman's child must retreat to a hostel away from her own children. She must be monitored regularly to ensure the integrity of the product. She may feel a sense of loss akin to giving up her own child for adoption. She may damage her health through excessive surrogating. She may find it impossible to bear further children of her own. She may be called a prostitute when she returns to her Third World village. She may see herself as a prostitute.

There have been cases of trafficking. There have been cases of default. If a child is stillborn or disabled, or if there is a miscarriage, or if an inadequate embryo has to be aborted, does the unsaleable outcome invalidate the contract? The surrogate was promised payment in exchange for a healthy child. She may be denied her money if her workmanship is poor.

Surgeons are paid not for success but because they are known to have done their best. Surrogates hired for artificial insemination are in a weaker position. The Indian clinic and its network of intermediaries have a legal obligation to the foreign principal who pays the bills. If the big boss does not like the results, the little boss might not get his cash. The little boss might accuse the birthing proletariat of contributory negligence. Where does the law stand on a false accusation of smoking in pregnancy? There are no unions. Lawyers want money. The surrogate knew the risks. It is coercion by consent. But what can she do?

The surrogate is being treated as a business asset. It reflects the lower status of women in the traditional Third World. Parents have long practised female infanticide because a girl is a low-return property. They have denied their daughters an education because the money must be set aside for a dowry. The debate about surrogacy is at least in part about the equality of respect. Yet it is also a debate about parenthood as a basic human right. The surrogate is receiving money because she is empowering an unknown other to raise a child. It is never a good idea to discard the baby merely because the bathwater has been in the vicinity of supply and demand.

Without an altruistic stand-in or a commercial surrogate the unknown other would have to live childless or to adopt. The unknown other might be a single homosexual, a same-sex partnership, an infertile couple, a post-menopausal woman, a would-be mother unwilling to undergo the trauma, dangers and stretch-marks of childbirth. Whoever the beneficiary is behind the veil, most reasonable people would say that most reasonable people should be able to have a family. The rights of the beneficiary must be respected. They must, however, be reconciled with the no less important rights of the surrogate. Thingification need not be the same as exploitation. Millionaire film stars are bought and sold as personality packages. They are treated as things, but they are treated well.

The surrogate enjoys a *quid pro quo*. The gratitude of the beneficiary almost certainly counts as part of her psychic income. So does the welfare of her own children or of a sister who will have the money to get married. For herself, she will be examined by medical professionals with whom, had she not become a surrogate, she would never have any contact. There may be an improvement in the domestic balance of power where the woman becomes the superior breadwinner. Enhanced respect goes a long way toward assuaging the infringement of self.

First and foremost, however, the debate about thingification without exploitation is a debate about pay. Remuneration for a surrogate in India lies between US$4000 and US$10 000. In the United States an equivalent surrogate would charge in the neighbourhood of US$32 000 to US$37 000. The difference could be in the ratio of 1:10. In India an uneducated woman in industry or agriculture would earn less than US$2 a day. In the United States an uneducated woman paid at the federal minimum wage would earn US$7.25 an hour. The difference, assuming the woman puts in an eight-hour day, is not far off 1:30. The disparities are neither fair nor unfair. They are what they are. That is how the market system works. That is how the agreed-upon game is played.

A mango in Sri Lanka costs less than a mango in the UK. A surgeon in Bangkok costs less than a surgeon in Singapore. A surrogate in India costs less than a surrogate in the United States. In each case the international tradeable commands a local reward. That local reward is not the same as the local reward in a different locality. Arbitrage gives rise to the gains from trade. Different means different. It does not mean that the Thai surgeon is being cheated, tricked or exploited. Nor does it mean that the Indian surrogate is being taken for a ride.

People who accept the market accept the thingification. The debate is not about whether a rich Sri Lankan should be entitled to pay a poor Sri Lankan a pittance for a mango. The debate is about whether a foreigner should be allowed to pay the local price for his mangoes, his surgeons and his surrogates or whether a fair-trade mark-up should be added on to protect the locals against the aliens who nip in and scrounge. A supplement could be added on to redistribute the surplus. It could cream off the exploitation. Multiple-tier pricing could restore equity to the swap.

The local price could be adjusted upward to ensure purchasing power parity. Street vendors in the Third World do this as a matter of course when they uprate the local price to the price that a tourist would be just willing to pay at home. Humbyrd proposes that the same heuristic of broad national category be employed to set a fair price for Indian surrogates selling to childless Americans. The Americans, going by the stereotype, can afford to pay over the odds: 'Nominal wages may be less to surrogate mothers in developing countries compared to their counterparts in developed countries, but the real wages should be equivalent' (Humbyrd, 2009: 117).

The non-standard price would mean that the payment would buy an equivalent basketful of commodities in the different countries to which the buyers and the sellers belong. It is in line with the principles of fair trade that are applied in socially responsive sectors of the coffee and other industries. Entry of a child into a signatory state could be made contingent on proof of index-linked compensation. The nominal wage is still set in the surrogate's home market. What makes it a fair wage is that it is then scaled up to match what money will buy in the foreign country in which the recipients reside.

The problem is that the beneficiaries do not all originate in a single home state. Global heterogeneities in the need for surrogates and the ability to pay imply that there will not be one reservation price but many: 'A fair price in one context would unavoidably be inducement in another' (Widdows, 2011: 89). Exploitation cannot be defined as payment below the going world price for the simple reason that there is no uni-valued world price, no meta-market equilibrium that fits all the beneficiary states. The fair-trade price would have to be a range. Indian surrogates will fight each other for the Swedes. They will turn down the Portuguese because their cost of living at home is too low.

There is a further problem, and perhaps a more serious one. Even a fair-trade price may be perceived as a thingification that offends against the social consensus. Most reasonable people would say that no price can ever be just which permits children to become indentured hands in unventilated sweat-shops. Is it possible that the surrogates themselves would see it as a violation of the ethical code that women must have any presence at all in the marketplace for body and soul? Not everything has a price. Free market or purchase power paritied, it can still happen that autonomous beings feel estranged and abused when they are 'induced to behave in a manner contrary to how they want to act' (Humbyrd, 2009: 114).

Duress is a state of mind. The dictator's standard of 'your money or your life' is a reminder that even in the free market not every equilibrium is equally congenial to both supply and demand. Power need not be in balance. When an illiterate price-taker faces a powerful monopolist, she knows that the cards are stacked against her. The condition is '*bi-laterally informed and voluntary*' again. The middlemen hold out for their commissions. The clinics grow fat on their windfalls. The market clearing price may in the circumstances be widely seen as a mechanism for laundering the inequity rather than a way of converting it into justice. Some people will ask for a minimum wage for surrogates and others will demand state welfare for the absolutely deprived. Some may even ask for the trade to be prohibited. Too much differentiation may be bad for a nation's health.

The market may be seen as the disease and not as the cure. Some people will assert that in the case of surrogates it is impossible to separate thingification from exploitation because to hire out one's body is instinctively to feel used. There is no reason to think that Humbyrd's fair price will feel like the surrogate's fair price when the air-conditioned Rolls-Royce speeds in to take the baby away.

6. Trade: the outputs

Trade was war in the Depression years of the 1930s. Beggar-thy-neighbour tariffs and competitive devaluations made the world economy red in tooth and claw. The bombs and the battlefields of the Second World War reinforced the message that life as well as livelihood would forever be at risk so long as myopic nations refused the plus-sum alternative of compromise and cooperation. The result was a post-war determination to convert swords into ploughshares that manifested itself at Dumbarton Oaks in the creation of the United Nations and at Bretton Woods in the International Monetary Fund and the World Bank. Then, in 1947, there was Havana.

Recognising that interdependent nations must first sell in order to buy, and persuaded that the international division of labour would universalise their comparative advantage, 23 industrial countries that had been spared the worst vicissitudes of the war met at Havana to discuss the formation of an International Trade Organization (ITO). It was not to be. Manufactures lent themselves to liberalisation but the United States Congress refused to phase out the US subsidies to agriculture. Havana had to settle not for an ITO but simply a GATT. The General Agreement on Tariffs and Trade only became the World Trade Organization (WTO) in the 'Uruguay Round' in 1995.

The GATT had successfully reduced barriers to trade in manufactured commodities if not in primary produce. The WTO felt that the time had come to extend the negotiations into the tertiary sector. In 1995 it adopted the General Agreement on Trade in Services. The GATS is the first set of legally enforceable rules ever negotiated at world level to free up the service trade (Adlung and Carzaniga, 2006).

The charter of the GATS is at once specialisation and dynamics, efficiency and expansion. It sets out 'to establish a multilateral framework of principles and rules for trade in services with a view to the expansion of such trade under conditions of transparency and progressive liberalization and as a means of promoting the economic growth of all trading partners and the development of developing countries' (World Trade Organization, 1995: 287). Services were the sunrise sector. Raw materials and finished products could no longer be taken to be the whole of trade.

This chapter explores the nature of a world consensus on the swap of invisibles. It is divided into three parts. Section 6.1, 'Joining the GATS', asks why formal adhesion has been sluggish despite the unquestionable potential. Section 6.2, 'Cross-border supply', is devoted to GATS Mode 1. It explains that services can go abroad even if the service providers remain rooted at home. Section 6.3, 'Consumption abroad', turns to GATS Mode 2. It is the way in which most people probably conceptualise the phenomenon of medical travel: 'Broadly defined, a "medical tourist" is one who travels to a foreign country to consume medical practices' (Howze, 2007: 1014).

There are two further Modes to the GATS. They are discussed in the following two chapters. Chapter 7, 'The inputs: commercial presence', explores GATS Mode 3. It says that a multinational can be active in medical services even as it can integrate backward into oil or forward into retail. Chapter 8, 'The inputs: labour', is concerned with GATS Mode 4. Focusing on the input with a pulse, Chapter 8 says that doctors and nurses in an open market need no longer be trapped within the walls of their citizenship. The world is a big place. Sick people are everywhere you look.

6.1 JOINING THE GATS

Countries which join the WTO are free not to join the GATS. They are free to supply and demand their services in the time-honoured manner that antedates the agreements. They are also free to keep some service sectors closed. Most treaties are one-size-fits-all. The GATS treaty is a buffet meal.

In the case of tourism, telecommunications and finance (which includes the subcategory of health insurance), 90 per cent of WTO members have opened up their services. In the case of healthcare it has been only 39 per cent. It is the same proportion as for education. A majority of countries seem to be putting off the all but irreversible commitment until their fledgling hospitals are up to the challenge from the first movers. The evolution towards world free service trade has been gradual. Developed countries have been quicker than poor countries to sign up. Even in the global mass market, the arguments of List for infant activities and Prebisch for import substitution may still be detected.

The largest number of health-specific access commitments has been for Mode 2, the smallest for Mode 4. The high result for Mode 2 is not unexpected. It is not easy to stop someone with a passport from going abroad. The low result for Mode 4 is also predictable. Migration is socially and politically sensitive.

Even within the categories, some signatories have insisted on exclusions and restrictions. They are allowed to choose and edit. All safeguards must, however, be in place before the nation signs up. Once a state has agreed to a clause, its contents are set in stone. This proof of commitment instils confidence in its trading partners and in potential investors. They know that the signatory will stand by its promises.

Countries can withdraw from the GATS after an initial term of three years. If they do so, however, they must pay compensation to all GATS partners adversely affected. Countries that refuse to pay run the risk of trade sanctions. If a member of the WTO does not formally extend its membership into the GATS, it does not live in fear of such retaliation. It can choose later on to suspend some stipulations. It can also employ non-GATS concessions like permission to invest as bargaining chips in future trade negotiations. These can later be exchanged, without multinational assent, for a *quid pro quo* such as a reduction in agricultural support.

Sitting on the hands keeps the options open. Conditions are changing. Countries are understandably tempted to test the water before they make a multi-period commitment: 'There is literally no policy change a government can make because of the GATS, or by making commitments under the GATS, that it could not make without it; but there are potential policy changes which it prevents' (Woodward, 2005: 513). GATS is restrictive even as it is enabling. Favouritism cannot be shown to home-owned enterprise nor discrimination practised against the foreigner. Governments sometimes fear the consequences of such clauses. They prefer to experiment with pilot schemes until they are confident enough to take the next step.

Postponement also meets the objection that not every constituency may have been consulted before the domestic market was dragooned into freedom. The Ministry of Commerce in some countries has acted without any input from the Ministry of Health. Some countries have continued to treat getting rich and getting well as two things apart. Public opinion is not always canvassed. Experimentation without a binding commitment leaves the door open to further debate at a national level: 'GATS commitments could also represent a serious obstacle to policy innovations, because many policies would need to have been correctly anticipated by each country at the time it made its commitments' (Woodward, 2005: 528). It is impossible to foresee the unforeseeable.

Fearing GATS but wanting integration, countries have an intermediate option. More than 250 regional and bilateral trade agreements have been concluded. Regional trade agreements (RTAs) and free trade agreements (FTAs) now dominate 30 per cent of world trade. The tendency to trade diversion is undeniable. The possibility of trade creation makes it into a positive-sum game. Especially attractive, elusive consensus is easier to secure:

> Often *liberalization is more easily negotiated at the regional level*, as it involves countries with geographical proximity, cultural ties, and similar levels of economic development. They also often involve a more limited number of participants and thus allow for greater reciprocity, as well as often being undertaken for *reasons other than purely economic ones*, such as strategic, cultural, and political reasons. (Smith, 2012: 180)

Bilateralism and regionalism are more malleable than rigid GATS:

> In a bi-lateral relationship, the amount of trade would be formalised: contracts would specify a specific number of patients to be treated in specific hospitals, prices can be negotiated directly with these hospitals and savings made from treating these patients abroad can be incorporated into the budget, allowing for better planning and organising of resources. (Smith, Martinez Alvarez and Chanda, 2011: 278)

Agreed-upon standards, restricted access and most-favoured fees would not be possible under a GATS-type multinational scenario 'where all countries can trade with each other and are not able to pre-establish this sort of precondition' (Martinez Alvarez, Chanda and Smith, 2011: 17). Tailor-made is more likely if the aggregates are small and each party's stake transparent.

India and Britain have a bilateral interest in the portability of state insurance and the availability of private beds. Canada, Mexico and the United States share a concentrated pattern of trade. The Association of Southeast Asian Nations (ASEAN) through the ASEAN Free Trade Agreement on Services (AFAS) has recognised the social and geographical contiguities. The GATS comes further down the shopping list when countries with common interests but at different stages of development negotiate to take selected barriers down.

6.2 CROSS-BORDER SUPPLY

Conceptually, the four Modes are distinct. In practice, they are complements and substitutes. A doctor, providing advice online to a foreign patient (Mode 1), may request his client to travel abroad to meet him face to face (Mode 2). He may decide to open a second practice abroad (Mode 3). He may decide to operate that foreign subsidiary himself (Mode 3 with a Mode 4 element). He may decide to travel abroad on a temporary basis to treat an individual patient. Foreign investment (Mode 3) can pay for distance medicine (Mode 1). Transnational manpower (Mode 4) can attract in transnational patients (Mode 2). Modes 1, 2, 3 and 4 are not free-standing. Rather, they are a bundle. They are a linked-up web of synergies.

In the real world the four Modes are symbiotic: 'Health-services trade should be considered as an integrated package to appreciate fully the potential risks and opportunities presented' (Smith, Chanda and Tangcharoensathien, 2009: 598). In theory, however, they are separate. This chapter, together with Chapter 7 and Chapter 8, examines each of the four building blocks in turn.

Mode 1 is distance facilitation. The service crosses the border. The patient does not. In that way Mode 1 is on all fours with the traditional model of a commodity produced in one country which is consumed in another. Even things in boxes can be researched and e-purchased online. About 23.6 per cent of Norwegians in 2007 had bought manufactured goods in this way (Wangberg, Andreassen, Kummervold, Wynn and Sørensen, 2009: 693).

6.2.1 Knowledge Crosses Borders

The historic focus of the GATT and the WTO has been on visible trade. The GATS is an acknowledgement that business has moved on: 'The growing importance of services in national economies and in international trade is largely due to an increase in the production of intermediate services (i.e. outsourcing). Firms increasingly delegate knowledge-intensive intermediate-stage processing activities to specialized suppliers in order to benefit from lower factor costs' (Lennon, 2009: 1). The current account is technology-neutral. Whether a report is packed in an envelope, ordered electronically or transmitted online, it is covered by the agreement to de-nationalise the exchange. Physical presence is not required. Territory and nationality are not important when virtual banking is conducted, e-insurance purchased or intellectual property faxed across.

Cross-border transfers of knowledge diffuse innovations and discoveries. Roemer and Roemer cite the examples of 'improved and effective methods of contraception, of techniques for obtaining safe drinking water, of low-cost refrigeration, of efficient transport and communication, of fertilizers and pesticides to enhance agriculture and nutrition, of the new therapeutic agents that can effectively treat leprosy, schistosomiasis, trachoma, onchocerciasis (river blindness), and other scourges of the developing world, once regarded as hopeless' (Roemer and Roemer, 1990: 1190). Know-how becomes a spillover public good. Poor people become well because cures, like diseases, do not stop to get their passports stamped.

Websites reporting on the quality of drugs and the performance of equipment are available on subscription or open access. They complement the hard-copy journals, only available after a lag. Doctors can register to be updated via email on scientific research in their field. They learn from journals about global best practice. The international media publicise new research on bird flu and saturated fat. Medical education can be delivered by distance learning. Knowledge can be refreshed and evidence-based medicine promoted. It presupposes a common language (usually English), a commonly accepted mode of teaching, adequate protection of intellectual property rights and, needless to say, trustworthy e-commerce that effects distance payment in an instant.

International communication and international exchange are cross-border contributions that the global economy is making to good health outcomes at home. Free trade improves allocation, promotes competition and raises living standards. Health status is enriched by affordable housing and better nutrition. It is a virtuous circle. A growing economy is in a better position to fund the public health infrastructure, curative and preventive alike.

Governments themselves act across the national boundaries. They seek to contain organ marketeering, test-tube cloning and chlorofluorocarbon externalities which pollute whole regions. Precisely because the public bads are multinational, the appropriate policy-tools such as taxes and subsidies will only be effective if they are implemented on a multi-polity scale. Cooperation between sovereign states, as Yach and Bettcher say, is truly in everyone's interest: 'In a world of shared global problems, the moral imperatives of addressing these problems also bring mutual benefits' (Yach and Bettcher, 1998: 741).

Drugs cross borders. They do so subject to the coercion by consent of the Agreement on Trade-Related Aspects of Intellectual Property Rights (TRIPS). Patents for new brand-name pharmaceuticals are granted for a period of 20 years and may be renewed. Sometimes the extension will be in connection with a bilateral free trade agreement or as the counterpart of other concessions ('TRIPS-plus'). The less-developed countries have been known to demand free entry for their primary produce in exchange. The debit side is that their hospitals pay a super-normal price, the government's drugs budget is depleted, and there is a trade deficit in Western medicines. TRIPS is difficult to reconcile with the home government's commitment to public health.

There is, however, a loophole. A waiver or 'compulsory licence' may be granted. Where it is, the reproduction and sale of a patented drug becomes legal even without the permission of the patent-holder. The exemption is an exception. The demand to mass-produce a generic must be backed up by evidence that (as with the AIDS cocktail or essential anti-malarials) a significant number of lives will be saved. The drug may be made available only in a less-developed country (not necessarily the country where it is manufactured). Even if it produces with the pass-through of the TRIPS special case, the supplier must still pay some compensation to the patent-holder. The world community does not condone theft.

TRIPS makes exceptions but normally it enforces the rule. Its critics complain that, precisely because it *de facto* restricts access and puts up price, it protects the innovators and the producers at the expense of sick people who ought to have priority. Its critics call for patents to be broken and the fruits of science to be made a public good. Its supporters reply that many familiar drugs would not exist today if a rent to an occasional great win had not been the incentive to conduct research and development. Health and profit may or may not be at variance. But this is not to deny that intellectual property crosses the borders, or that it does so within the framework of international agreements like TRIPS that lay down the rules of the game.

6.2.2 Medicine and Microelectronics

Some services such as the extraction of a tooth must be provided face to face: 'You can't hammer a nail over the Internet' (Blinder, 2006). Some, however, can go by a broadband link. Trading over distances is already altering the nature of world trade. Krugman, Obstfeld and Melitz regard it as the new frontier, the post-industrial revolution:

> About 60 per cent of total US employment consists of jobs that must be done close to the consumer, making them nontradable. But the 40 per cent of employment that is in tradable activities includes more service than manufacturing jobs. This suggests that the current dominance of world trade by manufactures . . . may be only temporary. In the long run, trade in services, delivered electronically, may become the most important component of world trade. (Krugman, Obstfeld and Melitz, 2012: 51)

The microelectronic revolution has altered the nature of trade. Services such as banking, brokerage and money transfer have crossed the borders for at least as long as the Medicis and the Fuggers, the City of London and the port of Rotterdam have been in business. Services are not new. What is new is the change in the composition of trade as a consequence of the new technological highway.

The US and UK are both net service exporters. Accounting, healthcare, legal services and other high-value items are prominent: 'In fact, the United States and the United Kingdom have run the largest and the second largest surpluses in services trade in the world in recent years' (Amiti and Wei, 2004: 20). Bhagwati, Panagariya and Srinivasan say that outsourcing of services, like trade in commodities, is a plus-sum game: 'Outsourcing leads to gains from trade and increases in the national income . . . Over time, high-value jobs can be expected to arise and expand' (Bhagwati, Panagariya and Srinivasan, 2004: 112). This is especially so since the basepoint is so low. Herman estimates that Mode 1 trade in health-related services currently accounts for no more than 0.01 per cent of gross domestic product (GDP) in the Organisation for Economic Co-operation and Development (OECD) countries (Herman, 2009).

Cross-border supply takes advantage of cheaper labour abroad. Both India and the Philippines have a pool of good English speakers able to interface easily with a voice on the telephone. It makes them well suited to outsourcing, often in facilities directly financed by foreign investment. Some of the operators will be working part-time while training in a medically related field. The outlay *prima facie* would appear to be cost-effective. Bhagwati has estimated that medical offshoring could save the United States alone as much as US$75 billion a year (quoted in *The Economist*, 2008). It would also relieve the pressure on scarce human resources, especially at night.

In the Philippines, offshore call centres employed 683000 workers in 2011 and generated about US$11 billion in revenue. This was 24 per cent more revenue than in 2010 (*Straits Times*, 2012: A15). In India, employment in activities specifically providing health services through Mode 1 increased from 30551 in 2000 to 242500 in 2005. Revenue rose from US$264 million to US$4072 million in the same period (Smith, Chanda and Tangcharoensathien, 2009: 594). It is a very rapid rate of growth indeed.

Local endowments of natural resources are ceding their pre-eminence to rootless exchanges that go through the air. Healthcare, where no two bodies are the same, has been swept along by the unseeable revolution. Especially quick to enter the new computer age have been back-office functions like hot-lines, claims processing, coding, legal services, data entry, data analysis, credit card billing, record-keeping, financial and accounting services, booking of appointments, maintenance of a medical library, transcription of medical notes, transcription of oral dictation, health insurance. It reduces the personal element but also the cost.

The outsourcing need not be to an outside organisation. Through vertical integration it can be to a fully owned subsidiary of the home-country parent: 'FDI in services thus often functions as a vehicle for trade in services' (Mortensen, 2008: 5). Sometimes, however, it is cost-effective to turn to an independent contractor, domestic or foreign. Neither an affiliate nor a subsidiary, the external associate fills a market niche. This is especially so where, as in India, there are existing strengths in information technology (IT).

India is hardly alone in this respect. The e-health industry in the European Union was estimated in 2006 to be worth US$27.7 billion. Chanda believes that Europe could potentially control a third of the global IT industry (Chanda, 2011: 3). Outsourcing can create new jobs in the richer and not just the poorer countries. It can produce a net gain in employment and exports. Public opinion is not always rational. A poll in 2004 revealed that only 17 per cent of Americans felt that outsourcing would be of benefit to the US economy (Bhagwati, Panagariya and Srinivasan, 2004: 94).

Telediagnosis, telepathology and teleradiology eliminate the delay when a sample or an X-ray must be sent by post. Clinical consultation, second opinions and remote monitoring can be flashed up on a screen without the need for the body-holder to be physically present. The shift from paper copy to digital imagery permits real-time teleconferencing across the continents and the time zones. Technicians can examine the laboratory samples, listen to the ultrasound, monitor the intensive care unit and interpret the scans. Doctors can pre-screen their patients and follow their recovery.

Clinical trials can be conducted abroad by pharmaceutical majors. Institutional tie-ups can be arranged that tap into the large population, wide range of diseases and diverse genetic pool of a big country like India. First surgery after approval can be performed overseas. Standards are the purview of independent review panels. Boards abroad like boards at home are able to protect the ethical code. Manufacturers follow the trials with care. The licence once granted, Mode 3 takes over and the multinational produces locally what local scientists have shown to be good.

Treatment itself can be digitised. With televisual contacts the specialist can perform minimally invasive laser surgery along a fibre-optic cable. Radiotherapy can be directed from Kolkata to a robot treating a cancer case in Kazakhstan. Third World villages gain access through a closed-circuit link to metropolitan centres of excellence and even to top-tier foreign expertise. Remote control, in short, becomes remote care. The division of labour goes worldwide: 'As telemedicine progresses, the adage that "all care is local" will recede' (Milstein and Smith, 2007: 141).

Whether the call centres, the telediagnosis or the core medical experience, what all the modes of Mode 1 have in common is a common reliance on the microelectronic infrastructure. Without the appropriate investment in telecommunications, Mode 1 would not be possible. The power grid must be rock solid. Connections must be rapid. There must be workable competition. IT professionals must be adequate in numbers and proficiency. Computer literacy must be near-universal. There must be postal and private delivery systems for healthcare products ordered online. Payment by credit card must be a social norm. With all of this, the cost must be affordable. Internet access in the Third World is more expensive than in the developed countries. The cost may be a deterrent. One inference is that the state must invest heavily in the information age. Unfortunately, it very often does not have the budget or the expertise to do so.

Privacy, liability and consumer safety remain problems to be solved. Within tolerable limits, however, data can be protected through laws and encryption. Information stored in the computer can be made secure even where it is sent electronically to other treatment centres, including treatment centres abroad. Trust in cross-border supply would be diminished if news leaked out about cosmetic surgery or drug addiction. Good passwords remedy a market failure.

Misinformation, substandard quality and breach of confidentiality are an ever-present threat in an unregulated internet nexus. The solution may be a multi-governmental register. Providers would be required to authenticate their name and address, the country in which they are based, the country in which any potential contract will be domiciled, their professional training, their qualifications and certificates, their collateral stake in ventures such as insurance underwriting or an online pharmacy. Practitioners offering a medical opinion could be expected to have an approved hospital accreditation or even a link to a medical centre in the patient's home territory. There could be industrial self-regulation in respect of advertising. There is never absolute certainty that information transmitted online will be accurate. Multi-governmental regulation can nonetheless go some way to weeding out the tricksters and the sharks.

6.3 CONSUMPTION ABROAD

GATS Mode 2 picks up the cross-border movement of the client base: 'Medical travel . . . refers to the international phenomenon of individuals travelling, often great distances, to access health-care services that are otherwise not available due to high costs, long waiting lists or limited health-care capacity in the country of origin' (United Nations Economic and Social Commission for Asia and the Pacific, 2007: 1).

6.3.1 The Gains From Trade

International travel is only an extension of the intra-national market. Plastic surgery costs twice as much in Los Angeles as it does in Knoxville, Tennessee. Within the USA, the price of a heart bypass varies from $15 000 to $100 000. Domestically as well as internationally, patients are already packing up their demand in pursuit of price, quality and product differentiation. The patient is already shopping for elective, non-emergency care. The world market is more of the same.

What cannot be known with certainty is whether domestic facilities are genuinely as good. Where services at home are more costly or of a lower standard, domestic patients will be well within their rights to say that not all substitutes are necessarily close. The denial of reimbursement might in the circumstances look suspiciously like a non-tariff barrier. As Cattaneo observes, there are circumstances in which value for money means discriminating against domestic supply: 'The cost of certain technologies might justify for some countries to continue sending patients abroad' (Cattaneo, 2009: 10n).

There is a great deal of money to be made from Mode 2. Patients come to Britain from the Middle East, the Far East and beyond. Over 30 per cent of the revenue of London's private hospitals is derived from overseas patients. In hospitals specialising in high-end procedures the proportion can go up to 70 per cent. Over 1000 specialists practise within a mile of Harley Street (Gerl, Boscher, Mainil and Kunhardt, 2009: 69). Hungary has more dentists per capita than any other country in the world.

6.3.2 Crowding Out

Medical tourists seek treatment in the urban private sector. In this they follow the local elite. The result is a redistribution of access and a strain on scarce capacity: 'With a limited pool of human resources and multiple sources of demand . . . there is bound to be a contraction in one sector as another expands' (Vijaya, 2010: 61). As many as 21 rural district hospitals in Thailand are functioning without a single full-time doctor. The dentist-to-population ratio, 1:15 000 in Thailand as a whole, is 1:22 000 in the deprived North-East. Many medical specialities in Thailand are not represented at all in the countryside. A subsidised health card for the rural poor is becoming an uncashable cheque. Doctors are relocating to the urban private sector where they can earn four to ten times more and where their workload is substantially less. Arunanondchai and Fink estimate that for an incremental 100 000 private patients, Thai or traveller, the result is an internal brain drain of between 240 and 700 medical doctors (Arunanondchai and Fink, 2007: 20).

Urban tertiary waxes. Rural primary wanes. About 35 per cent of the doctors in Thailand are in the capital. In India 59 per cent of the doctors are in cities, mainly large cities (United Nations Economic and Social Commission for Asia and the Pacific, 2007: 25). While this statistic says something about urbanisation, it says just as much about the doctors. Things will change. There are currently 6.5 doctors per 10 000 population in India. In Singapore there are 15, in the Netherlands 37. Nationally at least, the doctor–patient ratio in India is bound to rise.

The weighted workload exacerbates the shortfall. Foreigners are more demanding. Medical travellers will normally be seen by a super-scale doctor with at least ten years' experience. The consultation will be more interactive and more comprehensive. A full-time doctor spends between 1.4 minutes and 4.5 minutes longer with a foreigner than with a Thai (NaRanong and NaRanong, 2011: 338). The differentials add up: 'Due to its private nature, the resources needed to provide services to one foreigner may be equivalent to those used to provide service to 4–5 Thais. Thus the workload was equivalent to 3–4 million Thai patients' (Wibulpolprasert, Pachanee, Pitayarangsarit and Hempisut, 2004: 5). Thai professionals are in deficit at the best of times. In 2010 there were only 8840 dentists in the whole of Thailand. Medical tourism makes the deficiency worse.

Foreigners alone are not to blame. Pachanee and Wibulpolprasert conclude that 'international trade in health services is not the major contributing factor to the current internal brain drain. The increased demand from Thai patients in the private sector is more influential' (Pachanee and Wibulpolprasert, 2006: 314). Rich *bumiputras* and not just rich *farangs* are being moved to the head of the queue. It is the domestic and not just the export demand that is to blame for rising prices, hurried consultations, inadequate communication, inaccurate diagnosis and geographical maldistribution.

The pursuit of profit 'furthers the prioritization of advancements in treatment for people with access over expanding access for all' (Vijaya, 2010: 63). *De facto* privatisation upscales the client base but at the same time leaves the relatively deprived without even a general practitioner. Care inputs improve the outcome indicators: 'States with higher health worker density tend to have lower infant mortality rates and better health . . . Similarly, positive associations are observed for immunizations and attended deliveries' (Rao, Bhatnagar and Berman, 2012). A care shortfall will by the same token have an adverse effect. Timely diagnosis is delayed because the bottleneck expertise has gone to the towns. A lack of midwives raises the likelihood of maternal mortality. About 70 per cent of deaths each year in the Philippines, chiefly in hard-to-reach areas, are not medically attended. Some at least of those deaths would have been prevented if there had been early access to affordable local services.

The incomers and the elites may be sucking up the access. Public policy, however, has the power to lean against the prevailing winds. A hypothecated tax on commercial hospitals or foreign patients could cross-subsidise health insurance for low-income locals. Private providers could be required by law to supply emergency care, chronic wards and outreach clinics in isolated areas. They could be mandated to invest in public health, preventive medicine and the training of local paramedics.

They could also be compelled to provide free healthcare equivalent to some proportion (the Public Trust Act in India makes it 20 per cent) of their bedstock or total resources (Pennings, 2007: 507; Shetty, 2010: 672). Foreign-owned or locally owned, they would in this way be putting on display their conviction that the deprived must not be allowed to die where they fall. They would be stating that private facilities must not become a ghetto for the foreign or an enclave for the rich, but rather be integrated into the life of the nation.

The commitment admittedly has not always been honoured in the way that the statute intended. Charity beds have been hidden in charity wings lest a saleable image be spoiled by paupers in rags. Pro-poor facilities sometimes lack amenities and top-grade staff. Some doctors do not turn up for their public service shifts when there are full-fee foreigners who demand to be seen. Free beds in the absence of on-the-spot means tests can be allocated by contacts, politics and even bribes. Certain specialities and drugs can be too costly to offer to the destitute who cannot pay. Stem cell therapies are excluded because they are experimental. Cosmetic surgery is excluded because it is a luxury. Malpractice suits are inconceivable. The shortcomings are a fact. At the end of the day, however, charity beds are preferable to overcrowded wards and private hospitals have more technology than public. Trickle down is infinitely more ethical than no trickle at all.

Mode 2 brings patients into the country. The whole as well as the parts will reap the gain. There is import substitution: locals are treated locally who would otherwise have gone abroad (Ehrbeck, Guevara and Mango, 2008: 8). There is reflux migration: expatriate locals are attracted back by competitive salaries supported by high-grade technology. There are new jobs: unskilled locals find work as cooks, cleaners, drivers and porters. There are economies of scale: plant and personnel even in minority specialisms are kept fully employed. There is a regional multiplier. There is foreign exchange. There is economic growth. There is taxable capacity. If Mode 2 brings paying customers into the country, then Mode 2 is contributing to a larger resource pool upon which a health-conscious state can draw to blanket in the poor.

6.3.3 Measuring the Contribution

Medical tourists contribute to national income. The problem is to say how much they are worth. The price is ambiguous. The quantity is imprecise. Price times quantity is equal to revenue. Every economics undergraduate knows that. What the first-year textbooks do not say is what to do when the price as well as the quantity is in a locked box hidden by a veil.

It is difficult to translate patient numbers into revenue earned. Hospital bills are secret. All patients are unique. All professionals quote where they can a non-standard fee. In spite of that it is possible to make guarded calculations using the average price per diagnostic-related group. Often, as in Taiwan, a national insurance scheme will publish a schedule of fees. In the United States the equivalent might be the Medicare reimbursement rate. Prices in the state sector are often fixed centrally (NaRanong and NaRanong, 2011: 338). Most foreign patients are, however, treated in the private sector. There the cost per case is likely to be higher and less transparent.

Charges may not be the same for local and international clients. The cost per consultation may be higher where foreigners require translators and go in for time-consuming questions. The bill may not separate out the medical and the hotel-and-catering components. The diagnostic-related group may be subjective and debatable. Internal cross-subsidisation of one department by another, politics more than economics, may track the hospital balance of power. Taxes, subsidies, state infrastructure all confer an external benefit. Time, waits and queues are a private cost. The investigator will want to find out if the costs outweigh the benefits. It will not be an easy task.

Even if there are no guidelines or scales, charges can be approximated by typical estimates. These may be obtained from facilitators, insurance companies or an online search. Alternatively, they can be reconstructed through a focus group of doctors and administrators in private hospitals that attract a high proportion of foreign patients. Focus groups can be asked to put relative prices on common interventions so as to arrive at a representative measure.

Patient numbers multiplied by average expenditure give an indication of the revenue that medical tourism brings in. The evidence suggests that South Africa and Cuba might be earning between US$30 million and US$40 million each from medical travel. Malaysia might be earning US$167 million annually, Thailand US$400 million (some estimates go as high as US$850 million or even US$1.3 billion), Singapore about US$856 million, India from US$400 million to US$2.2 billion (Bookman and Bookman, 2007: 3; Smith, Chanda and Tangcharoensathien, 2009: 595). Israel might be earning over US$100 million a year, Jordan as much as US$1 billion (Connell, 2011: 132–133).

The figures vary widely. There is no indication of the alternative use that would have been made of the same endowment. There is no allowance for the costs that had made possible the benefits. Yet the figures on revenue are for all that positive numbers. Taken on their own terms, what they seem to say is that medical tourism is good for the national wealth.

Lautier found that health service exports in Tunisia in 2010 lay between US$500 million and US$1000 million. This was 0.88 per cent of gross domestic product (up from 0.38 per cent in 2003) and 14.7 per cent of the country's total tourism exports (Lautier, 2013: 16). About 10 500 new medical posts were created through health tourism (Lautier, 2008: 107). Approximately 27 000 derivative jobs were created in complementary industries such as catering.

The health tourism multiplier increases the number of professionals in post. In Korea, every 100 new foreign patients is the trigger for six new medical positions. In Thailand too, the inflow 'increases demand for physicians and other health professionals. By 2015, about 7 million outpatients and 0.4 million inpatients from medical tourism are estimated to be expected, requiring 200–300 extra physicians, which is about 20–30% of total private medical doctors or 9–12% of total doctors in Thailand' (Smith, Chanda and Tangcharoensathien, 2009: 599). Even though it is concentrated in the capital, still it represents a sizeable increase in the nation's doctoring stock.

Foreign patients are paying for care and are paying well. Medical travellers remain longer in the country. Their conditions are medically more complex. They are more likely to have an inpatient stay. Their length of stay is more likely to be above average. Lacking a local insurer or a local general practitioner, they are less likely to have a local benchmark. Where they are self-pay, they are less likely to have bargaining power comparable to that of a local group plan. It all shows up in the bill.

One study in Singapore found that the average tourist spends US$144 per day but that the average medical tourist spends US$362 (Turner, 2007: 314). In Tunisia the recreational tourist spends €300–€400, the medical tourist €2500–€4000 (Tourism-Review.com., 2007). In Costa Rica the Ministry of Health estimates that each medical tourist stays 11 days in the country and spends between US$6500 and US$7000. This is more than four times what an ordinary tourist would spend (Lee, 2012: 94). Another study, in the United States, found that 'international patients with the highest severity of illness stay 25 per cent longer than domestic patients with a similar severity of illness' (Johnson and Garman, 2010: 173). They spend US$47 000 per inpatient discharge. The equivalent figure for an American would be US$33 359.

The net impact goes far beyond the payment made to the doctors and the hospitals. There is also the knock-on effect for accommodation, shopping, laundry, taxis, meals and tourism, both for the patients themselves and for their companions. For Tunisia, Lautier calculated that, assuming a multiplier of 1.28, relatives and friends added a further 0.50 per cent to the GDP (Lautier, 2008: 108). Medical bills are not the whole of the induced expenditure.

In the Philippines, based on estimates for the tourism sector as a whole, the regional and the national multiplier are greater still:

> Tourism development can have strong poverty reduction effects in remote and rural areas. It has been calculated that for every foreign tourist that visits the country and spends about a thousand dollars, one job for one year is supported. Each US$1 spent by a tourist to pay for accommodation services gets multiplied 2.1 times. (Arangkada Philippines, 2009)

There are spin-offs to agriculture, industry, transport, pharmaceuticals and other complements. They feed through into economic growth. There are leakages as well: money will leave the country if tour companies, airlines and hotels are foreign-owned, or when tourists consume imported food and drinks. More optimistically, there is also an option demand. Tourists who come for the beaches might come back for the hospitals.

Worldwide, according to one survey, 83 per cent of patients travelled with a companion and 95 per cent spent money on sightseeing, shopping, restaurants or hotels (Medical Tourism Association, 2009: 34, 35). At Bumrungrad, the comparable figures were 75 per cent and 85 per cent respectively. They are lower because recorded foreigners are often resident expatriates (Medical Tourism Association/Bumrungrad International, 2010: 23). The benefits are high. The spillovers are higher. In Thailand, those accompanying the patient are believed to spend at least twice as much as the patient himself (NaRanong and NaRanong, 2011: 337). The earnings mount up. All of this is accomplished without the pollution that would have been created by manufacturing. Greenback technology is green technology. It is a healthy way to grow.

7. The inputs: commercial presence

Land only crosses the national frontiers when Singapore buys landfill from Indonesia and China cedes a disputed island to Vietnam. Other factors of production are more mobile. Chapter 7 is about capital. Chapter 8 is about labour. The world has developed beyond theories of comparative advantage which explain the gains from trade in the language of fixed domestic endowments. Nowadays it is inputs as well as outputs that are leaving home in pursuit of higher productivity elsewhere.

Commercial presence in health services is, worldwide, still marginal. The share of inward foreign direct investment (FDI) in health as a proportion of total inward FDI in services is believed to be low, at around 0.2 per cent for developed countries and 0.1 per cent in the Third World (Herman, 2009: 15). The growth rate tells a different story. FDI in healthcare is catching up.

This chapter is on health-related commercial presence. It is divided into four sections. Section 7.1, 'Market and hierarchy', explains why business firms exist. Section 7.2, 'Foreign investment', says why healthcare suppliers choose to establish treatment centres abroad. Section 7.3, 'Illustrations and examples', studies cases to make the principles clear. Section 7.4, 'Policy inferences', establishes what governments can do both to attract direct investment and to ensure that foreigners respect the host nation's priorities.

The statistics are imprecise and the definitions inconsistent. In some countries a local affiliate is called foreign-controlled where as little as 10 per cent of the voting shares are in the hands of non-residents. It is believed in the United States that a vocal minority owning as little as 10 per cent of the equity can be in a position to dominate (Krugman, Obstfeld and Melitz, 2012: 210). In other countries the threshold is as high as 51 per cent. Sometimes each subsidiary is treated as an independent entity. Sometimes fellow enterprises with a common parent are added together to measure the market penetration. Holding companies, straw-man nominees and associated affiliates make it difficult to identify the locus of control. The General Agreement on Trade in Services (GATS) was adopted before the database essential for estimating its success had been prepared. It is just as well. The wait would otherwise have been a long one.

7.1 MARKET AND HIERARCHY

The textbook case is exchange. An integrated hierarchy spanning multiple jurisdictions is as much an anomaly to the neoclassical economist as is a single-country organisation that dispenses internally with supply and demand: 'The distinguishing mark of the firm is the supersession of the price mechanism' (Coase, 1937: 389).

Concentration and globalisation mean that the school syllabus must be revised. Intra-organisational allocation often displaces the inter-organisational nexus precisely because in-house trade is the more efficient platform. An integrated structure internalises the transaction costs of information-gathering and bargain-striking. This can represent a considerable gain. A trading partner identified externally through bounded rationality might not be a very good trading partner. Real-world conjecture and guesstimate might not match up to the utility maximum brokered by an ideal-typical auctioneer. Searching and contracting are not without their costs. An integrated structure reduces those costs. It also creates new costs of its own in the form of diminishing returns to entrepreneurship, creativity and imagination.

The precise optimum cannot be known *a priori*. The choice depends, as Williamson points out, on the 'comparative costs of planning, adapting, and monitoring task completion under alternative governance structures' (Williamson, 1981: 1544). The economic balance is not immune from managerial and technological innovation: 'Changes like the telephone and the telegraph which tend to reduce the cost of organising spatially will tend to increase the size of the firm' (Coase, 1937: 297). Sometimes the market will be more expensive and sometimes the institutional hierarchy. Always, however, it is relative cost that pipes the tune. Own-brands, exchange, multi-product, single-product, franchising, consultants on piecework, long-term contracts, public–private joint ventures – all are up for grabs.

Relative cost plays an important role in corporate expansion. Both vertical and horizontal integration reflect the quest for the equilibrium scale.

In the case of vertical integration, the firm expands downstream into raw materials and components and forward into retailing and marketing. Its intention may be to safeguard a unique natural resource such as oil or to ensure its access to a protected market. The danger is that the company will lose internal economies if it spreads itself too thin. In the health-care industry, vertical integration can take the form of an international network of referrals and contacts. In line with the '*growing interconnectedness of transnational economies*', many companies 'strategically fragment their operations, such that a head office will reside in a nation with, say, a well-developed infrastructure, while its manufacturing sector may be outsourced to a nation with lower labour costs' (Behrman and Smith, 2010: 82). Medical procedures are performed abroad. Business administration remains at home. It means that regulators have a foothold in two jurisdictions.

Clinics abroad can serve as outstation feeders for the group's tertiary hospital. Pre-admission tests and post-operative follow-up in a satellite clinic remain within the seamless web of a single structure. The hub-and-spoke model increases the likelihood that the patients will travel to the foreign hospital abroad. If they did not, they might seek treatment in their own country; or another multinational might fill the market vacuum. Vertical integration seals in the first-mover advantage.

Companies with a large stable of affiliates can afford to spread risk through geographical and industrial diversification. They will also be facing the diseconomies of control. The more numerous the markets in which the subsidiaries operate, the more difficult it will be to coordinate their plans.

Internationally, firms may divide up the production process between areas that field cheap labour for manual routines and areas that pyramid high-end science on educated human capital: 'Shipping intangible research results around the world is less costly than shipping physical components' (Caves, 2007: 106). The local subsidiary becomes a link in a network. Assuming that transportation costs are economic and communication is free from noise, an integrated network can make an economical use of factor endowments. Where it decides that it is not doing so, it has the option of demerging the fringe units that put up the cost of the whole.

In the case of horizontal integration, the fixed overhead is spread over a larger number of plants. When additional sites are established, the marginal cost is low or zero since the deadweight of invention has already been written off. Within the firm the knowledge required for replication has the character of a public good. That is the advantage of the unified structure. Know-how that can be accessed free of charge by outsiders will normally be underprovided. The originator will have no incentive to take the initiative where a best-practice discovery can fall into the hands of a predatory rival.

Horizontal integration is attractive where the firm possesses intangible assets. Examples of such 'proprietary assets' (Caves, 2007: 3) would be microelectronic algorithms, surgical short-cuts, habitual routines, house secrets, patented designs, a registered trademark, a differentiated image. Intellectual property of this kind is difficult to license or sell. Its market value cannot be estimated until it is put to use. Outsiders who lease the blueprints and then fail to extend are able to retain the winning formula for their own use. To protect their rent from free riders the owner has no choice but to frustrate arbitrage by sealing in the sector-specific asset. The cloning of their original business is the expedient that they adopt.

Horizontal integration has the further attraction that it blocks off opportunistic behaviour. Contracts can never be complete. The unforeseen may happen. A self-interested trading partner may seek (perhaps deceitfully) to make a non-sustainable gain. Williamson observes that 'opportunism effectively extends the usual assumption of self-interest seeking to make allowance for self-interest seeking with guile' (Williamson, 1981: 1545). An example is what happens once firm-specific infrastructure such as a feeder railway has been installed. Asset-specificity leaves the factory open to bullying if an outside contract must be renewed and the bilateral relationship renegotiated. Without the feeder link, its clients cannot come in and its product cannot get out.

Besides that, franchising can be accompanied by quality debasement. Where this occurs, it devalues the company's name. It limits future sales of the brand worldwide. The cost-effectiveness of marketing is reduced. Internal organisation in such circumstances can be a better alternative.

An organised structure under a single top management is one answer to the problem of transaction costs and information leakages. Another would be a global value chain of independent producers which have developed the habit of ordering their output sequentially. Gap buys over a billion units of clothing but does not own a single factory abroad. Focusing on design, marketing and distribution – in a word, the name – it outsources its production to smaller suppliers to which it holds no title. Nike, similarly, makes use of contract where others would go for capital: 'Nike has slightly more than 20 000 direct employees, but its products are manufactured by more than 500 000 workers in over 700 factories in 51 countries' (Thun, 2011: 346). Lower transport costs and electronic communications make such non-proprietorial chains possible. An illustration in the field of health is the insurance company which has a number of hospitals in its sphere of influence but does not own even one. A preferred proprietor, a recommended subcontractor, can be a guarantee almost on a par with direct provision.

7.2 FOREIGN INVESTMENT

There are two routes open to foreign investors who wish to establish a local presence. The first is portfolio investment: the gain-seeker purchases shares in a listed company in order to secure the influence, the dividends and the capital appreciation. The second is direct investment: the business penetrates the market through the acquisition of (or merger with) an existing brownfield business or through the *ab initio* creation of productive capacity in a greenfield start-up. Portfolio investment is short-run and opportunistic: the speculator comes and goes. Foreign direct investment – FDI – is a longer-term commitment. The investor is not planning to flip the assets for a quick return. Nor is it certain that another investor would want them.

Pharmaceutical companies like Pfizer, Merck, Johnson and Johnson, GlaxoSmithKline (all US-based), Bayer, Schering-Plough (in Germany), Ciba-Geigy, Roche, Novartis (in Switzerland), AstraZeneca (in the United Kingdom) are high-profile organisations with registered patents and solid transfer value. They are among the world's largest (non-financial) transnationals. Pharmaceuticals make up 55 per cent (by value) of health-related products traded internationally. Of the top 20 corporations, all from Europe and the United States, each has more than 20 affiliates. They operate in more than 40 countries, developed and less developed. Globalisation of production within an existing multinational ensures that there will not be a perceived quality shortfall when costs are cut through the offshoring of drugs to a country like Singapore (where pharmaceuticals account for 8 per cent of total manufacturing output) or India. Buying Indian is seen as the same as buying Swiss. Besides that, India itself will one day be a mass market. Leveraging on exports, the companies get a toehold in rapidly increasing sales.

FDI is a long-term commitment. The question is why the organisation goes down this road. The traditional way to penetrate a new market is through arm's-length pricing and the shipment abroad of its output. That is the question: why does the corporation not simply manufacture at home and then export its wares?

One reason is the need to tap into customers on the spot. It is in the nature of a personal service that it must be supplied face to face. Some clients are willing to travel abroad. Others would prefer that their service provider should come to them. Cost is a consideration: while the very rich can afford to travel, the rising middle classes might only be able to afford private treatment if it is delivered near at hand. This is especially important where the service is delivered in steps. While some interventions are completed in a single visit, others require a battery of diagnostic tests in advance, protracted follow-up in the months and even years to come. A local facility has locational advantage. It is convenient for its client-base.

An entrant will often be able to capitalise on the absence of indigenous competitors. It may be able to develop a niche market in a narrow area such as colon cancer. It may be able to transfer sophisticated technology and advanced know-how that consolidates its reputation as a cut above the locals.

To remain the front-runner, it may have no choice but to go abroad. Market saturation in its core market might drive a one-line producer to complement its citizen pool with foreign patients in need of the same. The alternative might be high distributions or the transformation of a once-focused firm into a catch-all conglomerate without a competitive edge. A firm loses face if it is known to be expanding into marginal, even unrelated lines of activity, because there is no other way to grow. Excess capacity focuses the mind. Going abroad is the answer.

Some markets are sheltered. Tariffs and non-tariff barriers (which may include a high rate of exchange) artificially inflate the rate of return. Such walls attract the entrant to settle inside. Wishing to penetrate, the entrant might situate no more than the final stage of its production chain in its target territory. Residency is a sensible move. Although average tariffs have been reduced in successive rounds, there has been a growth in intra-regional traffic. The non-tariff concessions in economic communities will normally be confined to resident enterprise. Foreign-owned businesses will enjoy the advantages if they relocate.

International law facilitates the move. The free movement of medical equipment and supplies is guaranteed by the World Trade Organization (WTO). The WTO commits its members to the non-discriminatory universalisation of the most-favoured-nation principle. Foreign or local, all members must be guaranteed a level playing-field. Exchange controls at the same time have been relaxed. Exchange rates are less likely to deviate from the free market fix that reflects purchasing power parity. History is on the side of FDI. Globalisation lends support to the firm that invests abroad.

Entrants have advantages. Multinational enterprise brings in physical capital: it confers a positive externality where savings (as in the poorer countries) are low and foreign exchange scarce. Foreign investment brings in human capital: it imports specialist manpower, internationalises management and makes the transfer of technology a cross-border external economy. The benefits trickle down to domestically owned firms. Local managers trained and promoted in a multinational will be better placed later on to go into business on their own. Local doctors will be ready and willing to be headhunted by the state.

The stream of benefits goes both ways. Local knowledge is a major entry-barrier. Investors may prefer portfolio participation because FDI is too much of a risk. A compromise would be a joint venture that taps into local networks such as the Fresenius Medical Group. Headquartered in Germany, Fresenius collaborates with doctors and clinics in the United States to provide outpatient dialysis to more than 78 000 Americans. Through Fresenius Medical Care Asia Pacific it has additional affiliates in countries such as Singapore, Taiwan, Japan and China (Outreville, 2007: 306).

A multinational establishing a subsidiary or a branch overseas will face the one-time transaction cost of learning local practices, management styles and ways of doing business. Host-country executives already understand the usages and the language. This is especially important in the service sector. Their presence may defuse latent resentment, not least where the foreign company enters by taking over a going concern. Locals must, however, have had adequate training and experience. It is not always possible (especially in a Third World context) to find local manpower with high-end skills. Locals appointed, their integration into the incomer's corporate culture is not instantaneous. In the interim the company has no alternative but to incur the cost of posting its own professionals abroad.

Permits must be secured. Visas must be arranged. Local managers do not eliminate the hurdles but they may have the contacts to make the problems more tractable. Canada is familiar to US companies. Myanmar is not. Sometimes the multi-plant corporation will be able to respond more effectively if monolithic headquarters devolves power to the decision-makers on the spot. A tall hierarchy may be too remote for hands-on control.

Foreign direct investment is especially beneficial where it is part of a balanced cluster. Consider the situation in India: 'Indian hospitals import 70 per cent or more of medical devices and equipment, often at high cost, the root cause being the limited domestic manufacturing capacity . . . Apart from a few Indian or joint venture operations in this area, there is little domestic production' (Chanda, 2010: 136–137). There are obstacles to the development of the supplier industries. Local shortages mean that home manufacturers can afford to be high-cost. Home suppliers are sheltered by customs duties. The limited hospital market means that the producers of inputs cannot obtain economies of scale.

A hospital needs beds, latex gloves, surgical gowns and drugs: demand gives a stimulus to local manufacturing and pharmaceuticals. A health centre requires educated manpower: state schooling may be a complement. A factory wants internal economies: one buyer cannot demand enough equipment to justify a sophisticated subdivision of production. An industry wants specialised supplies: geographical concentration ensures local availability and cuts down on waits. Alfred Marshall emphasised that, alongside internal economies that reduce the unit cost of production, there are also external economies which each firm can enjoy precisely because of 'the concentration of large numbers of small businesses of a similar kind in the same locality' (Marshall, 1890 [1949]: 230). More competitors lower the cost of production. What all can do, one cannot.

A crowded matrix allows the suppliers to liaise face to face with their customers. Employees cutting their ties with one firm face lower search costs in moving to another. There are knowledge spillovers where staff employed by contenders and challengers talk shop over drinks or tennis. Informal exchanges about processes, products and innovations move the firms more rapidly along their learning curve. Ambitious outsiders, domestic and international, are attracted in. Knock-on jobs add new value beyond the core activity. Every cluster stands in need of hotels, schools, shops and watering holes. The multiplier primes all the pumps. The whole is different from the sum of the parts.

The invisible hand will in many cases be enough to bring into being the agglomeration of function. Marshall's examples of steel-making in Solingen and printing in Paternoster Square look forward to the capitalist networks of modern Hollywood, Bollywood, Wall Street and Silicon Valley. Sometimes, however, the state will choose to intervene. It was public money that initially attracted Hewlett Packard to Bangalore. It was the state that invested heavily in bioscientific research in Singapore in the Biopolis and Fisionopolis estates as well as the local universities. It was the state that planned for a whole spectrum of complements in special medical zones at Jeju, Cebu, Medellin and the Dubai Healthcare City.

The wider community shares in the upgraded infrastructure of airports and roads. Environmental dis-welfares must be addressed. Tourism must be coordinated with sewers. Hospitals must arrange tie-ins with hotels (Plentitas with Sheraton) and with airlines (Bumrungrad with Thai). The joint product must be marketed. WiFi and security must be provided. Public and private work together. Together they make up a mixed medical economy.

Constellations are economic. Whether they also have to be geographical is open to debate. Microelectronics allows both new ideas and business services to travel great distances. Just as banks and brokers sell worldwide, so a health centre can use Mode 1 to tap into a cross-border market. In some cases a cluster is rooted in a place because of local supplies of a natural resource. Not all business opportunities are, however, equally tied to giants in the earth like coal and iron. There is no reason for a call centre, an animation studio or a research institute or even the head office to be situated in California. Manila or Singapore may do just as well.

Yet there is an intermediate optimum somewhere between Paternoster agglomeration and amoebic multiplicity. Vertical integration in the global economy has empowered corporations to divide labour by country: 'Intra-firm trade represents roughly one-third of worldwide trade and over 40 per cent of US trade' (Krugman, Obstfeld and Melitz, 2012: 215). Serial offshoring allows them to capitalise on the competitive advantage of different regions. Each region promises the economies of physical agglomeration. No single region, however, covers all the stages in the production chain. The result is that the multinational has to keep moving the product along.

Entry from abroad challenges domestic cartels and price-fixing arrangements. It forces suppliers to keep their costs down. Entry is not, however, without its disadvantages. One of these involves capital. While some multinationals will be importing funds from their First World home, others will be borrowing in host-country markets, often with the host-country government as an underwriter. Domestic savings being scarce, the multinationals may be putting pressure on interest rates that will price local borrowers out. It is, of course, possible to argue that banks and other intermediaries in less-developed countries are not always capable of turning savings in agriculture into finance for industry. Lending to a multinational might in so imperfect a market be the best way of channelling resources into value-adding activities and not unproductive paper.

The foreign firm may be repatriating its profits rather than making the surplus locally available. Where it brings in its own staff and imports its own inputs, it puts further pressure on capital and exchange. Vertical integration exacerbates the drain. Transnationals often charge their affiliates an internally determined price for the licences and patents. These transfer prices on intra-firm payments can be used to reduce the local government's tax take.

A new entrant can undercut local producers. It can bankrupt them or drive them into a merger. While the disruption of long-established networks may be a stimulus to efficiency, it is also true that local firms are likely to be buying inputs from local suppliers. The redirection of business might trigger a knock-on contraction as local suppliers fail and supplies are increasingly imported. It is a fallen form of technology transfer where few or no local firms survive and the technology is merely lent to another spoke in the wheel.

FDI is foreign. It is also normally private. Being private, it is likely not only to cream off some burden from the state sector but to alter the proportions between the sectors. In that way it will accentuate the two-tier bias. In South Africa the private sector musters only 22 per cent of the hospital beds but absorbs 60 per cent of all healthcare spending (Crush, Chikanda and Maswikwa, forthcoming). In India 80 per cent of the hospitals (but only 5 per cent of the beds) are in the state sector. The private sector accounts for over 50 per cent of the bills and employs 80 per cent of all qualified doctors. Both absolute and relative values count. The private sector is well funded. The state sector lives from hand to mouth.

The entry of private providers alters the rules of the game. US FDI in the UK hospital sector is a case in point: 'A vicious cycle was generated in which the growth of private insurance spurred the introduction of private hospitals which ignited further growth of private insurance. The American hospitals both created and satisfied the demand for an alternative health system to the National Health Service' (Berliner and Regan, 1987: 1282). The National Health Service was not prepared for the challenge of profit-seeking American competitors with a commercial approach to insurance, management, accountancy and marketing. It could not match the new entrants' user-friendly service in areas such as luxury amenities, convenient scheduling, immediate admission, sophisticated technology. It did not offer the full range of specialist clinics for alcoholism, drug abuse, anorexia, bulimia. The result was that some UK patients privatised themselves and opted out. It was cheaper for them to visit an American hospital in the UK than to travel abroad.

Some FDI is private but still not for profit. Thus the Christus Muguerza Alta Especialidad Hospital in Monterrey, Mexico (affiliated to Christus Health in Dallas) ploughs back its surplus. As a Catholic non-profit organisation, the Christus group has invested heavily in altruism, commitment and the ideals of the Good Samaritan. It puts into practice its public service orientation, not least through the five social assistance clinics that it operates in deprived communities. The same may be said of the 93 Christian not-for-profit hospitals and clinics worldwide (a further 59 are in operation in the United States) that make up the California-based Adventist Health International. Most FDI nonetheless goes abroad for profit. An example would be an insurance company that builds or buys abroad because it costs less to get its clients patched up that way.

An increase in FDI may therefore be expected to increase the share of business and of the market orientation in health. It is a topic in the ideological transition. The relative privatisation of health, whether slower growth in the state sector or the outright sale of state-owned plant, represents a fundamental sea-change that socialists and social democrats will strongly resist. The National Health Service has a charter to deliver good-quality medical services to rich and poor alike. A private multinational is run with a view to profit and loss.

Profit and loss can be but need not be antithetical to good health. On the one hand, new services and medicines can become available more quickly in the private than in the public sector. The demonstration effect makes public patients want the new frontier for themselves. On the other hand, higher quality may be expensive, unneeded, supplier-induced, flat-of-the-curve. It can be public money wasted because public opinion is easily impressed and ill-informed. The vote motive can unleash an escalation in costs.

7.3 ILLUSTRATIONS AND EXAMPLES

World FDI amounted in 2007 to US$500 billion (Smith, 2012: 185). FDI in developing countries is over three times that of official development aid. Over half of FDI is in services. Health-specific FDI is less than FDI in oil or retailing. It is on a rising trend but it also has some way to go.

Much of the investment is genuinely multinational. An example is the Health Corporation of America. The largest healthcare provider in the world, it caters for half the private patients in the UK. Its hospitals include the Harley Street Clinic and its profits in 2011 were £61.7 million.

US corporations are the leading players. They are not the only ones. Ramsay Health Care based in New South Wales has 10000 beds and 120 hospitals in Australia, the UK, France, Malaysia and Indonesia. Bangkok Dusit Medical Services, the market leader in Thailand, has two hospitals in Cambodia and is planning a third in Myanmar. Bumrungrad, also based in Thailand, has 102 clinics in eight Asian countries, plus a 56 per cent stake in the Asian Hospital, Manila. Foreignness is a spectrum and not an either/or.

Trading on its reputation for efficiency, Bumrungrad managed but did not own the 450-bed Bumrungrad Al Mafraq Hospital in Abu Dhabi which it operated on behalf of the Health Authority of Abu Dhabi. Domestic supplies of capital and foreign exchange are adequate in Abu Dhabi because of the oil. What the locals do not have is a track record in combining managerial techniques, high-tech medicine and information technology (IT). Bumrungrad fills the gap in the life cycle of the country and, indeed, in the product cycle of an innovation. Outside management enables the flying geese to follow the leader until such a time as their evolving strengths allow them to take off on their own.

Africans too are investing abroad, and not just in their neighbours. Netcare, Life Healthcare and Mediclinic, controlling between them 83.4 per cent of private beds in South Africa, have invested in hospitals not just in Botswana and Namibia but also in the UK, Switzerland and the United Arab Emirates. The supernormal profits earned in South Africa by the three giant national networks generated the springboard capital they needed to go abroad.

The protected nature of the South African healthcare market made it possible for the oligopolists to collude. Imperfect competition may have been a blessing in disguise: 'Protectionism or rather the domination it allows may be crucial to MNCs [multinational corporations] from emerging countries' (Mortensen, 2008: 28). In Europe, on the other hand, it was not the imposition but rather the elimination of protection that was the greater incentive: 'Foreign ownership in medical practice activities comprises 24.39 per cent of all ownership, while foreign ownership in hospital activities is 10.38 per cent' (Herman, 2009). The reduction in barriers as well as the bulwark of enforceable contracts was a sound reason for the MNCs to invest European Union-wide. Privatisation, coincidentally, gave them an opportunity to take over some assets from the state.

The experience of India, Singapore and Malaysia is especially interesting. Together, these examples illustrate most of what can go wrong and what can go right when health-related investments flow in and flow out.

7.3.1 India

Private hospitals in India tend to have been founded with Indian capital. There is not a great deal of foreign direct investment in the sector despite the fact that India permits 100 per cent foreign ownership and does not limit borrowing on world capital markets. The bulk of foreign financing in Indian hospitals has been through private equity funds and the take-up of initial public offers. Some of the money came from non-resident Indians (Chanda, 2010: 129–130). FDI in the Indian hospital industry is still in its infancy.

It is hard to say where the Third World ends and the First World begins when a country with a GDP per capita in 2011 of US$838 is able to develop a competitive advantage in financial resources and state-of-the-art technology. Venture capital and family funding were there at the outset. The Apollo Hospitals Group, established in 1983 by Dr Prathap Reddy, was initially a family business. As soon as it had shown itself to be commercially viable, the capital base was opened up to the world. The Reddys now hold only 32 per cent of the equity. Foreigners have 41 per cent. Schroder Capital Partners holds a considerable stake, as does the Singapore government through its sovereign wealth fund Temasek (Oberholzer-Gee, Khanna and Knoop, 2005: 8).

Apollo, India's first and largest for-profit hospital chain, has 54 hospitals. Some are in India (Chennai, Bangalore, Hyderabad, Delhi), some in South Asia (Bangladesh, Sri Lanka), some in the Middle East. It receives over 50 000 international patients a year from 55 countries. It has a telemedicine station in Kazakhstan. It co-owns the Apollo Gleneagles Hospital in Kolkata with the brand-name Parkway group from Singapore. It has plans to expand into Europe (Malta), Africa (Libya, Ethiopia, Tanzania) and the Caribbean (Barbados, the Bahamas). Although India is far away, the Caribbean is only an hour's flight for the large concentrations of retired Americans in South Florida.

Apollo's business strategy goes beyond horizontal integration. It has put in place a vertical structure, using the primary care clinics it franchises in India and the health centres it operates in Tanzania and Mauritius as a source of referrals. It has also diversified into neighbouring activities. All of these are health-related. Apollo has a stake in a network of pharmacies. These alone, reflecting the prominence of self-medication in India, generate 40 per cent of group profits. It has a consulting service. Feasibility studies are conducted for clients in Asia, Africa and the Middle East. It has an interest in health insurance. It operates nursing schools. This is partly as a response to its own high turnover of nurses, about 25 per cent a year (Oberholzer-Gee, Khanna and Knoop, 2005: 3).

Apollo is the market leader. It is the world's third-largest private health provider. Other important Indian medical chains are Narayana Hrudayalaya, Manipal, Max Healthcare and Fortis Healthcare International. Together they not only provide high-standard care for middle-class Indians but they also dominate inward medical tourism and hospital FDI.

Narayana, based in Bangalore and largely owned by the Shetty family, received start-up funding from the long-established Shankar Narayana Construction Company. It has 5000 beds in 14 hospitals in India. Dr Devi Shetty says that he was inspired by the example of Mother Theresa to provide health insurance for the poor at 22 US cents a month and to charge a lower rate for the needy. Keen to follow Apollo into the Americas, Narayana is building a 2000-bed health city (with a medical school) in the Cayman Islands and is planning a 3000-bed hospital in Mexico City. The projects, costing at least US$2 billion, will be funded by private investors in India and the United States. The hospitals will be largely staffed by Indians. Work permits and recognition of professional certification were part of the deal.

The critical mass will come from the US market. Americans are attracted by the moderate prices, the good quality and the convenient location. The Cayman Islanders themselves, numbering a mere 55 000, would never have been able to ensure the economic throughput necessary for a tertiary centre. When the hospital is built, the locals and not just the tourists will be able to go to Narayana for their medical needs. The Caymans is currently spending $30 million annually on treatment abroad. It is hard currency that it cannot spare.

Fortis too, as with Apollo and Narayana, does both national and international business. Its growth has been fed by the purchase of ten hospitals in India from the Wockhardt group. Despite the German-sounding name, Wockhardt is an Indian family firm, founded in the 1960s by Habil Khorakiwala and later managed by his sons. Its core business is pharmaceuticals and biotechnological products which it manufactures in India and, overseas, in the US, UK, France, Germany and Ireland. Its hospitals were an add-on. They were pulling it into diversification that was actually retarding its expansion. Wockhardt wanted consolidation, Fortis market share. Both companies benefited from the sale.

Fortis is owned and operated by two brothers, Malvinder Mohan Singh and Shrivinder Mohan Singh. It has 39 hospitals in India, New Zealand, Canada, Mauritius, Sri Lanka, Vietnam, Dubai, Hong Kong and Singapore. It was keen to enhance its profile in Singapore through the purchase of the Parkway group. In the event, in 2011, the four Parkway hospitals, its primary care centres and its medical college were sold to IHH.

Indian hospitals have Indian roots. Alongside entrepreneurial dynasties like the Reddys, the Shettys, the Khorakiwalas and the Singhs, there has nonetheless been a limited amount of inward foreign investment, and not just in the software industry. Pacific Healthcare from Singapore, previously involved in a joint venture with India's Vitae Healthcare, holds a stake in Cure Heart in Bangalore and the Cosmetic Medical and Dental Centre in Mumbai. Parkway is a partner in the Asian Heart Institute in Mumbai. The Columbia Asia Group, an offshoot of Columbia Pacific, a Seattle-based investment company with hospitals in Indonesia, Vietnam and Malaysia, has 11 American-standard multi-speciality facilities in India. FDI in the Indian hospital sector is already there.

It is there but it is limited. Developing India seems to be generating much of its own healthcare capital. The prosperous North seems not to be making significant investments in an up-and-coming industry in an up-and-coming country. The process should be two-way. Tata buys the UK's Jaguar. Microsoft buys Korea's Thrunet. UK banks go into the US. American banks come into the UK. In spite of that the North is not investing heavily in India's healthcare sector.

The set-up overhead is considerable. The number of foreign hospitals potentially able to contest the market is, worldwide, necessarily limited. Infrastructure such as electricity is deficient. Urban land is expensive. Delays in processing paperwork are commonplace. Skill is scarce. Medical equipment is expensive. Insurance penetration is low. Delivery and finance 'are not transparent or accountable' (Peters and Muraleedharan, 2008: 2113). Plans for special zones and healthcare cities are still under consideration. Some investors, as Chanda discovered in a series of interviews, do not want to come in because they feel the business climate leaves much to be desired: 'It was noted by several respondents that the Indian government does not have a clear roadmap for the healthcare sector, has not considered it a core sector, and is perceived to have a non-transparent regulatory environment and corrupt and inefficient procedures for establishing business' (Chanda, 2010: 133). Whether or not the bias is justified is not relevant. Investment is driven by perceptions at least as much as by balance sheets. The perception is red tape and uncertainty.

Chanda has observed that liberalisation is not all that is required:

> A liberal multilateral commitment on FDI will not necessarily result in a surge of FDI inflows into healthcare unless other structural and regulatory issues are addressed. Furthermore, there is a need to ensure coherence in the negotiating and domestic policy stance across related sectors, such as across the health and insurance sectors or the health and education sectors. (Chanda, 2010: 142)

It is political economy and not only economics that is holding the FDI back.

Chanda draws attention to a further impediment, namely 'a lack of awareness' (Chanda, 2011: 7) in India and in foreign countries of the untapped opportunities. The domestic market is large and growing. Labour is relatively cheap. New airports are being built. There are unexploited economies of size. The international investor may be unduly concerned about the risks. There are also the prospects. Awareness is the key.

Regulatory issues cannot be neglected. Although India has a comprehensive system of laws and law courts (and a Right to Information Act, 2006), there is the backlog and the expense. As for the ministries, the system of

> administrative and bureaucratic controls does not seem to be functioning well. Public safety in the health sector is not assured . . . At a time when new technologies and pharmaceuticals continuously raise the stakes and the potential for harm to the public, India's regulatory approach does not appear to address the realities of India's highly unregulated health markets. (Peters and Muraleedharan, 2008: 2133)

There is, as so often in private medicine, evidence of unnecessary services, excessive caesareans, superfluous hysterectomies: 'According to Transparency International, the health sector is viewed by the public as second only to the police as the most corrupt sector in the country' (Peters and Muraleedharan, 2008: 2140). Minimum standards are not always ensured. Professional self-regulation is patchy. Regulation that is too loose will one day have to be tightened up. The fear of an 'inspectorate Raj' deters foreign direct investors. So does the iceberg of the poor which a populist administration could require the private sector to cross-subsidise.

Regulation is a problem. Hospitals doing an international business at least have an international stamp of approval from a body such as the Joint Commission International (JCI). The spread of insurance will introduce additional scrutiny that is absent where payment is out-of-pocket. Out-of-pocket is the typical means of payment in India. Private persons have less information and little power. The spread of insurance will weaken the hospitals' position. Performance-based contracts could be the result.

7.3.2 Singapore and Malaysia

The two largest private groups in Singapore are Parkway and Raffles. The largest group in Malaysia is Pantai. Both Parkway and Pantai are owned by IHH Healthcare Berhad, registered in Malaysia. IHH is Asia's largest healthcare multinational by market capitalisation. It is the world's second-largest listed private healthcare provider, after HCA Holdings in the USA.

The majority shareholder is the Malaysian sovereign wealth fund Khazaneh Nasional. Khazaneh holds a 100 per cent stake in a holding company, Pulau Memutik, which holds a 62 per cent stake in IHH which holds a 100 per cent stake in Parkway Pantai Limited (PPL) which holds a 100 per cent stake in the Parkway chain in Singapore and the Pantai chain in Malaysia, as well as IMU Health which operates a private health sciences university in Kuala Lumpur. IHH also has an 11 per cent stake in Apollo in India and a 94 per cent stake in IHH Turkey which has a 60 per cent stake in Acibadem Holdings which has a 97 per cent stake in Acibadem which, with 5.2 per cent of all hospital beds, is the largest private healthcare provider in Turkey. The non-Khazaneh equity in IHH is 27 per cent held by MKK Holdings (100 per cent owned by the Mitsui Corporation), 7 per cent held by Abraaj Capital (a Dubai-based private equity company) and 4 per cent in the hands of Aydinlar (a Turkish family trust) (IHH Healthcare Berhad, 2012: 315). IHH is a public–private corporation through which the Malaysian public sector co-owns a presence in the global private sector. What would Marx have made of that?

Khazaneh in Malaysia, Temasek Holdings in Singapore, are state-owned. A sovereign wealth fund has to strike a balance between health and return, the domestic patient and the cross-border traveller. The model is corporatist and collaborative through and through: 'Indeed, it is not possible to think about the emergence of the medical tourist industry and its initial development in Asia in the aftermath of the 1997 financial crisis without thinking about the role of the state' (Chee, 2010: 337). There can be multiple conflicts of interest. Temasek holds 4.87 percent of shares in the Raffles Medical Group (the same percentage as the Qatar Investment Authority) and 1 per cent (down from 12 per cent) in Bumrungrad. Yet they are in competition.

The Singapore private hospitals are active abroad. IHH has offices or clinics in India, China, Vietnam, Brunei, Hong Kong (where it is building a 500-bed hospital) and, beyond the Asia Pacific, in Turkey and Macedonia. Raffles has clinics in Hong Kong and Shanghai. It is exploring (with Kaiser Permanente) a 50:50 joint venture in the USA. The future will generate significant investment opportunities as population, expectations, income, insurance cover and median age go up in target countries. Means tests will make public services relatively more expensive. The gap with the private sector will in that way narrow.

The government sector internationally will not be able to meet the demand for doctors and beds. The Organisation for Economic Co-operation and Development (OECD) average is 3.7 doctors per 1000 population. In Vietnam it is 1.9. In Indonesia it is 0.6. The pressures for catch-up will be great and they will be irresistible. Singapore and Malaysia are in the right industry at the right time.

7.4 POLICY INFERENCES

Brownfield or greenfield, the outcome of start-ups and acquisitions is likely to be globally integrated networks that serve many masters and most of all themselves:

> In many instances, the decisions that firms make are based on global strategies for corporate success, rather than on the basis of conditions within any of the countries in which the firm conducts its business. As a result, multinational corporations highlight the tensions inherent in an economy that is increasingly organized along global lines and political systems that continue to reflect exclusive national territories. (Oatley, 2012: 158)

Politics is national. Business is international. As important as healthcare undeniably is, the danger is that there will be no one big enough to make the disparate players serve the interest of the whole.

7.4.1 Attracting and Retaining

Capitalism is a profit and loss system. Gamblers who are attached to their endowment should stay out of the casino. Instead they lobby the state to abandon impartial laissez-faire and come to their aid. Galbraith was sharply critical of special-pleaders such as these who seek to live well at the taxpayers' expense: 'There is much to the increasingly common observation that the modern economy features socialism for the large corporation, free enterprise for the small' (Galbraith, 1975: 172).

Businesses that ask the government to share their losses should be prepared to share their profits as well. Perhaps, however, they are already doing so. The multiplier effect of new investment on employment, national income, market competition, the balance of payments and company tax is an external economy which may snowball spillovers far in excess of the start-up subsidy. The possibility is there that new hospitals will yield a competitive rate of return for the nation and not just for the shareholders. Businesses are unlikely to neglect a lucrative market merely because the state is not overcompensating them with a hand-out. Also, as with all infant industries, state aid cannot be expected to run on forever.

Adam Smith was neither the first nor the last to point out that homeless capital can pack up and leave if disclosure is probing or regulation onerous:

> The proprietor of land is necessarily a citizen of the particular country in which his estate lies. The proprietor of stock is properly a citizen of the world, and is not necessarily attached to any particular country. He would be apt to abandon the country in which he was exposed to a vexatious inquisition . . . By removing his stock he would put an end to all the industry which it had maintained in the country which he left. (Smith, 1776 [1961]: II, 375–376)

Countries, like people, prefer more to less. The possibility of 'exit', the absence of 'loyalty', mean that the 'voice' of the foreign gain-seeker stands a reasonable chance of producing results.

The levers are many and they are familiar. Tax holidays can be offered to overseas entrants. Purchase tax can be rebated to non-resident patients. Export earnings can be made tax-exempt. Accelerated depreciation can be granted to hospitals that upgrade. Interest rates can be subsidised. Risks can be shared. Medical equipment can be allowed in tariff-free. Repatriation of profits can be permitted even if the nation has exchange control. State land can be made available at concessionary rents. Building can be encouraged in special economic or free-trade zones. Hospitals can be given funding to secure accreditation.

Work permits for skilled expatriates can be fast-tracked. Medical visas for intending patients can be multiple entry. Damages for medical malpractice can be capped by law. Marketing overheads can be shared with parastatal organisations or given double tax relief. A one-stop shop like the Economic Development Board in Singapore can be created as a shortcut through the red tape, the bureaucracy, the uncertainty and in some countries the side-payments.

More generally, the business climate can be made more market-centric and less political. Property rights can be scrupulously protected. Patents can be enforced despite the lack of evidence that protection leads to an increase in FDI (Smith, Correa and Oh, 2009: 688). Education can equip manpower with bottleneck skills. Deregulation, privatisation and liberalisation can release price competition from frustrating controls. Minimum wages, traditional demarcations, job security, on-the-job training, confrontational unions and disruptive strikes can all be made past history. Domestic entrepreneurs as well as foreign multinationals will benefit from a more welcoming business environment. Across-the-board policies defuse the charge that the incomers are enjoying reverse discrimination that makes it difficult for the locals to undercut.

Ideally, the host government and the foreign transnational will have broadly the same objectives and plans. Once domestic politics becomes global politics, it will not be easy to win the requisite consensus: 'Historically, decisions about production have been made by local business owners with reference to local conditions. When MNCs are involved, however, foreign managers make production decisions with reference to global conditions' (Oatley, 2012: 180). The government may want import substitution. The multinational may favour export-led growth. The government may want a pro-poor wing. The multinational may reply that its shareholders have no stake in local charity or public health.

The multinational may threaten to go elsewhere if the host country does not attract or retain it in the manner to which it would like to become accustomed. Rhetoric or reality, the fact is that governments that want to bring in hospitals are reluctant to see them leave. The multinationals, knowing this, are in a position to play one rival country off against another. The outcome of this games-playing bluff and feint can well be the 'race to the bottom': 'States must effectively clamber over one another in an ever-more frenzied attempt to produce a more favourable investment environment for mobile ("footloose") foreign direct investors than their competitors' (Hay, 2011: 317). The prediction is not necessarily the contraction of the state. There can be an arms race. Public spending can actually rise as competing nations escalate their complements in a bid to overtake the concessions being made by their rivals.

The balance of support will depend upon the balance of power. Power is global. Yet it is domestic as well. Domestically as well as globally, there will be winners as well as losers as a result of the rules that evolve. The scarce factor has the superior bargaining position. In many of the countries that are seeking to attract medical tourism, the factor labour is in surplus and immobile while the factor capital is rootless and fancy free: 'A neo-Darwinian survival of the fittest effectively guarantees that states must internalize the preferences of capital, offering ever more attractive investment incentives, ever more flexible labour markets, and ever less restrictive environmental regulations, if they are not to be emptied of investment, economic activity, and employment' (Hay, 2011: 317). Unemployment benefits have to be cut because business taxes have to be cut. Business taxes have to be cut because without a major injection of fiscal welfare the roving bandits will make good their threat to pack up their blackmail and move on.

One country by itself has only limited power to defend its national interest. Only a regional if not a global strategy can mount an effective challenge to the unsentimental businesses that seal in no long-term commitment. What all can do, one cannot. It makes intervention more difficult and reinforces the libertarian agenda. Political culture converges on the standard size because the normal price is the equilibrium price in a competitive market. An unexpected by-product is that it becomes more difficult to monitor the performance of elected officials. Whatever happens, their excuse is that the world economy is to blame.

Mobile capital holds all the good cards. Or does it? Capital goes where the returns are highest. In theory the migration of business should trigger a worldwide law of indifference whereby comparable industries score comparable profits. The pull of gravity is a familiar phenomenon in the case of portfolio investment. Whether it is true as well of FDI is more debatable. Once firm-specific plant has been shipped in and installed, it is difficult to disinvest and move across. Sunk costs weaken a company's bargaining position. Exit is expensive. Capital is immobile. It is especially illiquid where it has been adapted to local needs, where it is partially funded by the local government, or where it is integrated into a risk-sharing public–private partnership.

Besides that, there is the fear of the unknown where withdrawal from one market is followed by re-entry into another. Sometimes a tertiary hospital will already have a primary presence in a foreign country. Its referrals upwards may be viewed as a pilot sample. Extrapolation allows it to interpret new entry as an increment rather than a leap in the dark. Experience may be augmented by surveys in the same market and by case studies in others. These help it to determine if it would be more profitable to penetrate or to skim. At the end of the day, however, divorce followed by remarriage is still a risky proposition. Information is inadequate. Inertia is safe. Rhetoric aside, companies often remain where they are.

7.4.2 The Sovereign State

There is the invisible hand and there is the WTO. There is the free market and there is the international accord. There is also the sovereign state. It would be a mistake to write off the sovereign state as an anachronism and a throwback. As with all business deals, medical travel can only establish a presence if it plays by the rules laid down by the host. Even in an era of globalisation, the national Parliament, democratically elected, remains duty bound to respond to public opinion and to put the needs of the citizens first.

GATS membership is not an acquisition which takes over the Shop of State. Each member retains its residual rights. The proviso is that deviations from the common rules should be logged at the time of adhesion in the schedule of commitments. If previously agreed, signatories can limit the number of foreign entrants just as they can restrict the number of domestic operators. They can impose quotas on the employment of foreign nationals. They can levy a super-tax on foreign patients and the hospitals that treat them. They can specify a maximum or a minimum number of surgeries. They can lay down a maximum or a minimum number of beds. They can demand that incomer hospitals bring in state-of-the-art technology. They can insist on a threshold investment, funded abroad. They can discourage feeder clinics that function exclusively as referral centres. They can decide if development land can be purchased freehold by foreign-owned business.

Nation-states despite the GATS can decide whether foreign-trained professionals measure up to local standards. They can screen incoming manpower in the light of local needs. They can impose a ceiling on the proportion of equity held by non-nationals. In Thailand it is 49 per cent. In Singapore and India there is no limit. It is a reminder that the GATS does not preclude the freedom of manoeuvre. Legislatures within limits can still make their own rules.

Some rules proscribe. In some countries there are strict restrictions on multinational investment in defence, banking, broadcasting, the public utilities and even hospitals, where the sovereign government has determined that to issue a certificate of entitlement would be to flood the domestic market with excess capacity. Some rules prescribe. Joint ventures with government or local partners can be made compulsory. The state can demand that local directors be appointed to international boards, that research and development (R&D) be conducted locally to make the country knowledge-based, that profits be reinvested, that medical equipment be manufactured locally, that advanced technology be licensed to foreign competitors. Some rules coordinate. Export targets must be met. Import substitution must be promoted. Fees for technology transfer must not be used to evade local taxation. Whether proscription, prescription or coordination, the message is clear. The dodo is dead. The sovereign state is not. It is alive and kicking.

The Agreement on Trade Related Investment Measures (TRIMS) was made to limit restrictions that are not in the spirit of the WTO. One example is local content requirements that insist upon domestic components. Another is trade-balancing rules that limit a company's imports to the value of the domestically produced commodities that it sends abroad.

The TRIMS Agreement seeks to eliminate preference shown to domestically owned as opposed to foreign-owned companies. Agreement or no Agreement, many market distortions fall through the net. This is particularly the case with restrictions not explicitly enumerated in the protocol, restrictions subject to an opt-out clause and restrictions provided for under bilateral free trade agreements (FTAs) and regional trade agreements (RTAs). Restrictions will often be possible because discrimination can only be charged where the home and the foreign producer are delivering a 'like' service. In an age of market segmentation, product differentiation and monopolistic competition, it is true by definition that few services will be perceived as 'like'.

State-supplied services (except for government procurement and public–private joint ventures) enjoy an exemption. The GATS and the TRIMS raise no objection if the UK government gives most-favoured treatment to the NHS. The condition, in the words of Article 1 of the GATS accord, is that state services are 'neither supplied on a commercial basis nor in competition with one or more service suppliers'. The clause is not easy to interpret. Not 'in competition' is presumably intended to be read as not 'profit-seeking'. Taken literally, however, almost every state-supplied system will be in technical violation of the GATS.

State delivery, whether free at the point of consumption or made subject to a token user charge, is subsidised delivery. The same holds true where the NHS contracts-out its waiting lists to the private sector. The larger the state sector, the smaller the incentive for non-state hospitals to enter and invest. A state quasi-monopoly keeps the private competitors out. They will only be able to mount a credible challenge if their quality is significantly better or if they have differentiated their product into a minority line.

The state sector has the right to hoard domestic healthcare provision for itself. Yet it also has the freedom to encourage commercial alternatives in order to concentrate state spending on the most deprived:

> Public sector resources could, in principle, be released to improve healthcare for the poor if the wealthy pay for care from these new foreign enterprises. This, of course, counts on it being FDI through construction (FDIC) which entails the construction of new productive capacity, and not FDI through purchase (FDIP), which entails the purchase of existing productive capacity. (Smith, 2004: 2315)

The sovereign government has the right to specify the FDIC and the FDIP. It is not obliged to extend carte blanche to a foreign firm that wants to cream off the affluent minority from its state-operated network.

Even if it is a minority presence, private entrants might be regarded as a threat to social policy. Liberalisation is not without its risks. The NHS can ignore the provisions of GATS Mode 4. The private sector has to live with the influx of overseas nurses. Full globalisation is incompatible with full independence. The special treatment granted to state-supplied health allows the home government to manage its own affairs.

Further exemptions are permitted for the infant industries of the poorer countries. Special treatment is enshrined in Article XVIII of the original GATT treaty of 1947. It protects local industry from foreign invasion. Developed countries have some reservations about the length of the transition to the WTO cold shower. So do multinationals, many of them fleeing to the Third World because of the spider's web of directives at home. They sometimes complain that sophisticated regulation is beyond the capacity of some poor countries. Regulation, they say, makes a second-best into a muddle. Some poor countries retort that laissez-faire means neocolonialism that will inevitably stunt their growth. They welcome Article XVIII because without it they can never escape from the poverty trap.

8. The inputs: labour

One view is that enterprise will locate where the input it requires is available in abundance: 'Countries tend to export goods whose production is intensive in factors with which the countries are abundantly endowed' (Krugman, Obstfeld and Melitz, 2012: 121). A modified view is that the endowments themselves will cross the national frontiers. The previous chapter discussed the migration of capital, often under the aegis of a transnational company. The present chapter will discuss the international mobility of blood and bones. There is a link. Often a transnational corporation will practise rotation from the centre to the periphery and back again.

Before the world was one, the English Channel was a wall. Labour, gain-seeking and ambitious, was mobile between industries and sectors. Given enough time, workers would disinvest in sunset skills and retrain in the next big thing. But they would not go abroad. They would not relocate to produce the service in the consumer's own territory.

Times have changed. In the new global economy, the skilled and the unskilled move about freely in fields such as finance, football, information technology (IT) and education. Healthcare is yet another area where transferable how-to is being sucked in by a scarcity of can-do at home. Doctors and nurses, radiologists and researchers, are especially mobile. Both in the exporting and the importing countries, the statistics are bound to cause unrest. Elections are won and lost by popular reactions to GATS Mode 4.

This chapter examines the international circulation of medical manpower. Section 8.1 cites figures to show that the medical endowment is not evenly spread. Section 8.2 explains the pull and push of the external and the internal brain drain. Section 8.3 examines the unique status of migration in the poorer countries. Section 8.4 discusses the processes and the obstacles. Section 8.5 shows that training is lost but that remittances are gained. Section 8.6 suggests economic and social policies that might retain professionals in under-doctored areas while not interfering with the individual's freedom to go where most advantage is.

8.1 THE DISTRIBUTION OF MANPOWER

About 37 per cent of the world's healthcare workers are based in the World Health Organization (WHO) Americas Region. It accounts for half of the world's healthcare spend although it is home to only 10 per cent of the world's burden of disease. For sub-Saharan Africa the figures are 3 per cent, 1 per cent and 24 per cent, respectively. There is no solution in sight. African countries are producing no more than 10 per cent to 30 per cent of the healthcare professionals they require (World Health Organization, 2006: 8).

In the United States there are 24.2 doctors and 98 nurses per 10000 population. In the United Kingdom it is 27.4 and 101.3. At the other end of the spectrum there is Uganda where the figures are 1.2 and 13.1 and Cambodia where they are 2.2 and 7.9 (World Health Organization, 2012). To meet the WHO targets Chad would have to expand its supply of professionals by 900 per cent. The deficiency could be even greater depending on the standard of best practice that is selected (Woomer, 2011: 69).

The internal imbalance accentuates the international inequality. Dussault and Franceschini show that about 50 per cent of healthcare professionals in Nicaragua practise in the capital where only 20 per cent of the population lives. About 87 per cent of the doctors in Ghana are urban-based although 66 per cent of the population is rural (Dussault and Franceschini, 2006). Dovlo reports that there are two surgeons and only one gynaecologist in Ghana's poorest three districts – one-third of Ghana's land area and one-sixth of its population – but that 35 per cent of all medical professionals are based in two urban teaching hospitals (Dovlo, 2005). There is little or no private sector outside the main cities. In poor countries the opportunities for air ambulances and telemedicine are limited. While medical care is not the only cause, in Mexico the life expectancy is 55 years in the rural districts, 71 years in the towns.

The imbalance is inter-sectoral as well as inter-regional. In South Africa the private sector consumes 60 per cent of healthcare resources but services only 18 per cent of the population (Connell, 2010: 32). In Singapore 50 per cent of doctors work in the private sector although it treats only 20 per cent of the patients. It is not so much the medical tourists as the preferences of the urban and the demanding that are at the root of this dispersion.

Bottlenecks are a problem. Costly scanners cannot be operated because of a lack of trained professionals. It is often labour, not capital, that forces Emiratis to seek medical care abroad (Deloitte, 2011: 10, 12). About 80 per cent of the doctors and 90 per cent of the nurses in the Emirates are non-

Emiratis. They have been trained in a variety of professional cultures. The dispersion in heuristics makes effective management difficult.

A further difficulty in managing effectively is that, always on the look-out for better opportunities, uprooted professionals do not necessarily stay for long before making another move. A revolving door means a loss of organisational memory that can manifest itself in miscommunication and mistakes. The babel of cultures – 68 nationalities on the staff of a single London hospital, 40 nationalities on the staff of a single Saudi centre (Connell, 2010: 63, 65) – cannot do much for continuity, stability and solidarity. Turnover of medical manpower in the Emirates is between 13 and 15 per cent per annum. Kenyan nurses treat South Africa as a stepping stone to the UK National Health Service. Many professionals are using the Gulf, like Singapore and Hong Kong, as, stepwise, the first port of call on a journey that they hope will take them to the UK, the US or Australia. Moving on need not mean moving home. The effort they put in might be less than the investment that is made by a professional, local or foreign, whose goal is a career for life.

Worldwide, applying the World Health Organization's guideline of 2.28 doctors, nurses and midwives per 10 000 population, there is a shortfall of 2.4 million bodies. To that must be added a further shortage of 1.9 million complementary professionals (World Health Organization, 2006: 12). The deficit of 4.3 million can only get worse. Doctors will retire. Some of them will retire early. In the Organisation for Economic Co-operation and Development (OECD) countries about 30 per cent of doctors in 2009 were over 55 (OECD, 2011: 62). There is a high attrition rate among nurses. Replacement is not keeping up with the outflow.

The world's population on current projections will go from 6.93 billion in 2011 to 10 billion in 2100. The old and the very old will constitute a growing share of the growing total. They will experience more disability-days and require more attention. They will place an unprecedented strain on the professionals' time. Life expectancy and the old-dependency ratio are increasing. The declining fertility rate means that a higher proportion of young people will, without immigration, have to enter the medical professions simply to keep the numbers constant.

New expedients such as community hospitals, nursing homes and day-case clinics are being adopted to economise on inpatient stays. It is an uphill struggle. Rising participation rates mean that fewer women will be available at home to act as informal carers for the extended family. Urbanisation leaves the rural elderly stranded and alone. Old-people's homes will be needed to fill the vacuum. All things considered, professionals will be in increasingly short supply. This is particularly so if neglected constituencies such as the mentally ill and the destitute are given the services for which they lack the effective demand.

The American Medical Association predicts a shortage of 91 500 doctors and 260 000 nurses in the United States by the mid-2020s. The doctor shortage in the United States may reach 200 000 (Connell, 2010: 16). Shortage is a relative term. The United States, with 98 nurses per 10 000 population, anticipates it will not have enough. So does Sierra Leone where the equivalent figure is 1.7. Some 36 of the 47 countries in sub-Saharan Africa fall short of the minimum set by the World Health Organization of 500 nurses per 100 000 population (Connell, 2010: 16). In the United States in 2006, 126 000 full-time positions for registered nurses were unfilled. By 2020 the number of vacancies on present projections will reach 400 000 (Dussault and Franceschini, 2006).

The shortfall of doctors, nurses, pharmacists, physiotherapists and radiologists is likely to become more serious as incomes rise, expectations rise and insurance becomes more inclusive. Both rich countries and poor countries will have to recruit. Some at least of the vacancies will be filled by foreigners.

Market theory teaches that there will be a price effect and a quantity effect. Both can damage the well-being and productivity of the supplier states. On the price side, fewer professionals mean rising costs:

> Trade . . . takes place predominantly from areas of scarcity to areas of plenty, exacerbating rather than easing supply shortages. Factor price equalization . . . would be little short of disastrous for developing countries, where health systems operate within tight financial constraints, and health professional salaries may be as little as 2–3% of those in developed countries. (Woodward, 2005: 515)

On the quantity side, some at least of those migrants will be the cause of under-doctored black spots at home. It is a domino effect: 'Rich countries recruit foreign workers to fill rural positions and professionals leave rural areas to fill in the gaps in cities in the exporting countries' (Dussault and Franceschini, 2006). Brong Ahafo has more greenery than Accra. Accra has more sunshine than Tyne and Wear. Why then do they not stay where they are?

8.2 PULL AND PUSH

Migration is brought about by pull and push. On the one hand the professionals want something better, self-perceived. On the other hand they want to escape from a situation that does not match up.

8.2.1 Pull

Austerity budgets and excessive training leave some countries with an oversupply of doctors and nurses: 'Recently in Scotland, one-half of physiotherapist graduates were left without employment due to a lack of entry-level posts, encouraging some of them to apply for jobs abroad. Unemployment rates among physicians were reported to be at 5 per cent in Switzerland, 5–10 per cent in Spain' (Wiskow, 2006: 22). In Mexico 15 per cent of all doctors are unemployed, underemployed or inactive (Dussault and Franceschini, 2006). In Ghana if all Ghanaian doctors working abroad were immediately to return home the government would only be able to provide employment for one in seven (Rutten, 2009: 307). Too many doctors were trained by the medical schools. Too many posts were lost due to macroeconomic stringency. Migration is demand and not just supply. Fiscal deficits had to be corrected. The alternative to unemployment might have to be employment abroad.

Young doctors are the more likely to leave. Their incomes will be lower and their tenure less secure: 'An Internet-based survey among Polish physicians found that one-third of all Polish doctors between 25 and 35 years old, equivalent to 10 000 physicians, planned to work in Western European countries' (Wiskow, 2006: 20). In Western European countries they knew they would find work in their profession. Between 1997 and 2003, 80 per cent of new National Health Service doctors and 73 per cent of new NHS nurses were recruited internationally (Pond and McPake, 2006: 1450).

Employment aside, there is remuneration. Higher pay, private or foreign, will often be the deciding factor: 'Migration is largely a response to real and perceived inequalities in socioeconomic opportunities, within and between states' (Connell, 2009: 55). People want to better themselves. The disparity can be huge. Nurses from the Philippines earn on average US$45 780 per annum in the United States. They earn US$2000 in urban areas in the Philippines. They earn even less in the countryside: 'This translates into enormous earning potential; nurses exporting abroad can make in 1 year in an American hospital what it would take them over 20 years to earn at home' (Brush and Vasupuram, 2006: 182).

Within the European Union (EU), Eastern Europe pays less. There the reserve army has been known to push the pay-grade below the subsistence minimum:

> Salaries in the Czech Republic were four to eight times less than in Western European countries . . . Polish doctors were paid an average of 6200 euros a year, while they could earn ten times more in a West European country such

> as Germany. A young hospital doctor in Poland . . . could not live from this and was dependent on financial support from his/her family or by taking up a second job. (Wiskow, 2006: 22)

The President of the Czech Medical Chamber saw clearly what the open market would mean: 'We will face a serious problem. A number of Czech hospitals will be on the verge of closing because of a shortage of physicians. And it won't be just single cases' (Mareckova, 2004: 1443). Some of the health professionals who move to other EU member states will never return.

Jobs and wages are common considerations but still not the only ones. Economic migration is tempered by 'professional and social aspirations that highlight the influence of the cultural environment' (Alonso-Garbayo and Maben, 2009). An example would be the Philippine nurses who relocate from the Gulf to the NHS because of 'religious and gender-related issues' (Alonso-Garbayo and Maben, 2009). Money made them go out. Other things made them go on.

The onward journey recalls Maslow's hierarchy of needs. Economics is necessary but not sufficient: 'Human life will never be understood unless its highest aspirations are taken into account' (Maslow, 1970 [1954]: xii). Professionals want self-actualisation. They want responsibility. They want upgrading. They want on-the-job exposure to quality capital, modern drugs and reliable infrastructure. They want in-house training and formal education. They want a career structure and promotions based on merit.

Sometimes they are attracted by a better environment for original research. Sometimes they want to sample varied lifestyles, locum a 'grand tour' and see the world. Sometimes they want to build up a contributory pension. Sometimes they want to rejoin family members and friends who have planted new roots abroad. Sometimes they want to put down new roots of their own.

Many nurses leave their children behind. The implication is that they are intending to go back. It is not always so. Some nurses see their attachment abroad as the first step in relocating the whole family to the USA. The husband becomes the trailing spouse. Temporary residence becomes permanent residence and eventually citizenship. Their children will have better education and better career prospects in the West. It is a new form of rootedness. Where cultural Bangladeshis have Americanised children, the generation gap will be an obstacle to circular migration.

This is not to say that nurses and doctors are insensitive to money, only that the pull is more than finance alone. In a study in 2007 of the reasons why non-European doctors had come to the UK, as many as 77 per cent of the respondents (most of them from India) gave as their main reason the training opportunities in the NHS. Only 7 per cent said that the main reason had been better pay. The same proportion said it had been the work environment (George, Rozario, Anthony, Jude and McKay, 2007). They wanted to learn. They went abroad to add on the skills. They saw the spell as a sabbatical to acquire new knowledge. They were not obliged to remain abroad for the rest of their career.

The mobility of labour is a complement to the mobility of patients. Bumrungrad employs only Thai doctors. Many of them, however, have trained or worked abroad. Patients trust Thailand, India or Panama because so many of their professionals have certified their skills in a First World setting. Outward Mode 4 makes inward Mode 2 possible.

8.2.2 Push

It is push as well as pull that is making them rush for the door. Professionals complain of low job satisfaction, low social standing, a lack of holidays, systemic favouritism and endemic corruption. Staff might have to resort to under-the-counter payments or illicit resale of prescription drugs to make ends meet. Some will be away because they are simultaneously running a business outside. Some will be exhausted because of double shifts when fellow professionals go abroad, colleagues become chronically ill and the burnt-out retire early.

Under-resourcing means risk. There is the ever-present threat of cross-infection where the hospital cannot provide a mask. There is the danger of HIV where the hospital cannot afford protective gloves against a potential needle-stick. Migration is not the only cause of the manpower deficiencies. In some African countries death is the main cause of exits. In South Africa, 14 per cent of health workers are infected with AIDS. Every patient is viewed as a possible source of infection. As Palmer notes with exemplary understatement: 'Staff time is lost through funeral attendance' (Palmer, 2006: 31). Many health workers themselves have no health insurance.

Turnover and attrition compound the stress and the overwork. Rising productivity is a euphemism for rising case loads. A study of one polyclinic in Zimbabwe revealed that cases per midwife had doubled in only three years. As for Malawi, 'one hospital in ten is closed due to lack of staff; in some, shortages of midwives result in hospital cleaning staff carrying out deliveries' (Gerein, Green and Pearson, 2006: 45, 46). Staff work harder. Specialisms become unbalanced. Patients are abusive and violent. Bureaucracy stifles autonomy. Management is seen as controlling, unapproachable, distant, unappreciative, centralising, opaque and impersonal. It is an uphill struggle.

Morale must suffer when stunted professionals know they are not living up to their ethic of care. Mathauer and Imhoff, in a series of interviews conducted in Benin and Kenya, found that it was not just low salaries but perceived default that left overqualified practitioners dissatisfied with their lot:

> The study shows that health workers overall are strongly guided by their professional conscience and similar aspects related to professional ethos . . . Many health workers are demotivated and frustrated precisely because they are unable to satisfy their professional conscience and impeded in pursuing their vocation due to lack of means and supplies and due to inadequate or inappropriately applied human resources management (HRM) tools. (Mathauer and Imhoff, 2006)

Medical people want to help. If they are not given the drugs, the computers, the medical equipment upon which that help depends, they may be pushed to go abroad.

8.2.3 Going Home

There is pull and there is push. There is also home.

Connell found that one-third of students training to enter health-related occupations in Tonga, Samoa and Fiji were doing so explicitly because they wanted to leave (Connell, 2009: 71). In India 80 per cent of trainee nurses in one nursing school had applied to overseas recruiters even before they completed their education (Connell, 2010: 90, 145). One estimate is that 63 per cent of India's nurses and 54 per cent of India's doctors are looking to get out: 'As long as striking global disparities in nursing income persist, it will be difficult to stem the haemorrhage of nurses emigrating' (Hawkes, Kolenko, Shockness and Diwaker, 2009).

That, however, does not mean that they would never go back. A study of student nurses at a private hospital in Kerala found that 80 per cent of would-be emigrants were expecting to return (Hawkes, Kolenko, Shockness and Diwaker, 2009). A study of student nurses in Uganda revealed that three out of four, after a limited period spent working abroad, had every intention of going back (Nguyen, Ropers, Nderitu, Zuyderduin, Luboga and Hagopian, 2008). A similar survey in Sri Lanka made it not 75 per cent but 5 per cent. In Kenya it was 55 per cent (Connell, 2009: 97). Intentions aside, 52 per cent of Indian doctors who trained outside remained outside. That leaves 48 per cent who went abroad to study but later came home to roost (Gupta, Goldar and Mitra, 1998: 219).

Health workers remain at home because home has its plus-points too. Inertia, place, a familiar culture, a common language, devotion to one's country, a service ethic, fear of homesickness, a house with a plot of land might all be reasons for not venturing too far. There are international restrictions that make labour less mobile than capital. There are forms to fill in. There might be a non-transferable pension pot, an extended family, young children, aged parents, a network of friends, the risk of rootlessness if a second move succeeds the first, a position of seniority that might not be matched abroad.

Health workers already abroad must wrestle with the same considerations and more. Hours and workloads in the foreign country might be excessive. Pay and conditions might be inferior. Money that looked good in the Third World might not look as good in the light of First World prices. Resentful locals might blame the foreigners for flooding the market and forcing down the wage. Dress and prayer-times might lead to frictions. Temporaries might be passed over for training and promotion. Social security might be confined to the resident population. System-years in the new country might not be transferable to the old one.

Emigrants do return. There may simply be no further need to work abroad. Politics may have become more stable. Tribal preference may have been superseded by meritocracy. A civil war may have come to an end. Economic growth may have civilised the infrastructure. Electricity, waste disposal, running water, good roads may be making life in the homeland less of an obstacle course. The life cycle may be causing the reflux. Retirement at home may be more congenial than growing old with strangers.

Doctors go back when they have accumulated enough savings for a house or a shop; or because of new opportunities in the burgeoning private sector; or because medical tourism opens up new jobs; or because improved equipment gives the specialist a chance to make the most of his skills. Medical professionals in any case are seldom seriously poor. So long as the money is enough, they might reason, there is no real need to follow the rainbow abroad.

8.3 THE THIRD WORLD

GATS Mode 3 is a net inflow into the poorer countries. GATS Mode 4 is a net outflow. A temporary absence of up to five years evolves into a permanent loss when a foreign professional makes a new home abroad. The statistics do not distinguish between short stays and long. The professionals themselves do not plan things out. Most proceed gradually, one step at a time.

If there were more development in the Third World there might be less slippage and more reflux. That is the future. The present is less encouraging. The Empire is striking back.

8.3.1 Origins and Destinations

The destination countries are normally the ones coloured white on the map: the US, the UK, Canada and Australia. The flow is overwhelmingly South to North. Only 11 per cent of medical professionals from rich countries are making a move to the underdeveloped Third World. A minority will be medical missionaries and Good Samaritans like Florence Nightingale, Dr Livingstone and Albert Schweitzer. Some will be from non-governmental organisations (NGOs). Many will be naturalised expatriates returning to the country of their birth. It is one of the advantages of the luxury private sector that it attracts the people called *balikbayan* in the Philippines and *viet khieu* in Vietnam to go back. Dr Prathap Reddy, founder of the Apollo chain, had previously worked for 15 years in the United States. Dr Naresh Trehan gave up an income of US$2 million in Manhattan to found the Escorts Heart Hospital in India. About two-thirds of doctors at Apollo in 2005 were Indians who had returned to India from the US or the UK (Oberholzer-Gee, Khanna and Knoop, 2005: 4).

Some Southerners come back. Far more Southerners do not. Western patients treated in the Third World will have seen Indian or Mexican professionals in the First. In 2009, 33.7 per cent of doctors in the United Kingdom, 35.1 per cent in Canada, 42.9 per cent in Australia, 46.9 per cent in New Zealand and 24.5 per cent in the United States were of foreign origin (O'Brien and Gostin, 2011: 22). Origin is not the same as nationality: although 33.7 per cent of doctors in the UK were foreign-born, only about 18 per cent were still foreign nationals. In Saudi Arabia no more than 12 per cent of the doctors and nurses are citizens. There are over 85000 migrant doctors and nurses in Saudi Arabia. In the UAE it is 10 per cent. In Kuwait the share of local nurses is only 6 per cent (Connell, 2010: 50).

Most of the incomers – 64 per cent – received their healthcare training in low-income or middle-income countries (Hagopian, Thompson, Fordyce, Johnson and Hart, 2004). The main exporters are India, the Philippines, Mexico, Pakistan, the Caribbean and sub-Saharan Africa. There are approximately 60000 Indian-trained doctors in the United States. They make up 5 per cent of the US physician workforce. In the UK the share is 11 per cent. The Philippines is the second-largest source of foreign-trained doctors. There are about 20000 Philippine doctors (2.1 per cent of all doctors) in the United States. Canadians make up 1.1 per cent, the British 0.4 per cent (Smith, Chanda and Tangcharoensathien, 2009: 597).

A fifth of the teachers in American medical schools are foreign-born. Four-fifths of the nurses in the United States, one-half in the United Kingdom, were born abroad. Nurses from the Philippines alone account for 14 per cent of all nurses in the United States (Mattoo and Rathindran, 2006: 83). Since 1990, over two-thirds of graduating nurses in Jamaica have emigrated. More Bangladeshi nurses now work in the Middle East than in Bangladesh (Kaelin, 2011: 32).

About 30 per cent of doctors trained in Ghana and 20 per cent of doctors trained in Uganda now work in the United States and Canada. For sub-Saharan Africa as a whole, between 6 and 10 per cent of all registered doctors are practising in North America and a further 6 per cent in the UK (Hagopian, Thompson, Fordyce, Johnson and Hart, 2004). Approximately 23 per cent of doctors trained in sub-Saharan Africa have taken jobs in OECD countries. There are 65000 in total (Rutten, 2009: 298). In Asia in 2006, of doctors trained locally, 12.8 per cent in Malaysia, 9.7 per cent in the Philippines, 10.2 per cent in Singapore, and 3.3 per cent in Thailand were working in OECD countries (Kanchanachitra, Pachanee, Dayrit and Tangcharoensathien, 2012: 79).

One-third to one-half of health professionals trained in South Africa in the 1990s, and 61 per cent of all doctors trained in Ghana between 1986 and 1995, subsequently emigrated (Chanda, 2002: 160). Over half – 56 per cent – of doctors born in Kenya now do their doctoring outside Kenya (McPake, 2012: 135). For Liberia it is 43 per cent. There are said to be more Malawian doctors in Manchester than in Malawi.

Pakistan currently exports almost half of the 5000 doctors it graduates each year, Bangladesh two-thirds, Sri Lanka 25 per cent. For Mozambique, Zimbabwe and Kenya, the number leaving is more than 50 per cent (Connell, 2010: 49, 50–51). Some are prepared to work as nurses to go abroad. Although the absolute numbers may be small, the high proportion knocks a sizeable dent in the doctoring stock.

South Africa, from the 1960s to the 1990s, lost between 44 per cent and 47 per cent of its medical graduates, 42 per cent of them to the USA, 45 per cent to Commonwealth countries. Between 1925 and 1975 the loss had been only 14 per cent. Of those who remain in South Africa, 76 per cent reside in urban areas (Weiner, Mitchell and Price, 1998: 59).

The countryside and the country are being hollowed out. Even so, the brain drain must be seen in perspective. African-trained doctors employed in OECD countries account for no more than 12 per cent of the doctor shortfall in Africa. In South-East Asia the percentage is even lower, at 9 per cent (O'Brien and Gostin, 2011: 21). If Africa and South-East Asia want to have more doctors, there is no alternative but to train more doctors. Stopping the brain drain by itself will not do the trick.

8.3.2 Migratory Capital

Doctors must be trained and retained. They must also be given doctoring work to do. A doctor playing a game is no different from anyone else. Supply is as nothing without the demand that makes the professional spring into action.

In Ghana 43 per cent of posts for doctors and 26 per cent of posts for nurses in 2003 were unfilled (Bach, 2003: 5). In 2006 approximately 13 per cent of all Ghana-trained nurses and midwives were working in developed countries (Lori, Rominski, Gyakobo, Muriu, Kweku and Agyei-Baffour, 2012). In Kenya one-half of all nursing positions in 2010 were unfilled although one-third of all nurses in Kenya were out of work (Connell, 2010: 37). In Trinidad and Tobago and in Jamaica the figure is also one-half. In Thailand the regional health centres have 6000 vacancies that they cannot fill. In India the community health centres face a shortfall of 67 per cent in paediatrics, 56 per cent in obstetrics, gynaecology and general surgery (Hazarika, 2010: 249). In the Philippines there are 30000 unfilled nursing positions (Bach, 2003: 4). The country that is supplying nurses to the world is experiencing a shortage of nurses at home.

In Malawi in 2006, 65 per cent of nursing posts were vacant despite the urgency of the need. Life expectancy at birth was 37 years in Malawi. One million of its 16 million citizens were suffering from AIDS (Palmer, 2006: 28, 29). Per capita expenditure on health was US$12.4 per capita. One-third of that came from donor aid.

Demand-side, posts are frozen because the budget is not there. Supply-side, jobs go unadvertised because no fish will bite. Specialist units shut down: 'Operating theatres for cardiac surgery at one of the most expensive hospitals in Malaysia have not been used since 2005 because of a shortage of cardiac-thoracic surgeons and expensive equipment is unused since there are too few specialists' (Connell, 2010: 126). A cardiovascular unit in the Philippines had to close when experienced nurses were selectively poached and could not be replaced. Operations are put off because there are too few anaesthetists or intensive-care nurses. Qualified professionals simply cannot be found:

> A centre for spinal injuries in South Africa had to be closed the very day its two anesthetists were recruited to Canada as the centre was unable to find replacements for them . . . Two hundred hospitals have been closed in the Philippines due to a shortage of health care professionals . . . Around 10000 nurses on average leave the Philippines each year. (Kaelin, 2011: 32, 33)

The Philippines is the world's largest exporter of nurses, just as India is the world's largest exporter of doctors. The Philippines has a long-standing culture of work abroad. There are approximately 163 756 Philippine nurses working outside the Philippines. It is estimated that about 68 per cent of all Philippine doctors and 85 per cent of all Philippine nurses will at some stage have worked abroad (Kanchanachitra, Pachanee, Dayrit and Tangcharoensathien, 2012: 79). They go principally to the UK, the US, the Middle East and Singapore.

The Philippines is not the only country to be educating with a view to employment abroad. Mainland Chinese students come to Singapore for courses offered by Australian nursing schools. The fees are lower than in Australia. The graduates acquire a qualification that is recognised for work in Australia. Training includes cancer care, heart disease, geriatrics and the 'how-tos' of sophisticated technology. These skill sets are not a first priority for rural needs at home or for a career in public health.

In Albania, where nursing has traditionally been women's work, half the nursing students are currently men. They are going to nursing school so that they can emigrate. In Warsaw there is a college offering a six-week course in English and English healthcare for dentists wishing to work in the United Kingdom (Wiskow, 2006: 21). There are nursing schools in India, St Vincent and elsewhere that prepare students for the US and the UK nursing boards. Medical qualifications are an investment in a better environment. They are a passport to a more congenial life elsewhere: 'Acquiring education and training in the health sector is tantamount to acquiring cultural migratory capital' (Connell, 2010: 93, 154). The prospect of working abroad raises the status of nursing at home.

8.3.3 The Carousel Effect

Emigration affects the quality as well as the quantity of the competence. Raw numbers do not tell the whole story. Kaushik and his colleagues, tracking a sample of Indian medical graduates, found that 'individuals receiving two awards, or more, were 35% more likely to migrate . . . Elite medical schools contribute disproportionately' (Kaushik, Jaiswal, Shah and Mahal, 2008: 42). Senior staff with valuable experience are particularly attractive. The high-flyers will be the first to be headhunted. It is the refugees from natural selection who will at the margin be left to treat the sick and mentor the students. Quality as well as quantity will be affected by the sift.

Where there is no money to fill the vacancies, the brain drain is also a brain gain. Without the safety valve of a job abroad, the educated and the disappointed could destabilise the political order. Where there is money but no take-up, the situation is different but still profoundly unsatisfactory. The nation that exports becomes the nation that imports. When home professionals go abroad, replacement professionals come in. They are not always as good.

It is a game of musical chairs. UK doctors go to Canada. Canadian doctors go to the United States. Indian doctors go to the UK and Canada. South African doctors migrate to Australia. Sub-Saharan doctors migrate to South Africa. Doctors from Eastern Germany fill a gap in Western Germany. Doctors from the Czech Republic fill a gap in Eastern Germany. Doctors from Slovakia fill a gap in the Czech Republic. Doctors from non-EU Moldova and low-pay Ukraine come in to fill the posts.

Doctors from Iraq go to Denmark because the Danes have gone to the UK. Nurses from Jamaica go to Bermuda because the nurses from Bermuda have gone to the US. Economics talks. The moving staircase moves up. The poor are recruiting from the poorer. A Thai doctor takes the conveyor belt to the capital. A Lao doctor speaking Thai takes his place in a rural clinic.

It need not be full-time. Polish doctors fly into the UK at the weekend to work the unsocial hours that the locals do not want. Nurses from Botswana spend their 'sick leave' in South Africa (Connell, 2010: 60). Sometimes semi-skilled auxiliaries are drafted in, unsupervised, to take over their duties. In most (but not all) cases, the immigrants lack the training and experience, the linguistic and cultural capacities, of the emigrants that they are replacing.

The immigrants get the job done. They may not get it done as well. It is a 'carousel effect' but it is also a cascade. At the bottom of the pecking order there are the hard cases who were rejected by the treatment centres at the top: 'Who on this medical merry-go-round arrived back in Tanzania (where there are currently 2.3 doctors per 100 000)? The answer is very few doctors indeed . . . The medical carousel unfortunately does not turn full circle, as it has in the past, so the poorest nations experience all drain but no gain' (Eastwood, Conroy, Naicker, West, Tutt and Plange-Rhule, 2005: 1894).

It is an equilibrium. It is not an optimum. The poorest of the poor find at the end of the day that there is no musical chair left for them: 'The nurse population ratio in Europe is ten times higher than in Africa or South-East Asia; it is likewise ten times higher in North America than in South America' (Kaelin, 2011: 31). They cannot retain and they cannot recruit. Phrases like 'poaching', 'snatching', 'looting', 'pirating' and 'stealing' describe the resentment that is building up at the gap in staffing that Patel calls 'the great brain robbery': 'India has fewer than 3000 psychiatrists for its one billion population compared with one psychiatrist for every 9000 people in the United Kingdom, a 27-fold difference. Despite this inequality, the NHS has launched a scheme to recruit senior psychiatrists and other specialists from India and other developing countries' (Patel, 2003: 926).

The NHS brings in the desperate even as it tries for the glamorous. Incomer staff are over-represented in mental institutions and geriatric wards. Someone has to do the job. Outsiders service the public sector when the insiders find something better to do. At the bottom of the pecking order are rural women in remote villages. They must give birth without a skilled attendant because the law of gravity has shunted them to the end of the queue.

8.4 THE MIGRANT PROFESSIONAL

Intra-national migration is a concomitant of economic growth. People move from the countryside to the towns in pursuit of a better life. In the process they release surplus labour from low-productivity agriculture, generate new savings for self-sustaining growth and access modern skills which contribute cumulatively to structural change (Todaro and Smith, 2009: 115–122, 344–354).

Intra-national migrants must overcome their fear of the unknown. They must escape from that maximin uncertainty which traps them in tried-and-tested replication. International migrants face even greater obstacles. Not only must they uproot themselves from long-established networks and family attachments, they must overcome a multiplicity of obstacles, cultural and legal.

Standardised medical training and handed-on short-cuts make it easier to adapt to the heartland of the former colonial power. Culture is a shared possession. An overlapping history explains why people from the Philippines make the United States their destination of choice. Language too is a unifying factor. It facilitates entry and acculturation. Regional accents and dialects will be acquired on the job. Grammar and syntax require background knowledge. It is one reason why the Commonwealth-educated go to the UK, the Algerians to France, the Angolans to Portugal.

Inability to communicate holds people back. Eastern Europeans who do not speak an international language must attend intensive catch-up sessions. A second language can, of course, be an advantage. Puerto Rican doctors are bilingual in Spanish as well as English, the Mauritians in English and French.

The process of changing countries is itself not straightforward. Entrants need an employment pass, a visa and a medical examination. Their certificates must be notarised. The police must confirm that their record is clean. Where the employer does not package in the passage and the hostel, the employee personally will have to manage the transition. Entrants will have to answer advertisements in a foreign language or work with recruiting agencies that are not always reliable. If the worker is illegal or has overstayed, he is vulnerable to tricksters against whom there is no redress.

Even workers on permits may have unenforceable contracts, ambiguously worded. The worker whose stay is tied to a single employer is especially open to exploitation. There is perpetual uncertainty about continued residence. There is a fear that complainers will not be renewed. Unionisation is discouraged. Multinational unions for nurses and auxiliaries do not exist. Prior socialisation at home is an external economy. It often makes immigrants more deferential and less assertive.

Incomers may experience isolation that is only partially offset by a pre-existent support-system of relatives, friends and former classmates. A network helps the newly arrived to find a job and settle in. It spreads up-to-date information and on-the-spot 'where-tos'. There is only so much an established migration route, a proximate destination and a critical mass of past travellers can do to make new people feel at home. In new centres of migration there may not even be an existing beachhead.

There is racial imbalance which some will put down to non-rational discrimination. In the UK the proportion of non-white consultants is highest in emergency and geriatric wards (the least popular clinics), lowest in surgery (the most prestigious speciality) (Bach, 2003: 19). In the US the new and the foreign are disproportionately represented in the deprived inner city where the white middle classes do not want to work. Is it the stereotype or is it the proficiency that pigeon-holes them as second-rate?

In the UK, some immigrants are ill-informed and even incompetent. Three-quarters of the doctors struck off the medical register in 2012 were trained abroad. One doctor, working as a stand-in, administered ten times the recommended dose of diamorphine. The drug was not commonly used in his country. The patient died (Leach and Donnelly, 2013: 1). His other patients, of course, did not die. There is the odd anecdote but no real proof that poorer areas have a lower health status specifically because an above-average proportion of local practitioners were schooled in Uganda, Trinidad or even New Zealand. What is known is only that some foreigners are butchers and that some foreigners are not. Much the same may be said of the locals. It is hard to spin much saloon-bar indignation from that.

To protect the patients from the butchers, some countries insist on local reaccreditation. In the absence of a common medical curriculum and a harmonised standard of practice, professional associations set a complex relicensing examination that in a bad light closely resembles a non-tariff barrier. The language of the test is itself a hurdle. While foreigners are allowed to practice medicine in Thailand, the examination (even for doctors intending to concentrate on international patients) is conducted entirely in Thai. In Taiwan it is conducted in Mandarin.

Registration is protracted and expensive. The result is that some specialists will have to work as general practitioners, some doctors as nurses, some nurses as nursing auxiliaries, some nursing auxiliaries as hospice attendants. Safety is important and information asymmetry is a danger. Yet it is also true that waste must result from the restrictive practice of national standards that are pitched too high.

The GATS does not require the mutual recognition of professional qualifications. Standards being so variable, they are exempt from the provisions of the WTO's most-favoured-nation clause. A common medical passport would make the meaning of the qualifications transparent. The benchmark might be the professional examinations of a vanguard country. Examples are the US Medical Licensing Exam (USMLE) and the National Council Licensure Examination for Registered Nurses (NCLEX-RN). Regional associations like the Association of Southeast Asian Nations (ASEAN), the North American Free Trade Agreement (NAFTA) and the EU recognise that mobility is not meaningful without harmonisation. ASEAN, despite opposition from national medical lobbies, has made Mutual Recognition Arrangements (MRAs) to facilitate the flow. Incomers still need an employment pass. There is no guarantee that they will obtain one.

Even so, the barriers to a genuinely free market in medical skill should not be exaggerated. Many doctors (including those active in medical tourism) have obtained licences and certificates in multiple jurisdictions. In the future there will be a permit, comparable to the international driver's licence, which will allow the doctor common-carrier access to an open medical highway. The competencies will at first be the Western ones as passed on in the Western schools. Later the gateway may be different. It may be more pluralistic and more tolerant.

8.5 REMITTANCES AND TRAINING

It is a trade-off between benefits and costs. Nationals working abroad are sending money back home. At the same time they are taking out scarce skills for which their fellow citizens have paid. Both the remittances and the training contribute to the well-being of the country. To acquire the one is, however, to sacrifice the other. It is all a question of choice.

8.5.1 Remittances

Expatriation of labour makes possible the repatriation of savings: 'Remittances account for 24 per cent of Nicaragua's GDP [gross domestic product], while in Turkey, remittances are four times larger than the country's inflow of foreign direct investment' (Dussault and Franceschini, 2006). Immigrants working in the UK are believed to be transferring at least £11 million a day (£4 billion a year) (*Weekly Telegraph*, 2009: 7). Of all the resources flowing into the developing countries in 2009, foreign direct investment (FDI) accounted for US$359 billion, overseas development aid US$120 billion, portfolio investment US$85 billion and documented remittances US$307 billion (World Bank, 2011: 17). Documented remittances are believed to be the second most significant source of funds from abroad.

Remittance flows to the Third World are about 70 per cent of total global remittances. The true amount is likely to have been much more. Unrecorded transfers are sent through relationship-based networks like the *hawala, barakat* or *hundi*. Often cash is brought in by a relative or friend visiting for a break. A study done in Egypt found that unofficial remittances were one-third to one-half of the total (Adams and Page, 2005: 1648).

In the case of Africa, about 75 per cent of remittances are sent informally. It is more efficient. At least 10 per cent of money remitted through the banking system disappears into fees and commissions (Doyle, 2013). Besides that, documented gifts might have to be declared for tax. Informal remittances, being invisible, are not taxed. They do, of course, stimulate the regional multiplier. Economic growth in that way expands the net tax take.

Remittances made up 12 per cent of the GDP of the Philippines in 2010. They amounted to US$21.3 billion, considerably higher than the US$7.5 billion that was sent back in 2003. About 10 per cent of the Filipino population are at any one time living outside the country (Bach, 2003: 4). Remittances to India in 2010 were US$55 billion, in 2011 US$66 billion, at a time when its FDI was US$36 billion. For China remittances were US$51 billion (World Bank, 2011: 13). For the 47 countries of sub-Saharan Africa they were US$51.8 billion. Overseas development aid to Africa in the same year was $43 billion (Doyle, 2013). In 2003 remittances to Africa had been only US$5 billion (Hagopian, Thompson, Fordyce, Johnson and Hart, 2004).

Some families consciously breed children for remittances. A study in Tuvalu elicited the declaration that an only son is one son too few: '"One is not enough. If he goes away to work, there is no one to look after me here.

If he stays and cares for me, no one earns any money overseas'" (Connell, 2009: 56). Frequently there is a gendered division of labour. Sons go abroad to earn. Daughters stay back to care. Having family members in several foreign countries diversifies the portfolio. The Gulf may be up even though Australia may be down. A good mix stabilises family incomes at home.

Remittances sent back to poorer countries make possible the education of the migrant's children and other family members. They cover the medical bills of an elderly parent. They reduce 'the level, depth, and severity of poverty in the developing world': 'A 10% increase in per capita official international remittances will lead, on average, to a 3.5% decline in the share of people living in poverty' (Adams and Page, 2005: 1646, 1660). Remittances bankroll an entrepreneurial relative who wants to start a business. They fund the purchase of expensive durables such as a refrigerator. Productive investment vies with conspicuous consumption. Land is purchased. Money earned abroad pulls up the price at home. Remittances in that way may make it more difficult for local people to buy a farm.

The township is split between the 'been-to' and the 'never-went'. The new divide fuels a latent resentment where the more educated move up and the more traditional till the rut. Widening social distance may work against the solidarity of the community. It may, on the other hand, be a new inequality that reflects the success abroad of racial minorities and pariah castes that have historically been excluded (de Haas, 2007: 13). Out-migration followed by remittances may be the solvent that attacks the complacency of an ossified and intolerant status quo.

Remittances enhance the social standing of women where it is the woman who goes overseas. A Filipina nurse working abroad contributes more to the family budget than her husband who is still on the farm. It alters the household balance of power. In exchange the extended family helps out with childcare and assumes responsibility for the old. The societal *quid pro quo* is the functional equivalent of a non-existent welfare state. It cannot, however, be denied that the supply of informal carers goes down when large numbers of women leave home in order to earn.

Remittances are an embodiment of intra-family duty and altruism. They are finely tuned on specific family requirements. There is no slippage into bureaucratic overheads. They can be a large proportion of the salary earned abroad. As for the correlation with education, however, there is no consensus. Some studies find that skilled workers, partly no doubt due to their higher market value, tend to remit more: 'Migrants with a university degree remit $300 more yearly than migrants without one' (Bollard, McKenzie, Morten and Rapoport, 2011: 155). Other studies find that, because skilled workers are more likely to be accompanied by their spouse and children, they in practice remit less: 'Low-skilled migrants tend to remit more because their migration is more temporary in nature and they are more concerned with returning home' (Adams, 2009: 99). There is no agreement on the relative magnitudes; length of absence may have an effect on the willingness to give (Mendoza, 2013: 1350006-12); and cross-country pooling may in any case mask the very real differences between one culture and another. The evidence does not lend itself to categorical pronouncements. It is not possible to distinguish in the statistics between remittances from cognates on short-term contracts and agnates permanently settled abroad. Nor is it possible to identify remittances that originate with medical professionals working away or transfers that are earmarked for health-related expenses at home.

8.5.2 Training

Remittances sent back are the benefit. Training gone abroad is the cost. The remittances and the training are loosely linked. Possibly the remittances from migrant nurses will outweigh the money spent to form their skills (Rutten, 2009: 308). This is one reason why countries such as the Philippines, India and Finland deliberately overeducate in order to prime the brain drain.

The financial overhead is a strain. About 25 per cent of doctors in the United States were trained in foreign medical schools. Many of those medical schools were highly subsidised (Cohen, 2011: 11). Before the medical school there had been foundation education at primary and secondary level. It all adds up. Each professional quitting Africa costs the continent on average US$184 000 (Rutten, 2009: 305). In South Africa the loss of investment in medical manpower has been estimated at US$1 billion. This is equal to one-third of official development aid to that country (Rutten, 2009: 306). It is the same as the total overseas debt of the whole of the continent.

It has been described as yet another instance of the inverse care law. The poor pay the taxes. The rich use the skills. The locals sacrifice. The foreigners profit. It is a perverse transfer which most benefits the individuals and the countries which have the least need of support. The African Union estimates that low-income African countries subsidise high-income developed countries to the tune of US$500 million a year through the medical education they support. Another estimate suggests that wasted training is costing the Third World a total of US$552 billion (Connell, 2010: 142). Ghana alone has spent £65 million since 1998 on the training of doctors, £38 million on the training of nurses, who later went to the UK (Rutten, 2009: 305).

This should be seen in the light of the £250000 that it costs to train a doctor in the UK. The amount is four to six times more than the equivalent sum in India. As with international trade in textiles and bananas, so with international trade in doctors and nurses. World resources are better allocated when the UK imports and India supplies. More to the point, the Indian sunk cost is a left-behind bygone that the British are not expected to cover. Foreign doctors do not bill the United Kingdom for the total social cost of their training. They are willing to work for the marginal private cost alone.

Cost aside, there is also time. It would take five years and more to educate an English school leaver up to the requisite standard. The Indian professional only needs to jump on a plane. Mobility of labour converts the adjustment process from production to transfer. It keeps down the slippage and the uncertainty. Five years and more is a long time. A lagged response might engender a cobweb mismatch. The young Englishman might himself take British bygones abroad. All things considered, it is better economics to ride free on the foreigners' embodied expense. It is better economics to buy a ready-made Indian off the shelf.

Not all doctors in the First World are bought in from the Third. More than a quarter of foreign doctors in Belgium are from the Netherlands. Norwegians are half of all foreign doctors in Denmark (Connell, 2010: 57). That said, the bulk of the movement is undeniably South–North. About two-thirds of the foreign doctors in the United States, three-quarters in the UK, come from the less-developed countries. It is development aid from the Third World to the First.

Yet it is not just foreign countries that derive the benefit. Within a single country there can be an inverse care law in the distribution of the public subsidy. What happens in India is what happens across the world: 'When medical staff trained in public institutions for fees of about 500 rupees ($11; £6; €9) a month move to work in private health care this represents indirect support for the private sector of some 4000m–5000m rupees per year' (Sengupta and Nundy, 2005: 1158). Some private hospitals are owned by foreigners and some are owned by Indians. Irrespective of the ownership, the public hospitals are finding it hard to claw back a socially approved share in the educational subsidy. The inference is that the state might have to get involved.

8.6 STATE AND LABOUR

New skills and remittances are the benefits. Bottlenecks and shortfalls are the costs. The poor countries are losing manpower to the healthcare superpowers. They do not stand a chance: 'Migration is seriously affecting the sustainability of health systems in many developing countries' (Eastwood, Conroy, Naicker, West, Tutt and Plange-Rhule, 2005: 1893).

8.6.1 The Rich Countries

The world is not flat but skewed: 'The richest countries in the world are attracting some of the most skilled and talented migrants in the international labor market' (Mendoza, 2013: 1350006-1). Half of all educated professionals go to the United States. The figure rises to 85 per cent if Canada, Australia, the UK, France and Germany are added in. The US and the UK alone swallow up each year more than half the tradeable nurses. The rich countries perceive that they are experiencing a shortage of skill. One solution is to expand the domestic medical stock. The other solution is ride free on imports because underinvestment is the cost-effective choice.

The evidence confirms that the richer countries have not hesitated to compromise on self-sufficiency precisely because the poorer countries have been there to fill the posts:

> Since 1998, foreign-trained nurse entrants to the US nurse sector have increased at a rate faster than that of US-educated new nurses. This has not been the result of a lack of interest on the part of would-be nursing students in the US, as more than 11 000 qualified students were denied admission to nursing schools in 2003 as a result of limited capacity. (Nguyen, Ropers, Nderitu, Zuyderduin, Luboga and Hagopian, 2008)

Locals were being denied the opportunity to train. It makes perfect sense. Why grow grapes in Scotland if it is cheaper to ship them in from the South?

To stem the inflow the Northern schools could increase their intake. It would be expensive. In 2011 the average annual income in the Philippines was £3284. In the United Kingdom it was £26 000. The reservation price for the foreigner is less than the opportunity cost for a local. It may not be in the best interests of the richer countries to train their own people. It may be cheaper to rely on international differences to keep the wage bill down.

Medical people like all people need an incentive to work. Money is one such incentive. It is not the only incentive but it is always there. Even the most dedicated have families to feed and school fees to find: 'In the UK, increasing nursing pay would seem to make the single largest contribution to resolving the labour market imbalance that is draining poor countries of their health staff' (Pond and McPake, 2006: 1453). Economically speaking, the nursing shortage is self-inflicted. It is low pay and not just training places that are keeping locals out of the trade.

Higher pay is not sustainable in the long run in the absence of higher productivity. The job function must be retooled and re-engineered in order that it might validate a competitive wage. That upgrading in itself will raise the prestige of the occupation. It will make health service jobs more attractive to entrants who would in earlier times have rejected them as exhausting, dirty and routine.

In earlier times many women treated nursing, like teaching and office work, as a stop-gap that passed the time before marriage and family. Twenty-somethings were willing to accept lower pay since nursing for them was not a career for life. Later, women became more receptive to jobs outside the home, while a more open labour market meant that they could compete with men for a wider range of occupations. Nursing in the UK remains 90 per cent female. The increasing participation of men is demonstrating nonetheless that even the traditional breadwinners are making it their first choice. Higher pay, higher status, genuine career prospects all mean that nurses have good reasons to attain a higher level of professional excellence.

Tasks are being rethought. Nurses devolve form-filling and clerical duties to nurse-assistants. Surgeons devolve routine procedures to nurse-practitioners. Graduate qualifications raise the academic profile of the profession. In the long run the rise in productivity may make the rise in pay self-funding. If it does, then economists, feminists, nationalists and mercantilists will be in agreement on one thing at least. The staffing deficit with the rest of the world can be corrected by eliminating the shortfall at home.

8.6.2 The Poor Countries

Pay rates will tend to converge in the long run. The law of one price is the logical consequence, at least in the economics textbook, of free markets and speculative arbitrage. The factor price equalisation theorem will not provide much comfort to sick people in the *ulu*, the *bled* or the bush when their only neurologist decides to relocate. In the short run, the Third World must be protected against itself. That is why Third World governments frequently petition the World Trade Organization (WTO) for floodgates that ration the flow.

An outright ban would be an infringement of the basic human right to travel and work. A country does not 'own' its citizens. Respect for persons dictates that dental technicians as well as political dissidents should have the freedom to sample the world. The elimination of the safety valve would deprive poorer families of much-needed remittances. The signalling mechanism would be distorted. The spillover from overseas exposure would be blocked out. Professional attachments upgrade human capital. New techniques enrich the quality of service. Medicine is knowledge. Knowledge does not stop at the border posts. Where professionals go abroad and then return, an outright ban would mean that the community never enjoys the top-up benefit that would have augmented the value of the foundation investment.

What may be contemplated may nonetheless be a tax on the negative externality of educated professionals who fail to deliver at home. The tax, proposed by Bhagwati in the spirit of Pigou (Bhagwati, 1979), would at once discourage the emigration of skill and secure compensation for the home-country's loss. Yet there is a problem. An emigrant already paying income tax in his new homeland may find it inequitable to pay income tax in his former homeland as well. A country that opts for a Bhagwati tax might therefore impose a once-for-all lump sum upon exit instead. The bill is settled. The sunk cost lies where it falls.

The clean break is especially attractive in the light of the information costs. A Bhagwati tax on foreign income would be difficult to implement in the absence of a common, global tax return. Without a single declaration, different countries could use different definitions of income or make discriminatory assessments of residents, citizens, former citizens, permit holders. Avoidance and evasion would travel free on the transactions costs and the multiplicity. At the end of the day the tax might not raise enough revenue to warrant the expense.

The ban is command-and-control. The tax is the managed market. There is also the bond. The bond is a legal contract and a rule.

Subsidised training gives the home country a lien. Professionals who go abroad for further study could be required to post a bond that will only be refunded on their return. The importing country could refuse to employ defaulters who jump bail and stay away. Students who obtain their medical education in public-sector facilities could be obliged to work for an agreed number of years in public-sector clinics. Some of those clinics will be in deprived areas.

Bonds can also be offered to foreigners. Singapore offers scholarships to trainee nurses from China. In return they are obliged to work in Singapore for a period of years after they qualify. Chinese speakers blend well into the Singapore culture. The bond allows for substantial acclimatisation. Some of them will stay.

Bonding is least inconvenient at an early stage in the conscript's career. The commitment expires before marriage, children and a housing loan make a well-paid job more urgent and mid-career national service patently unattractive. Women most of all, but also men, might not enter medicine if they felt that delayed postings might interfere with their child-rearing role.

A related option would be for the government to cancel all student loans where the professional remains for an agreed-upon number of years in the home country. The arrangement is not ideal. Repayments are normally concentrated in the early years of the clinician's career. They delay the brain drain by three to five years but they do not prevent it. Writing-off will not be relevant to the mid-career professional whose debt has been amortised even as his skill-set has matured into its prime.

Besides that, there is a marked class bias. The affluent are more likely to repay their loan prematurely or not to take out a loan at all. Students from a prosperous background will often have family support. The education they receive is included in GATS Mode 2. Training abroad and working abroad, there is no question of a bond. Some countries have made at least two years of voluntary service a precondition for a medical licence. It is a risky strategy. Doctors who have trained abroad at their own expense may be deterred from returning home.

Where bonds fail, managed mobility might succeed. Driven solely by ethics and conscious that they are acting against their own national interest, First World countries could narrow the channel by limiting the number of university places, student internships and professional attachments they offer to Third World applicants: 'Obtaining a training post in another country is the usual vehicle by which doctors migrate' (McPake, 2012: 135).

The First World, wishing to collaborate, could also ensure that short-term permits are strictly non-renewable. The rule would be that fixed-term visas cannot be converted into an unrestricted stay by doctors from the Third World who do not want to leave. The rule might be part of an inter-governmental agreement (a 'mobility partnership') that allows for the rotation of staff and the twinning of hospitals. A developed country might offer a developing professional a one-time contract or fellowship for a fixed term of five years. The condition would be that the final year (accompanied by paid repatriation) must be spent in his country of origin.

Revolving cohorts would spread the exposure while containing the loss. Foreigners, admittedly, may liken it to an un-welcome mat designed to stigmatise the resented. Forcing the *Gastarbeiter* to see themselves as no more than a temporary second-best would not do much for their self-esteem. As Max Frisch observed, people, even foreign people, are not really things: 'We imported workers and got men instead.' On the other hand, short-termism would reassure local protectionists that foreign talent had come in to fight a clearly defined fire and would thereafter be moved out. As long as the jobs are permanent but the workers are variable, local people will be less likely to object to flagrant outsiders who put pressure on the infrastructure.

Temporary movement is fully in the spirit of GATS Mode 4. An example would be Cuban bilateral aid. There are 25000 Cuban doctors in over 68 countries. They alleviate shortages and cement contacts. No doubt there is politics involved. In the 1990s in Zambia one doctor in every five was a Cuban. Cuban doctors promote goodwill. Then each cohort goes home and a new batch of Cuban doctors arrives.

A First World country may unilaterally choose the path of global justice. Examples in the United Kingdom would be the Pacific Code (2007) and the Commonwealth Code of Practice for the International Recruitment of Health Workers (2004). Seeking to limit hires from low-income countries, these codes exhort the NHS to abstain from aggressive and proactive procurement. The NHS should be especially careful about outmigration where a poor country has outstanding debt or where its medical services will be seriously disrupted.

The NHS can still recruit with the explicit consent of the developing country, or within the framework of an inter-governmental exchange. Managed migration is not absolute. Doctors and nurses who apply without being headhunted may still be hired. So may Third World professionals who are already working within a trade bloc or regional alliance such as the European Union. Adherence to the agreement on ethical hires is voluntary. There are no sanctions apart from adverse publicity. The private sector is not bound by the codes.

The stock is depleted by the outflow. It is a very small stock. Even if there were no drain through migration, there would be a strong case for new medical schools to bring the quantity and quality of medical professionals up to the international norm. About half the countries in sub-Saharan Africa have only one medical school or no medical school at all. University teaching does, moreover, build on science teaching in the secondary schools. In poor countries, and especially in the poorest areas, a foundation in science is simply not there.

Medical aid from the First World could take the form of building and equipping the medical schools. The debt confers legitimacy: the North is effectively reimbursing the South for the education lost when an expensive professional restocks a richer state. The calculation of a wrong put right is necessarily inexact. No one knows how long the doctor will stay away; or how much of his education was publicly financed; or what remission should be granted for the remittances that were made possible by the seed corn. It is not clear if the emigrant as well as the receiving country should make a contribution; or if new skills acquired in the new country should be a chargeable item. There is much in restitution that does not lend itself to the last decimal place. When in doubt, however, there is a good case for first principles. Building a medical school in a poor country is right and proper in itself.

Donor countries could sponsor eminent lecturers (often on secondment), in-service upgrading, top-up certificates and even a postgraduate programme. Collaborative research on dengue, malaria and other tropical diseases, often neglected in richer countries, could be conducted. Teaching in the local dialect as well as English would make education more accessible. Perhaps the intake should discriminate in favour of women, including married women with children. Apart from the social and medical advantages, affirmative action would retard the brain drain. Indian male doctors are 12 per cent more likely to emigrate than their female counterparts (Kaushik, Jaiswal, Shah and Mahal, 2008: 42).

Private medical education could also be encouraged. It is a risky strategy. Because unsubsidised schools would charge high fees, self-funding students would have an incentive to work with the elite or to work abroad. A private school will adapt its curriculum to focus on hospital-based curative care in the Western mould. Young doctors cannot afford to specialise on family doctoring and low-tech medicine. The hawkers and the farmers are not the market niche that repays the debt.

New medical schools should be situated in the under-doctored hinterland and not just the capital. The Third World is disproportionately agricultural. Doctors are disproportionately urban. The result of the internal brain drain is an internal inequality. In the Northern Region of Ghana there is one doctor for every 85 957 people, and no paediatrician. In Accra the ratio is one doctor for every 5806 people (McPake, 2012: 139). For Ghana as a whole there are nine doctors per 100 000 population. Of those doctors, 87 per cent live in cities although 66 per cent of the population lives in the countryside. Most of the doctors are based in the south. So are the medical schools. In Ghana 43 per cent of women are giving birth alone or with a non-skilled assistant: 65 per cent in the rural areas, 35 per cent in the towns (Lori, Rominski, Gyakobo, Muriu, Kweku and Agyei-Baffour, 2012). The maternal death rate in Ghana is 350 per 100 000 births. In Italy it is 3.9.

Medical schools in the provinces would attract a greater proportion of local students. An area-specific nucleus of friends, relatives and memories will make it easier for them to resist the temptation of better pay in the towns. The usual market correctives do not apply. The attrition rate is less. In Uganda it was found that students from rural areas were less likely to be lost abroad (Nguyen, Ropers, Nderitu, Zuyderduin, Luboga and Hagopian, 2008).

The community is the organism and not just the atom. Social policy should not neglect the whole merely because market economics makes so much of the part. Traditional healers could be integrated into the network of cure and care. General practitioners could delay retirement to remain with their patients. Local midwives could be on tap in the villages. Local pharmacies could give advice on drugs. Schoolteachers could double as first-aiders. Non-governmental organisations and charities could provide medical supplies. Students could be required to do a compulsory placement in a village.

Rural posting can have unexpected consequences. In Thailand a sample of students in an urban medical school revealed that two-thirds of them wanted to return to the rural area where they had been placed (Wibulpolprasert and Pengpaibon, 2003). The network in any case is not rural alone. Telemedicine increasingly provides a superhighway to top-tier diagnosis. Distant specialists are only an email away.

Students from rural areas can be attracted by special scholarships, hostel places and a book allowance. Priority can be given to them when they apply for postgraduate education. Retention, however, will always be a problem. In order to ensure that professionals do not desert the forgotten, the public sector will have to make use of financial and non-financial incentives. The list extends to differential capitations, hardship allowances, longer holidays, continuing education, long-service awards, tuition write-offs, tax allowances, accelerated promotion, rural–urban rotation schemes, study leave, transparent assessment, a car loan, subsidised housing, opportunities for research, support from paramedics on the principle that a barefoot doctor will often be enough. Experience gained abroad could be recognised through appointment at a higher grade. A job could be found for a spouse. A private practice with a supplementary income might be allowed.

Intrinsic motivation should not be neglected. A cross-national 'dictator game' involving 1064 student nurses in Kenya, South Africa and Thailand found that nurses shared 30 per cent of their controlled cash windfall with their deserving fellows. Other samples in other experiments gave only 10 per cent. Women, the over-35s, and respondents with children were above the average, as were respondents from Thailand where solidarity and harmony are core social values. Helping the community, helping others, matters (Smith, Lagarde, Blaauw, Goodman, English, Mullei, Pagaiya, Tangcharoensathien, Erasmus and Hanson, 2012: 168). Recruitment and retention will be most likely to succeed if the package appeals to the medical professional's above-average endowment of altruism and compassion.

Returnees might be permitted to retain a subsidiary affiliation overseas. Schools equivalent to those in the towns could be provided for the doctor's children. Disamenities such as power outages and potholed roads could be corrected. Better equipment could be provided in rural health centres. Paramedic support could be guaranteed.

A reverse brain drain can be stimulated through policy instruments such as these. The aim would be to bring professionals back home from abroad, to ensure that they are not over-represented in the domestic private sector, to attract them into under-doctored areas. The plan would be to prevent either overstaffing or understaffing; and also to respond sensitively to local preferences. The lion in the path is, however, the cost. Payment at international rates puts a strain on labour-intensive budgets. Local scarcities and unsatisfied demand will empower the private sector to pay what it must by charging what it can. Higher fees draw in more professionals but they also deter the poorest of the poor from consuming what they need.

The service is fundamental and the spillovers are self-evident. The state will have to become involved. Kaelin compares a coordinated effort to keep the doctors at home to a military task-force instructed to prevent the loss of life (Kaelin, 2011: 39). Yet there is something else. The higher the proportion of doctors that are attracted into the neglected areas, the lower the proportion of doctors that are available to meet the needs of the medical tourists.

Our nation is caught between a rock and a hard place. On the one hand we want the isolated and the impoverished to enjoy good health. On the other hand we want the foreign exchange to come in and the national product to go up. It is a fight to the finish between sociology and economics. Ethics, perhaps, provides the answer. Ethics teaches that the restoration of function is not the means but the end. Ethics teaches that the restoration of function is always and everywhere good even if the function that is being restored is the function of a foreign barbarian who smells of garlic and reads upside down.

9. The ethics of medical travel

The deontology may be sordid: no one but a Bad Samaritan walks away from a mugger's victim merely because the mugger's victim has already been mugged. The consequentialism is a different matter: a triple bypass in India is preferable to no bypass at all even if the attending surgeon has no service ethic but his fee. The need justifies the greed. Without the triple bypass a human life would prematurely have been snuffed out.

Economic utopians are natural communitarians. They have an atavistic longing for William Morris's Nowhere when production was driven by mutual aid and the goods in the shops were free. Real-world individuals are more frequently natural pragmatists. They like the meat, the beer and the bread so much that they are prepared to ignore the venality of the gain-seeker's stance: 'Give me that which I want, and you shall have this which you want, is the meaning of every such offer; and it is in this manner that we obtain from one another the far greater part of those good offices which we stand in need of' (Smith, 1776 [1961]: I, 18). We want the meat. We pay the money. We want the roses. We put up with the thorns. Why should a triple bypass in India be any different?

This chapter provides the answer to the question. Section 9.1, 'A market for health', suggests that the commodity care may be a thing apart. Section 9.2, 'The Categorical Imperative' and 9.3, 'The Collective Conscience', ask if there can be an absolute standard when the moral benchmark is so often a function of time and place. Section 9.4, 'The national mix', shows that medical travel imports forbidden fruit into the citizen's choice set and alters the outcome of democratic politics. Section 9.5, 'The tyranny of the majority', suggests that medical tourism provides something for everyone if the minorities are prepared to spend money in a foreign market. Section 9.6, 'Justice', explores the possibility that health travel will increase the social distance between the haves and the have-nots. It asks if the body-holder should convert from Titmuss to Hobbes and buy a gun.

9.1 A MARKET FOR HEALTH

Health status is not for sale. Life expectancy and disease-free life years cannot be bought off the peg. What is an economic tradeable is healthcare. The demand is a derived demand. An immunisation is demanded not for itself but because it keeps the germs at bay. An invasive intervention is bought not for final utility but because it drives grim death from the door.

Healthcare can be bought and sold. Yet the market, domestic or international, is not the familiar one. The commodity slips like water through the demand-and-supply mesh.

Everyone knows what a pineapple is. Healthcare is more difficult to circumscribe. If an injection produces good health, then so too does a tax on cigarettes, a bracing jog, a Dead Sea swim, a spa massage, a supportive friend and an apple a day. Nor does the injection come with a money-back guarantee. A defective refrigerator can be returned. An unsuccessful operation can end in paralysis, disfigurement or death. The doctor–patient contract is not a promise that the client will be returned to ideal-typical well-being. Knowledge is imperfect and outcomes are uncertain. Regret sits in whenever the knife comes out. All that the agreement specifies is that the customer will put his money down and that the shopkeeper will do his best.

Bestness itself is not easy to recognise. Customers know from experience when an orange is juicy and when a melon tastes fresh. The unique atom has learnt by doing when he articulates a personal and private choice. The situation is different when the commodity is the Patagonia Syndrome and the buyer simply hasn't a clue. Ignorance makes it difficult for the body-holder to diagnose the asymptotic, to spot the malfunction, to trace through the scenarios, to choose the alternative that is best suited to the job. The care provided, the body-holder cannot be certain that it was the most satisfying, the most cost-effective option. Unknowledge is a threat to personhood when the person is in the dark and his heart feels queer.

Information is asymmetric and expectations are non-rational. Markets underperform in such conditions. Confused, anxious and in pain, the sovereign principal will often hire a fee-for-service agent to tell him what he wants. The consumer may be the best judge of his own pineapples but cancer care is different. In the market for biopsies, scans and chemotherapy, the shopper has to be led by the expert adviser who knows best.

The consumer may not even want to have a choice. Differentiation opens up too many possibilities. Stranded at the crossroads and frightened by the kaleidoscope, the awareness of ever-multiplying opportunity costs makes the patient increasingly aware that it is all but impossible to optimise.

The doctor takes over the treatment. The people next door pay all or most of the bill. So long as there is an insurance plan that pools the grouped contingencies, the frightened risk-averter has the reassurance that he has prepaid his worrying probabilities. He has entered into pure communism sold to him through the capitalist free market.

Communism by consent deviates significantly from the textbook market. The financial burden becomes a shared bygone. The potential interventions become a buffet meal. Moral hazard tempts the risk averter to avert fewer risks. Insurance reduces the disincentive to self-inflicted ill health. The economic burden becomes greater because of a drug called insurance. The doctor is not unaware of what the removal of the financial barrier will mean for his professional and his economic freedom. Guaranteed payment alters the nature of the choices he can make.

The doctor has a professional ethic that commits him to disinterested service. Money can warp that selfless devotion. Supplier-induced demand might become the business plan. The doctor might sell marginal tests or useless treatments that waste the wealth and imperil the health of the sovereign consumer who has to pay. The doctor can take advantage of the patient's ignorance to abuse the trust that was placed in him. Where there is an appeals mechanism, he may protect himself against a malpractice action through defensive medicine that still further puts up the cost.

Money can warp the ethic. What is striking is how often it does not. Most doctors choose medicine over banking at least in part because they want to help the sick. As doctors they have internalised the Hippocratic Oath. They know that their remembered code, policing itself, would curse them with a spoiled conscience were they to supply unneeded interventions purely to reap the pecuniary *quid pro quo*. Money is a part but not the whole of their remuneration. The market for pineapples is guided by an invisible hand that knows no benevolence but only self-love. In the case of pineapples the rule is *caveat emptor*. Medical care is different. In the case of care, medical ethics will frequently stay the scalpel and correct a market failure.

Doctors, moreover, are required to conform to the standards of their professional bodies and the government regulators. The barrow-boy at the roadside has the economist's freedom to price aggressively and innovate relentlessly. The doctor has to live by his conventions. Practice variation and the shortcomings of evidence-based medicine make the doctor dependent on the learned heuristic and the shared response. Personal recommendations mean repeat business. A maverick who strays too far from the locally validated best practice will be putting his reputation within his network on the line.

In common with the professional consensus, the social consensus takes a view on the pursuit of interest and gain. The wider community identifies a bedrock minimum, a threshold entitlement that no decent human being should have to do without. The World Health Organization was unambiguously in line with the unimodal consensus when it committed itself from the beginning to good care as a non-negotiable right: 'The enjoyment of the highest attainable standard of health is one of the fundamental rights of every human being . . . Governments have a responsibility for the health of their peoples' (World Health Organization, 1962 [1946]: 1).

Not just the World Health Organization but also the United Nations (in its Universal Declaration of Human Rights, 1948) and the Council of Europe (in the European Convention on Human Rights, 1950) have proclaimed that every human being has 'equal and inalienable rights' that, extending beyond the law and the vote, must include adequate access to medical services 'indispensable for his dignity and the free development of his personality' (United Nations, 1948 [1950]). The right to health is not freedom from the state but rather freedom through the state. It is the freedom to become, the freedom to unfold.

The right to health is more than good health alone. A facilitator as well as an absolute, it is also the precondition for the right to work and the right to achieve. Like education, adequate health is an enabling input. It is a means as well as an end. An employee who is frequently ill or who is debilitated by poor circulation will not qualify for on-the-job training and the rapid promotions to which he would otherwise have been entitled. His integration in the wider social organism may be put at risk.

The right to health is grounded in the respect for persons. A natural right, it is a logical deduction from the definition of what it means to be fully human, neither stunted nor repressed. Joined to that is the idea of a citizenship right. Fundamental care is a part of the social contract. It is the minimum tolerable endowment that the members of the community guarantee to their fellow team-mates. Pineapples may be earned. Luxury medicine may be left to laissez-faire. Basic care, however, is different. It is ascribed. It is a sacred trust.

Different people will call different things basic. The sick role is not set in stone. Respect for persons dictates that the multiple subjectivities and the idiosyncratic predilections must not be looked quizzically in the mouth. Even so, it is the common culture and the integrating collectivity that puts the 'normal' into 'normal functioning', the 'irreducible' into 'irreducible need'. A unique collectivity will call some things top-ups and electives but others the shared minimum below which no fellow team-mate should be allowed to fall. No one but a scoundrel merchants good health to his parents or cost–benefits his children for a tonsillectomy. No one who sees the majesty of the adventure shared will send a premature baby cold-bloodedly to the scrap heap. The sociology of medicine is not the theology of business. When the National Health Service defaults on its social umbrella, it is all who live in Arthur's kingdom who feel that they have been let down.

Diseases spread. One person's cough becomes another person's tuberculosis. Public bads are super-territorial. One nation's mosquito becomes another nation's malaria. Epidemics and infections, unlike oranges and pineapples, violate the fundamental ethical precept that costs should not be imposed on third parties who have not given their assent to the game. Health services are the public utilities that promote positive externalities while protecting the common territory from plague. The common territory has globalised itself beyond the nation-state. Rickets and squints drag down the pace of economic growth in an interdependent world where every Alter is every Ego's supply and demand.

The spillover is growth but it is also humanity. Where fellow toilers cannot reach the socially specified minimum, warm-hearted neighbours chip in to ensure the basic package. The reason is empathy rather than exchange. A decent endowment of the basics is agreed upon by the consensus. The reason is the hard-wired human ability to enter into the imagined happiness and misery of others. People feel bad when others feel bad. That is how people are made.

Healthcare is not a commodity that lends itself naturally to the narrow self-seeking that succeeds so well in so many other areas of social life. Rational as they may be in the marketplace for pineapples, people are swayed by their passions when they are confronted with the possibility of illness or death: 'Disease reminds us of the fragility of life and the limits of human existence . . . The solidarity we show with the ill by caring for them has come to have deep religious and moral significance in many cultures' (Daniels, 1985: 49). People believe that healthcare is more fundamental to the good life than pineapples. They surrender to the mystique that it is the medicine man who stands between themselves and suffering their way towards a preventable death.

9.2 THE CATEGORICAL IMPERATIVE

There are no physical laws in ethics. There are no eternal constants comparable to the objective, non-ego constraints of Newton's apple or King Canute's tides. What there are in ethics are subjective 'ought-to-bes'. Some of these principles are so familiar and so powerful that they recur across the boundaries of geography, economy, ideology, creed and culture. Newton's apple falls as if guided by an invisible hand. Kant's Imperative, like Newton's gravity, is a point of equilibrium on which the moral codes tend to converge.

Kant's Categorical Imperative has an intuitive appeal even to persons who have never read a word of Kant. Kant says: 'Act in such a way that you always treat humanity, whether in your own person or in the person of any other, never simply as a means, but always at the same time as an end' (Kant, 1785 [1961]: 96). Virtually every religious or civil code says the same. The reason is simple logic. Without mutual respect the life in common would degenerate into a struggle for survival in which every man would be a wolf to every other.

The Categorical Imperative serves a practical purpose. It affords multi-period protection precisely because it enjoins imperfect beings to do unto others as they would wish others to do unto them. Justice is blind. The constitution is all. Rule-utilitarianism keeps weakness of will in check.

Promise-keeping is an example. Self-interest narrowly understood tempts each fallible Adam to default on his commitments. If, however, all were to follow each into the self-seeking fallacy of composition, then myopic opportunism would mean that credible undertakings could no longer be given. Grassroots trust would give way to Big Brother whose policemen ensure that the trains run on time. It is Leviathan or it is self-restraint. The Categorical Imperative is self-restraint. Interest as well as ethics leads the would-be free riders to submit.

In-period consequences are not within the remit of the categorical and the constitutional. Act-utilitarianism would degrade the universal rule to the status of a 'hypothetical imperative'. It would make amoral outcome the sole judge of oughtness. It leaves no other standard of virtue but instrumentality: 'We should have no other reason for praising a man but that for which we commend a chest of drawers' (Smith, 1759 [1966]: 271). Consequentialism is not enough to distinguish right from wrong. Deontology is the *sine qua non* if fallible Adam is not to become imprisoned in an insoluble dilemma of conjectural variation.

Unlike the rules of hygiene or the rules of the road, the precise content of the ethical code is not laid down for all time. All that is eternal and unchangeable is the meta-principle of respect, equality and autonomy. Supplier-induced demand and cynical price-gouging would clearly be a violation of the standard. So would the concealment of relevant facts when informed consent is being sought for a clinical test. The Categorical Imperative is more than a social convention. It is an encoded statement that patients and doctors alike have the same endowment of equal moral worth.

Religions often say that the rules are the rules because they are the irrefragable fruits of Divine Intervention. The vision of God as a Supreme

Legislator is especially evocative in the Old Testament when God reveals his Ten Commandments to Moses; the people of Israel, strict constructionists, respond by saying 'all that the Lord has spoken we will do' (Holy Bible, 2001: Exodus: 19:13). Elsewhere, the United States Declaration of Independence legitimates its moral absolutes with an appeal upward to a Higher Authority: 'We hold these truths to be self-evident, that all men are created equal, that they are endowed by their Creator with certain unalienable Rights' (*Declaration of Independence*, 1776). The Creator is a Great Teacher. The Bible is a Great Book. Fundamentalists who have revelation have no further need for philosophy.

Thomas Jefferson, with his fellow Enlightenment revolutionaries, declared that they were taking their case against a predatory despot to the Supreme Judge of the world. In fact, they were pleading just as strongly for the secular rationality of the Categorical Imperative. What else can it be but the Golden Rule when the Declaration of Independence promulgates an equal right to life, liberty and the pursuit of happiness? In that respect the Declaration of Independence is at one with the Sermon on the Mount: 'Whatever you wish that others would do to you, do also to them, for this is the Law and the Prophets' (Holy Bible, 2001: Matthew: 7:19).

The Law and the Prophets have no real warmth for the war of each against all. They know precisely what is required of fellow citizens for peaceful coexistence: 'You shall not steal', 'you shall not murder', 'you shall not desire your neighbour's house' (Holy Bible, 2001: Deuteronomy: 6:7). The Ten Commandments are, literally, set in stone. Confucius, who had not studied the Law and the Prophets, applied the same common sense in time of civil war when he told his disciples that the 'single word which can be a guide to conduct throughout one's life' can only be this: 'Do not impose on others what you yourself do not desire' (Confucius, n.d. [1979]: 135).

The Golden Rule seems to recur in all times and places: 'The golden rule is close to being a global principle – a norm common to all peoples of all time' (Gensler, 2011: 95). Gensler sees it as nothing less than 'a good one-sentence summary of what morality is about': 'The golden rule captures the *spirit* beyond moral rules. It helps us to see the point beyond moral rules. It engages our reasoning, instead of imposing an answer. It counteracts self-centeredness. And it correctly applies ideals like fairness and concern' (Gensler, 2011: 89). Existentialists like Camus are too quick to say that if God is dead then everything is possible. The Golden Rule can be personified as a man with a beard. Crucially, the Golden Rule does not require a belief in a man with a beard to command allegiance to 'self-evident truths' and tribal 'shall nots' which do not sway with the wind.

Interpretation of the law makes the lawyers rich. Does killing extend to killing in self-defence or in war? Is a person who hates himself honour-bound to hate his neighbours just as much? Does respect for persons include respect for plants, animals and irreplaceable natural resources that future generations will require for their sustenance? The debate is about the applications. It is not about the permafrozen core. The Categorical Imperative is a binding universal. Everyone except for the zero-sum aggressor must regard it as just.

9.3 THE COLLECTIVE CONSCIENCE

Durkheim did not visit God's filing cabinet to find out what moral man is obliged by universal nature to do. Instead he canvassed public opinion in his local High Street and in the shopping centre where the know-it-alls sit as judge and jury. There was no other means at his disposal to ferret out the holy writ: 'Man is a moral being only because he lives in society, since morality consists in being solidary with a group and varying with this solidarity. Let all social life disappear, and moral life will disappear with it, since it would no longer have any objective' (Durkheim, 1893 [1964]: 399). To act morally is to act in conformity with the habits and conventions of the surrounding social organism. It is the blood, the heart, the stomach and the feet that hand the lungs the script. Mill's sovereignty of the factored-down is as much a figment of the imagination, Durkheim believed, as Augustine's notion that God's Will is alone the origin of naked Adam's uncompromising code.

The norms are the norms of a unique reference group: 'To act morally is to act in terms of the collective interest' (Durkheim, 1895 [1964]: 6). The product of social interaction and the economic base, common customs are circumscribed by time and place. Then and there, and until things change, 'oughtness' can be derived from 'isness'. Coal is always black and swans are always white. Mores and ethical absolutes must, however, be consumed quickly, and always on the spot: 'Moral concepts are embedded in and are partially constitutive of forms of social life. One key way in which we may identify one form of social life as distinct from another is by identifying differences in moral concepts' (MacIntyre, 1998: 2).

Moral concepts are relative and specific. One man's meat is another man's poison. One man's cannibalism is another man's food chain. One man's Latin is another man's Greek. In Rome even little children can speak Latin. When in Rome do as the Romans do. But it is only a local tradition, a here-and-now means to an end. It is not a meta-ethic. It is not the Law and the Prophets. It is only the way we do things around here.

There is the universal and there is the specific. Martin Walzer makes a useful distinction between the two perspectives. At the core, he says, there is the 'thin' morality. On this both the cannibals and the Romans are likely to converge: 'It is everyone's morality because it is no one's in particular' (Walzer, 1994: 7). The 'thin' sphere is a minimalist code. It is a general narrative by means of which we can 'have moral expectations about the behavior not only of our fellows but of strangers too' (Walzer, 1994: 7). At the periphery, he continues, there is the 'thick' morality. It puts flesh on the skeleton precisely because it embeds the 'thin' code in a non-standard community: 'Morality is thick from the beginning, culturally integrated, fully resonant, and it reveals itself thinly only on special occasions' (Walzer, 1994: 4). The 'thin' code is the trunk. The 'thick' code is the branches. It is hard most of the time to see the trunk for the leaves.

The 'thick' code is shared memories, folkways and historical associations. It is the moral anthropology of a single tribe. An ivy-covered worldview empowers discrete individuals to formulate their overlapping needs: 'People don't just have needs; they have ideas about their needs; they have priorities, they have degrees of need; and these priorities and degrees are related not only to their human nature but also to their history and culture' (Walzer, 1983: 66). Other tribes will have their own house-brand intellectual frameworks. Domestically or internationally, the tribes do not all think alike.

Jews need food for physical survival. Jews also need communally validated food if they are to survive socially in their walled-in group. If a Jew does not conform to the expectations of the Jews whom he defines to be his fellows, he will be ostracised and cast out. Just as hurtful, he will stigmatise himself since he will know that he has been guilty of violating the constitution that has given him his self. In society or on his own, the tribesman who has broken the bonds of the band will be as out of place as a pig in a drawing-room. No one wants that. Ethical pluralism is the result.

Adam Smith says that the benchmark in the shopping centre will never be consumer sovereignty or idiosyncratic taste. Deciding what to wear, naked Adam must and will be guided at the crossroads by the costumes and props of the historical context that has given him his social language. Freedom is not unlimited unless the insensitive individualist is prepared to make himself a figure of fun: 'A man would be ridiculous who should appear in public with a suit of clothes quite different from those which are commonly worn, though the new dress should in itself be ever so graceful or convenient' (Smith, 1759 [1966]: 284). In France the lower classes can with perfect propriety wear wooden shoes and sometimes no shoes at all. Not so in England where even the lower classes are expected to wear leather shoes. Surrogacy or no surrogacy, private rooms or citizenship-class wards – it all depends on 'the peculiar manners and customs of the people' (Smith, 1776 [1961]: I, 132).

The Chinese use chopsticks. The Germans eat *Knoblauch*. The Punjabis speak Punjabi. In Slobovia they practice euthanasia. In North Bodoh they do not. Since different communities have different standards, global convergence on a single rule is not on the horizon: 'There will continue to be many communities, with different histories, ways of life, climates, political structures, and economies' (Walzer, 1983: 48). Walzer regards the philosopher's fiction of collective amnesia behind an impartial veil of ignorance as 'thin' but not 'thick'. Unsituated automatons purified of pre-existent bias cannot be found. It is too late for that: 'Admission and exclusion are at the core of communal interdependence' (Walzer, 1983: 62).

I am I because We are We. The I and the We dwell together in '*communities of character*, historically stable', in 'ongoing associations of men and women with some special commitment to one another' (Walzer, 1983: 62). The life in common puts its stamp on the one-off monad's freedom of choice. In return it gives the free-floating isolate the freedom to belong: 'One of our needs is community itself: culture, religion, and politics. It is only under the aegis of these three that all the other things we need become *socially recognized needs*, take on historical and determinate form' (Walzer, 1983: 65).

9.4 THE NATIONAL MIX

Bedrock morality is the Categorical Imperative. The existential overgrowth is the Collective Conscience. In every society the two standards must live together side by side. The 'thin' and the 'thick' must work together to produce a unified medical culture. Success is not guaranteed.

Each person has a property in himself. His moral autonomy must be respected: 'Over himself, over his own body and mind, the individual is sovereign' (Mill, 1974 [1859]: 69). Yet each person is simultaneously a member of a team. To claim his right he must acknowledge his duty: 'Your body is part of the national capital, and must be looked after, and sickness causes a loss of national income, in addition to being liable to spread' (Marshall, 1981 [1965]: 91). J.S. Mill is saying that discrete Ego alone holds the freehold to his own body and mind. T.H. Marshall is asserting that the deeds and titles remain in the hands of the passenger on the Clapham omnibus and the patient in the waiting-room. Marshall's window on the world is not the same as that of Mill.

Some cultures will be closer to J.S. Mill and 'freedom from'. Reasoning that only the wearer can know where the shoe pinches, they will say that the individual alone can assign cardinal and ordinal utility to his tastes and preferences. They will argue that the decentralised free market enjoys especial 'oughtness' in the field of medicine where there is always risk as well as hope. Other cultures will be closer to T.H. Marshall and 'freedom to'. Believing that all health systems are national health systems, they will state that the nation must spend freely on translating a paper entitlement into doctors and hospitals but in exchange the patient must forgo his breakfast fry-up and eat an apple a day.

There are things that they do and we do not. They sell priorities to the highest bidder. We believe in waits and queues. They treat abortion as a woman's right. We treat induced death as cold-blooded murder. They state that a body or a cadaver may reasonably be sold piecemeal as scrap because liberal democracy is predicated on devolution and exchange. We state that a non-rational taboo may not ever be violated even if the transaction would keep another human being alive.

Our way is an embodiment of our consensus: 'Our health care financing system reflects who we think should pay for health care and how much. Our systems for licensing, accreditation, malpractice, and regulatory approval of medical technologies reflect the quality standards we desire. Our public and private health insurance systems reflect the risks we can tolerate' (Cortez, 2008: 73). Our way is our way. Their way is their way. Consensus is *non disputandum*. Creative destruction, like charity, begins at home.

Medicine, like consensus, is a shared possession. It did not spring fully formed from Adam's rib. Basic science and professional education are a product of the historical ratchet. Not a free good but a handed-on commitment, they have been subsidised by generations past and encumbered by them with obligations.

Some cultures treat bygones as forever bygone. They see care as a mercantile start-from-here into which rootless postulants buy entry-tickets in the form of medical fees. Other cultures deny that the present can ever throw up a fresh or an *ab initio* response. They are convinced that doctor-missionaries have an unwritten bond to repay the stranger gift. Such cultures believe that doctors long dead are marching alongside doctors newly minted. Blood long gone is whispering to the lineal descendants of Harvey and Lister that they are forever embedded in Burke's intergenerational chain:

> As a result, when they accept the privilege of a medical education, medical and nursing students enter implicitly into a covenant with society to use their knowledge for the benefit of the sick. By entering into this covenant they become stewards rather than proprietors of the knowledge they acquire . . .

> Stewardship is a better metaphor than proprietorship for medical knowledge and skill (Pellegrino, 1999: 251)

The attitudes and the techniques are what they are today because of what they were before. They are inherited and they are common. 'What is' becomes 'what ought to be' given time. Medicine is one of many areas of social life in which the done thing is magnified into a venerated norm. The ritual does not require any further intellectualisation than that.

Some care systems are private and commercial. Passing the strict test of Darwinian survival, they condition the reflexes to the idea that profit-seeking, rational choice and *caveat emptor* are the American Dream. Other care systems are national and solidaristic. Evoking the memory of the Good Samaritan who did not default, they convey the message that affiliation and friendship mean an unequivocal duty to take full responsibility for our own. Reality is habit. An illustration is cumulative causality in the United Kingdom's National Health Service (NHS).

The National Health Service was conceived in the Second World War when Buckingham Palace and the impoverished East End alike were subjected to the citizenship contingency of Hitler's bombs. One Nation in peace was one consequence of One Nation at war. It led to the creation of a Health Service in 1948 that was committed not just to healing the sick but also to the perpetuation of social values like benevolence, obligation, trust and ascription. The Health Service, Titmuss stressed, was always more than the doctors and the hospitals alone: 'The most unsordid act of British social policy in the twentieth century has allowed and encouraged sentiments of altruism, reciprocity and social duty to express themselves; to be made explicit and identifiable in measurable patterns of behaviour by all social groups and classes' (Titmuss, 1970: 225). Allowed and encouraged. Thus does the circular flow of mind and matter ensure that the familiar and the validated will play a pivotal role in the social reproduction of right and wrong.

Few people if any learn the ethics by which they live from great books. Most people take their personal code from family and friends, the street and the city, nationhood experiences and revered role-models. Comprehensive education, television soaps, military service bring the tribesmen more closely together. So does Titmuss's NHS. It is both an institution and a metaphor. It is the exemplar of a rolling balance where the gift is at once the child and the parent of the gift. Budget Day is always Christmas when we buy beer for our fellows and they buy beer for us.

Common experiences make the tribesmen think as one. As Walzer puts it: 'Mutual provision breeds mutuality. So the common life is simultaneously the prerequisite of provision and one of its products' (Walzer, 1983:

65). The doctor must not assume that he can starve his fellows of social service by going abroad. The doctor like the rest of us is in and of his *Gemeinschaft*: 'I see no reason to respect the doctor's market freedom. Needed goods are not commodities' (Walzer, 1983: 90). Solidarity is not a neoliberal choice. The Collective Conscience, like the Categorical Imperative, is not up for grabs through an auction sale.

Some cultures are in favour of market-based hands-off. Some cultures are in favour of social democracy's resolute hands-on. The Collective Conscience does not take sides. Ideologically neutral, the Collective Conscience sees no conflict of principles so long as each moral code relates to a unique social consensus. Where there is a gulf is between the followers of Durkheim and the disciples of Kant. The Categorical Imperative embodies a commitment to human dignity and respect for persons. The Collective Conscience maintains that ordinary human beings know best. The Categorical Imperative may or may not be safe in their hands. Nothing is guaranteed.

Tolerance, neither eternal nor irreducible, may end up the prisoner of time and place. Misfits and non-conformists will in the circumstances be strongly tempted to circumvent their own national way. They will see some purpose in taking their non-standard deviance to a parallel system where the exception has been made the rule: 'Patients are opting out of our health care system and the delicate equilibrium of policy choices that it represents' (Cortez, 2008: 73). When in Rome, do as the Romans do. It is an incentive to track down the Romans and flee from the Greeks. Some patients are going private. Some patients are going abroad.

9.5 THE TYRANNY OF THE MAJORITY

Burkett describes the outsourcing of moral choices as an overall gain: 'In some ways, this is a political "win–win" because the people who want the procedures have access to them and the dominant public policy restricting the procedures is upheld' (Burkett, 2007: 237). Tawney argues that irrevocable 'self-evidents' and unquestionable 'shalt-nots' dictate that no one but a moral outlaw would dare to say *de gustibus*: 'Man is condemned to live in twilight; but darkness is darkness, and light is light. What matters is the direction in which his face is set' (Tawney, 1939: xviii).

Burkett says that tolerance of diversity is, morally speaking, win–win. Tawney says that the tolerance of the intolerable is, morally speaking, lose–lose. Trapped between the win–win and the lose–lose, the student of medical travel cannot do better than to fall back upon the wise Adam Smith who arrived at the following conclusion: 'There is nothing so absurd . . . which has not sometimes been asserted by some philosophers' (Smith, 1776 [1961]: II, 405).

9.5.1 Well-Being Goes Up

It is politically win–win. Because sovereign parliaments enact different laws, the cacophony of morals becomes a supermarket of services. Individual autonomy is upheld. Social mores are upheld. National laws are enforced at home but not abroad. There is something for everyone if the consumers are willing to shop around.

Social policies that satisfy the median voter do not satisfy the fringe. Where political democracy is at variance with its meta-principle of respect for persons, medical travel may be the validated escape. Money talks. Money gives the medical minority a chance to speak and be heard. The missed out are empowered to vote with their fees. The excluded are given the opportunity to pay twice for their care. The fringe is permitted to top up the tax-funded menu with a banned substance that the median voter regards with the deepest disgust.

Without medical travel the exceptions and the footnotes would be crushed by the tyranny of the majority. Because of medical travel there is a demand-led marketplace for morals. The willingness to pay may be seen as the practical embodiment of the Categorical Imperative. Guido Pennings compares it to fiscal federalism which respects the median but gives the fringe a chance to breathe:

> The purpose of national regulation should not be to prevent those who disagree to perform certain acts or make use of certain interventions or services. Prohibitive laws can only determine which services are available on the territory. As such, the law expresses the moral values of the majority within a community; nothing more, nothing less . . . Allowing people to look abroad demonstrates the absolute minimum of respect for their moral autonomy. (Pennings, 2004: 2691)

Respect for their moral autonomy might not extend to abortion on demand in the Vatican sick-bay. What it does mean is that the home jurisdiction grants its minorities the freedom to source for the procedure abroad. This is not 100 per cent moral autonomy but neither is it Big Brother who vaporises all dissent. Repressive tolerance is a workable compromise that defuses the frustration. The alternative, as Pennings says, could well be 'moral warfare': 'Imposing a moral opinion on persons who do not share this view carries the risk of conflicts which threaten peace and cooperation in society' (Pennings, 2002: 340). Country-shopping reduces the felt unhappiness that would have resulted if citizens had not been granted the right to purchase abortion or euthanasia (like pork and alcohol) in a different jurisdiction that lives by different values.

Social division breeds resentment. To that extent it is as much an externality as a smoking chimney or a polluted creek. Even chronic alcoholics have feelings. Even chronic alcoholics do not want to be sentenced to death because the median citizen drinks fresh milk instead.

The median citizen might oppose the release of scarce resources for self-inflicted conditions. Consensus might dictate that people who take risks with fast cars, fast food and fast friends should be treated last. The consequence is that a socially responsive healthcare system will be obliged to refuse liver transplants to chronic alcoholics because the beer-drinker's lifestyle is not to the milk-drinker's taste.

The chronic alcoholic will be resentful that the milk-drinkers have cast him out. Invoking the Categorical Imperative and calling for the Golden Rule, he will find that he has the Hippocratic Oath on his side. The professional ethic by which medical practitioners steer their craft teaches them to be tolerant and non-judgmental when a sick person cries out to them for help. They find it difficult to discriminate when a sick person is bleeding on the street. As Ho puts it: 'To use moral responsibility as a criterion would undermine the physician/patient relationship and the functioning of medicine in general' (Ho, 2008: 78).

Doctors because of their ethic find it difficult to stigmatise the self-destructive. In the treatment centre if not in the High Street they tend to assert that current conditions may not be bloodhounded for a past dereliction. Decoupling rights from duties, they say that documented body maintenance can never be made the gatekeeper to care. Public opinion is not on their side. Ho reports that in one study 71 per cent supported priorities that moved in step with deserts. The world is a big place. The remaining 29 per cent can take their passports and their wallets and go abroad (Ho, 2008: 78).

9.5.2 Well-Being Goes Down

Chronic alcoholics can go abroad for the new liver that the social consensus had denied to them at home. Medical travel for them defuses the divisive externality of social exclusion. Yet the road less travelled involves spillovers as well. Just as the tyranny of the majority can breed resentment, so the freedom of the minority can impose a cost. Deviation from the drill is not a victimless crime.

A post-menopausal woman who obtains fertility treatment abroad is putting pressure on her nation's scarce schools and child benefits: violating the home culture's norms, should she restore to her disapproving fellows the self-invited subsidy? A mother-to-be who without permission terminates a birth is stealing 40 years and more of potential labour power: will competitor nations compensate her countrymen when their rate of economic growth slows down? A traditional couple who gender-select their child are depriving history-to-come of a balanced breeding stock: where will the marriage partners come from if the population is not to shrink? A specialist who supplies cosmetic surgery to aliens is not a generalist who treats emergencies in an outstation: will the foreign body reimburse the local body for a necessity not provided because a luxury had banked the priority? Minorities experience regret when the majority stands between them and their revealed preference. The majority, however, experiences regret when the minorities break the majority's rules. On the one hand there is umbrage. On the other hand there is bile. The escape valve may be a private benefit but still the antipathy is a social cost.

There are losses from trade even as there are gains. Some of the losses can be assigned a pecuniary value. It may be possible to quantify the consumption diverted when altruism becomes damped and organs for transplant acquire a monetary value; or to estimate the public health implications when would-be parents are not screened pre-*in vitro* fertilisation (IVF) abroad for a history of drugs, alcoholism, violence or insanity. Some of the losses are more amorphous. Fugitives who opt out of the central value system are calling into question the collective discipline that makes the fellow citizens into a *sui generis* rather than a higgledy-piggledy agglomeration. Medical travel will be a temptation too far if it allows the travellers to pay a fine for the privilege of rejecting their common history.

A commitment to One-Nationhood may be encoded in the delivery system. This is the case with the UK NHS which has the non-medical function, both horizontal and multi-generational, of integrating British citizens in the values and ideals of an ongoing community. Culture-specific signifiers like old age, mutual aid and the sick role are codified in the institutions. New hips in Chennai are not the same as new hips at home since at home the new hips are packaged in a common experience with the latent function of integration and inclusion. Boss and worker, black and white, old and young lie side by side in the same ward. The beds are their university. The take-away from their university is that, toffee- nosed or hoi polloi, we all have joints and sometimes they hurt.

That sense of belonging, that cocoon of cohesion, can be put at risk when a privileged elite fast-tracks itself to a foreign country: 'Some argue that medical tourism allows wealthier patients to escape the rules imposed by society and breach a social contract with our health system' (Cortez, 2008: 75). Wealthier patients get new hips. Poorer citizens still suffer from being old. Wealthier patients do not need to sleep next to blacks, labourers, pensioners and social democrats. A private room privatises their utility-function. Wealthier patients want to escape the consensual equity of waiting and queues. The willing and the able can afford the means-tested alternative of rationing by price.

The NHS was designed to be classless. Medical tourism stratifies the treatment by income decile: 'Relatively few, relatively wealthy, individuals can buy their way out of moral dilemmas' (Blyth and Ferrand, 2008: 108). Our Collective Conscience prohibits abortion as it prohibits infanticide. The rich are allowed to purchase remissions that allow them to sin abroad. The poor are obliged to bring up their unwanted children at home.

Differential access goes against the moral principle of equal treatment for equal need. It makes the moral principle into a consumer durable which a common culture may choose to accept or to reject as it sees fit. Social actors who deny that the tail may legitimately wag the dog will make their position clear. Alongside the tyranny of the majority there can exist the tyranny of the minority. It is no less real for being clothed in the language of tolerance and respect.

9.5.3 Policing the Deviant

A country that regards its moral standards as never-varying absolutes might not be prepared to turn a blind eye to the escape route that circumvents its norms. Our society has reached consensus that female genital mutilation is as repellent to what we are as gang-rape or paedophilia. Our citizens find it insulting that the suburbs can purchase additional seats for their stretchered sick when the slums are forced by austerity to lie where they fall. Our Collective Conscience may be strong but that does not mean that it is universal. Closing the loophole is, however, more difficult.

Sometimes the home country and the foreign country will see eye to eye on right and wrong. War criminals are regularly extradited without a statute of limitations. Supranational legislation and extraterritorial jurisdiction are possible where the offence is so heinous that countries unite in condemning it as a violation of human rights. Lower-level infractions that do not warrant reference to the International Criminal Court are in practical terms the real void. Where the offence is cannabis and not genocide, a tourist is not likely to be arrested at Harwich if he has gone to Amsterdam to smoke.

It can be done. Doctors asked to perform a procedure that is perfectly legal in their own country could be asked to log with Interpol the name and address of each foreign national taking out a kidney transplant. Women under suspicion of having committed egg-freezing or abortion abroad could be required to undergo a gynaecological examination on their return. The military could board ships in international waters if it were believed that floating doctors were performing ultrasounds on scan-barred citizens. Nationals using the internet to source for xenotransplants or euthanasia could be denied a passport and mandated to seek counselling.

Immunosuppressants could be refused if there were proof that the virus had been contracted through prohibited activity. Commercial surrogacy could be banned outright. Parents of surrogate babies born abroad could be stopped from bringing them home or registering them for citizenship. A consensus that endorses the respect for persons may not feel entirely comfortable with a Draconian prohibition that makes a new-born infant into a stateless orphan. Yet it can be done.

A foreign country is not, of course, bound by the home country's rules. A law that cannot be enforced is no law at all. Unless the foreign country can be persuaded to go against its own moral consensus there is not a lot the home country can do. As Cohen points out, detection itself will be difficult: 'Especially for practices that are legal and indeed profitable in the destination country there will be no incentive to inform authorities in the patient's home country' (Cohen, 2012: 16). Destination countries might help out by confining procedures like assisted suicide to their own nationals. More often than not they will supply whatever they think it acceptable to supply. They will leave the home country to cope with its moral pluralists as it sees fit.

9.5.4 A World Common Culture

Economic evolution is not favourable to the Spirit of the Place. The world is flat and planes move fast. One prediction is that national standards will draw ever closer together in the wake of unstoppable globalisation. The social consensus goes worldwide. Wherever you look, the framework of discourse looks increasingly like Manhattan.

International trade engenders international protocols. Business conferences harmonise conventions on fraudulent advertising and unfounded exaggeration. The World Health Organization promulgates guidelines on public payment and minimum provision. The World Trade Organization opens up protected markets. The World Bank argues for economic liberalisation and responsible bond-issue. Bilateral agreements and regional alliances impose a threshold minimum of safety, security and quality.

Professional bodies coordinate the recognition of medical qualifications and the portability of health insurance. Joint Commission International (JCI) accreditation demands the mimicry of Western ways and United States medical schools. Foreign investors and transnational businesses favour company law that is recognisably the same. Civil-society coalitions make common cause across the national borders in support of a healthy environment and uncontaminated food. It all adds up to a homogenised core. Arbitrage smoothes out the variance. Wherever the medical tourists go for their surgery, they have reason to expect that the medical experience will be broadly in line with the best-practice code.

Regulations are not new. Tawney was only one interventionist among many to have welcomed them as an essential complement to individual freedom: 'The mother of liberty has, in fact, been law' (Tawney, 1966 [1949]: 169). Cattaneo makes a similar point: 'Trade promotion in the health sector is therefore not about deregulating, but better regulating, and sometimes even regulating more' (Cattaneo, 2009: 3). What is new is the relative standardisation of the laws and conventions. The regulations are less and less the manifesto of a unique country's distinctive institutions. They are more and more a common property in an interdependent world.

It introduces a whole new dimension to the debate about medical travel as a bulwark against oppression. If countries gradually converge on common laws and conventions, the health refugee may find that he has nowhere to go for a bought kidney or even a narcotic painkiller. There will always be Ayurveda in India and service with a smile in Thailand. The tourism will always differentiate the countries. As for the central medical experience, however, the danger is real that there will be fewer bolt-holes where the medical traveller can escape from the tyranny of the majority.

Yet it is not just the dispersion of the rules that is of concern to the tailing minority. It is also the strength of the rules. Trade and communications do not mean that one-size-fits-all must necessarily be a cultural straitjacket. Economics can be the solvent of social discipline. Not a straitjacket but a spectrum, one-size-fits-all can be loose, general and permissive. Seeking unanimity, nations might simply gravitate to the laws and conventions of the most liberal member. It is not Tawney. Neither, however, is it the tyranny that forces the minority to purchase its abortions abroad.

Health travellers are more likely to come in where fewer procedures are ruled out. Competition among host countries for the floating patient pool is itself a good reason for host countries to re-examine their moral absolutes. If foreign rivals are legalising the stem cells and the super-drugs, then it will cost jobs at home if the state errs on the side of caution. The result is the familiar race to the bottom. The country that licenses the greatest number of procedures is the country that creams off the gain. Money focuses the mind. The speakeasies are the precedent. Where there is a profit there is a way.

A market culture makes shoppers resentful of legislation that constricts their choice-set. Reductionist individualism is not in line with communitarian values that perpetuate the conservatism of an ongoing collectivity. Respect for persons may mean respect for communities of persons and not just for the desocialised one-off: 'We take on responsibilities to others by virtue of our own social roles and responsibilities' (Snyder, Crooks, Johnston and Kingsbury, 2013: 237). New duties are created as a consequence of participation in a shared and interdependent global socioeconomic order. Perhaps so; but the argument will have less than no appeal to asocial isolates who see no need to play by the rules. Sociology has been pushed out by economics. Nowadays the sociologists are driving taxis in Paris and busking for loose change.

Enlightenment self-interest, individual rationality and entrepreneurial search are becoming the consensual hard core. They are evolving into the only name on the ballot. Heather Widdows deplores the new hegemony which she sees as a kind of moral neo-colonialism, a false paradigm which is completing capitalism's historic mission of cross-border conquest: 'Unlike moral colonialism of the past, values are not presented as superior, but as universal, requiring not conversion to an alternative (presumably better) value system, but recognition of universal values' (Widdows, 2007: 306). The rules become similar and they become loose. The minorities will not need to travel for care. Sooner or later they will get their abortions at home.

9.6 JUSTICE

Money talks and patients travel. Medical travel opens up the world. But is it just? Ronald Labonté says that it is not. Governments, he says, should shift 'the trajectory of globalization away from purely economic objectives that benefit elites, towards health and human development goals that benefit everyone, especially the poor' (Labonté, 2003: 16). The title of his pamphlet is as uncompromising as its conclusion. It is *Dying for Trade: Why Globalization Can Be Bad for Our Health*. It cannot be fair that some sparrows fall while other sparrows fly. Our health is a common acquisition. Equity must not be sacrificed to efficiency and the thingification of the soul.

9.6.1 Rawls

A benchmark and a starting point is *A Theory of Justice*. In *A Theory of Justice* John Rawls conducts a thought-experiment to pinpoint the essence of acceptable social distance. He suggests that a unanimous verdict may be secured in the 'original position' ('purely hypothetical') that lies behind a 'veil of ignorance' (Rawls, 1971 [1999]: 19, 54) so thick that no one can estimate his own probable stake. Lost in unknowledge, Rawls predicts, anxious man will rationally gravitate to the 'difference principle'. It specifies that inequality can only be justified if the Gini coefficient works to the benefit of the bottom deciles who have the least: 'Social and economic inequalities are to be arranged so that they are . . . to the greatest benefit of the least advantaged' (Rawls, 1971 [1999]: 266).

Maximin makes sense. Frightened individualists situated behind a thick veil of unknowledge strive not to maximise their endowment but to minimise the disutility that would result from their worst-case scenario. No one situated behind the veil can afford to be an adventurous entrepreneur or a thrusting risk-lover. They do not know and they cannot guess. Unable to judge where their own greatest advantage lies, they take out Rawls-type insurance because a loser looks much like a winner in the dark.

Self-seeking man recognises that the Hobbesian *bellum* is inferior to accommodation and restraint. General rules are essential. These will typically reflect the plus-sum orientations of respect for persons, promise-keeping and the succour of those in need. Justice based on unanimity is reminiscent of Kant: 'The veil of ignorance is implicit, I think, in Kant's ethics' (Rawls, 1971 [1999]: 121). It is absolute consensus, invariant and stable. It is not social consensus, a function of time and space. There are no here-and-now conventions. There cannot be. The veil of ignorance precludes any access to the specific norms by which our tribesmen live.

Rawls treats society as a going concern: 'A society is a cooperative venture for mutual advantage' (Rawls, 1971 [1999]: 109). He is not a sentimental nationalist in the Hegelian mould but rather a hard-nosed investor shadowing the choice-calculus of 'free and rational persons concerned to further their own interests' (Rawls, 1971 [1999]: 10). In order to attain their utilitarian objectives, self-defined, they have a non-negotiable need for an endowment of 'primary goods' in the form of liberties, rights, opportunities, income and wealth (Rawls, 1971 [1999]: 54). All 'free and rational persons' have the same need. Equity is equality. Inequality is only tolerable where the difference in allocations is an across-the-board gain: 'Injustice, then, is simply inequalities that are not to the benefit of all' (Rawls, 1971 [1999]: 54).

Health does not figure explicitly in Rawls's list of 'primary goods'. Norman Daniels has suggested that it is implicit nonetheless. Daniels argues that basic health is the precondition if people are to be empowered to succeed. He believes that the economist's act-utilitarianism only trivialises the distinction between the foundation for choice and the in-period decision that is built upon it: 'Health is not happiness, and confusing the two over-medicalizes social philosophy' (Daniels, 1985: 29, 43).

Kaelin too sees health, like education, as the springboard to something more. He writes as follows about the healthcare minimum: 'Rawls is very clear about the importance of a minimum, needed for the active participation in the life of society. This minimum includes health care. Basic health care, thus, is non-negotiable and a government deliberately undermining it is violating the first principle of justice' (Kaelin, 2011: 38).

If it is, then there is a lot of violation about: 'While the language of human rights appears often in the global discourse, its inclusion in health systems efforts beyond rhetorical pronouncements is minimal' (Gruskin, Ahmed, Bogecho, Ferguson, Hanefeld, MacCarthy, Raad and Steiner, 2012: 337). Perhaps the reason is that ordinary people, neither philosophers nor politicians, do not really care whether healthcare is a right or a commodity. As far as Henry Dubb is concerned, his knee hurts and he wants to see a doctor. And that is all.

9.6.2 From Rawls to Medical Travel

The veil of ignorance is a whole-world veil. The richer countries are in clear violation of Rawls's justice to the extent that they starve the poorer countries of the 'primary goods' that the deprived most urgently require. Medical travel is no more than a new manifestation of an age-old imbalance. Walzer traces it back to the unequal distribution of economic power: 'What is at issue now is the dominance of money outside its sphere, the ability of wealthy men and women to trade in indulgences, purchase state offices, corrupt the courts, exercise political power' (Walzer, 1983: 120). Walzer believes that all morally minded persons will be opposed to 'political tyranny or the oppression of the poor' (Walzer, 1994: 5n). At home or abroad, absolutes are absolutes and injustice is wrong.

A state that is passive when its medical manpower goes abroad may think it is promoting individual freedom when the truth is that it is doing precisely the opposite: 'Along the lines of Rawls' theory, the migration of nurses makes an unfair world even less fair . . . The depletion of nurse stocks especially in sub-Saharan Africa and also in the Philippines leads to a break-down of even the basic health services' (Kaelin, 2011: 38). Sick people need attention. The attention is being depleted by the GATS. Mode 4 is not in keeping with the Rawlsian ethic.

The dereliction will be that much more serious if immigrant professionals end up servicing not the least but the most advantaged in destination countries that are themselves among the most privileged. In the private sector, in US Medicare, in the UK National Health Service, in

Third World cities at the cost of Third World farms, the pattern is the 'inverse care law': 'The availability of good medical care tends to vary inversely with the need of the population served' (Tudor Hart, 1971: 412). The upper income quintiles get the tests and the physiotherapy. The lowest income quintiles get a prescription for a generic if they get anything at all.

Poor countries belong to the Rawlsian least-advantaged. In India the infant mortality rate is 48 per 1000 live births. In the United States it is 7. In India there are 6.5 doctors per 10000 population and nine hospital beds. In the United States the figures are 24.2 and 30. Total per capita expenditure on health in India (purchasing power parity-adjusted) is US$124 per annum. In the United States it is US$7960 (World Health Organization, 2012: 54–55, 59–60, 104–105, 129–130, 137, 144). The Rawlsian theory is a universal theory. International as well as intranational, it suggests that the world's left-behind should enjoy an equitable share of the world's basic entitlements irrespective of the place where they happen to reside.

There is not enough to go around. In India 47 per cent of children under six are experiencing chronic malnutrition (Yamin, 2009: 2). A country like India may be making a mistake when it brings in health tourists who eat up the patrimony of the locals.

The developed countries buy. The less-developed countries sell. Some see it as bilateral gains from trade. Whittaker sees it as stratified exploitation 'across class, wealth, race and nation . . . Subaltern bodies across the globe service wealthy first world patients' (Whittaker, 2010: 404). Charity begins at home. Meghani says bluntly that the correct thing to do is to shut the door: 'American patients ought not to avail themselves of India's limited medical resources . . . It is a case of those who are significantly better off poaching the meagre resources of those who are substantially compromised' (Meghani, 2011: 25).

The Indians are severely deprived. The Americans have good doctors and hospitals at home. The practice of Americans crowding into India for care cannot in the circumstances 'be considered morally acceptable' (Meghani, 2011: 25). The World Bank neoliberals and the borderless medical tourists share 'moral culpability' (Meghani, 2011: 25) for the deficit in access that is costing poor Indians their lives.

To a Rawlsian it does not make sense. A needy American and a needy Indian are both needy. It cannot be justice to level-up the impoverished Indians by shutting the door to impoverished Americans who, like the impoverished Indians, are so impoverished that they cannot pay their countrymen's price. Americans are not in any case the only foreigners. Impoverished Yemenis sell their property in order to afford a last-ditch stand in Mumbai. It would be extremely ungenerous to treat an impoverished Yemeni as a bloated plutocrat.

If, moreover, bloated plutocrats are to be blamed, then they can be blamed much closer to home. The lowest wealth quintile in India has a child mortality rate three times that of the highest. The domestic elite can afford the best. The slums and the interior cannot. Redistribution of life-chances, if this is what the opponents of medical travel are suggesting, ought logically to extend beyond the foreign market to the dollar millionaires at home. They absorb an above-average share of their country's healthcare commons.

Luxury hotels on the beachfront were never intended for the poor sleeping rough. It is the same with caviar-class hospitals that cater principally to the elite. The deprived cannot be crowded out for the simple reason that the deprived had never been crowded in. Health tourism, as Cohen says, does 'not necessarily diminish access for *poor* Indian patients': that 'would remain steady at virtually none' (Cohen, 2011: 9). But that does not mean that the poor in India are condemned forever to sleeping rough.

9.6.3 The Economics of Levelling Up

It would be malicious and spiteful to deprive sick foreigners of the care they need. The politics of envy is never very attractive. Throwing money at the needy is more appealing. Government spending on health, in India only 30.3 per cent of the total, could rise towards the USA's 47.7 per cent or even the UK's 84.1 per cent (World Health Organization, 2012: 136, 140). The additional resources could be targeted on the Rawlsian less-advantaged. Poorer countries might wish to ensure that charity really does begin at home before they take steps to keep the rest of the world out.

If undersupply is the result of underfunding, then the money must be found. It will not be easy. It is simply not there: 'To illustrate, if Malaysia were to spend the same per-capita amount of money on healthcare as Switzerland, Malaysia's health expenditure would be roughly equal to its gross domestic product (GDP), leaving no money for food, housing, clothing, or transportation. For Thailand, Indonesia, and Cambodia, health expenditure would be, respectively, twice, five times, and thirteen times the value of national GDP' (Arunanondchai and Fink, 2007: 2). If health expenditure is to rise, then the GDP must also rise. Public finance depends on growth. The natural increase is the *sine qua non*.

It is not certain that taxable potential will be translated into taxes or that taxes will be channelled into pro-poor health. Resources might disappear into corruption, administration and superstar technology that are needed for the eradication of tuberculosis and polio, to fund national insurance for the desperate have-nots, to pay for a sanitary water supply, occupational health, comprehensive vaccination and birth control. Growth is not a universal panacea. It is, however, the necessary condition for healthcare levelling up.

Many things are possible where value is being added and budgets are secure. Since it is the public sector and not the private sector that takes action on free clinics and water-borne vectors, stagnation and austerity do little to enhance the safety net or to promote the Millennium Development Goals that were agreed upon by the United Nations in 2000. In the area of health, the United Nations proposed a reduction of three-quarters in the maternal mortality rate and of two-thirds in the mortality rate of the under-fives. It reached consensus on universal access to reproductive health. It agreed that the spread of killer viruses like AIDS had to be stopped and reversed within 15 years (Phillips, 2011: 442). Goals like these cannot be attained without funding. Growth and not just aid generates new money for the integration of the poor.

The World Health Organization acknowledges the concern, in both developed and developing countries, that 'trade objectives may override those of domestic health sectors and thus impede the realization of local goals' (World Health Organization, 2005: 7). Another perspective would be that trade objectives do not impede but rather facilitate the local purpose. Health tourism shows how it can be done. Outsourcing creates jobs through the electronic link. Foreign patients prime regional expansion. Local professionals are trained and retained. Labour-intensive jobs are created for the unskilled. Capital, scientific knowledge and practical expertise are attracted in to a local hub. Recreational tourism gets convalescents and relatives out into the countryside. Trickledown and the demonstration effect raise the standard of care for the locals. It need not be a zero-sum game.

Development in poor countries can be a moving staircase that frees the poor from malnutrition and damp. An initial inequity in the hospitals may in the long run buy considerably more fairness in medical care. Cosmetic surgery for the rich may be the way in which the poor pay for their appendectomies. The fiscal dividend may be the cost-effective route to inclusion. It may be the margin that makes more healthcare spending possible.

The wealth of nations may not, however, open all the doors: 'Changes in the share of income that accrues to the poorest fifth of society are not systematically associated with the overall growth rate of the economy' (Dollar and Kraay, 2004: F26). Globalisation fares no better: 'There is simply no association between changes in trade to GDP and changes in the Gini measure of inequality or between changes in trade to GDP and changes in the income share of the poorest quintile' (Dollar and Kraay, 2004: F27). Trade is positively correlated with growth. What is not clear is the way it is correlated with absolute and relative deprivation. Philosophers and politicians talk big. The fact, however, is that they do not know.

10. Conclusion: commodification

Some things are commodities. Some things are not. The social consensus generally accepts that pineapples, motorcars, English textiles and Portuguese wines are economic tradeables that may legitimately cross the frontiers of property and price. The social consensus generally denies that a vote, a verdict, an exemption from military service or a licence to practise polygamy may reasonably be rationed to the highest bidder at an auction sale. People can rent themselves out to a hectoring boss. People cannot sell themselves into slavery by consent. The distinction, as every working stiff will know, is not clear-cut. Borders are conventional ruts. They seem arbitrary at times but they are what they are.

On the one hand there is the marketable: 'Economics really does constitute the universal grammar of social science' (Hirshleifer, 1985: 53). On the other hand there is the super-marketable: 'Blocked exchanges set limits on the dominance of wealth' (Walzer, 1983: 100). 'Commodification' is the term that describes the new boundary-lines that are being marked out by encroaching capitalism.

Commodification is an evocation of what happens when uncompromising liberalism contests unaccustomed and unconventional areas of social space. Prisoners purchase upgrades to more luxurious cells. Foreigners buy a 'green card' or a passport. Speculators auction permits that license noxious pollutants. Universities merchant admissions and hawk honorary doctorates. Citing examples like these, Sandel reflects that imperial economics has gone on the rampage and that no domain is safe: 'There are some things money can't buy, but these days, not many. Today, almost everything is up for sale . . . Markets – and market values – have come to govern our lives' (Sandel, 2012: 3, 5).

Today, almost everything is up for sale. Healthcare and medical travel are no longer insulated from the ideological hegemony of a *Zeitgeist* that defines success by the strict market test. Kidneys are marketed. Blood is bought. Children are sold. Queues are jumped. Sperm is swapped. Soviet Communism having imploded, Wall Street's 'Greed is Good' is all the Writ that is Holy.

Some observers welcome the freedom to choose. They see no reason why the shopper should be imprisoned in the Royal Free Hospital when

Bumrungrad can take the pain out of the wait. Other observers are more cautious about the mixing of the opposites. Mammon dwells in one place. Caesar dwells in a different place. What is appropriate for pineapples need not be appropriate for health. Schwartz argues strongly that it is time to call a halt: 'The continued spread of economic objectives and tactics into domains of life that people have traditionally regarded as governed by other goals and rules are turning social life into a jungle. Economic imperialism must be stopped' (Schwartz, 1994: 366).

This chapter does not conclude that medical travel must be stopped. It does not say that medical travel is as degrading as a Christmas mass where the priests tout salvation for whatever the traffic will bear. All it says is that a social transformation is taking place and that it seems to have a lurch: 'Without ever deciding to do so, we drifted from *having* a market economy to *being* a market society' (Sandel, 2012: 10). The invisible hand has voted for a lurch. The rest of us would now like to have a vote as well.

The debate is about the synthesis of the opposites. Will the winning dog gobble up the weaker dog? Will, alternatively, the Good Dog and the Bad Dog find common ground where they can coexist and share? This chapter explores the pluses and the minuses of the dogs. Section 10.1, 'Unblocking exchange', describes the transformation of shared conventions into private utilities that can be bought and sold. Section 10.2, 'The paradigm shift', discusses the causes and spread of the new consensus. Section 10.3, 'The doctor knows best', says that the doctor does not know best. Section 10.4, 'The political lead', asks if parliaments have the will to mould medical travel in the social interest.

10.1 UNBLOCKING EXCHANGE

The borders are being redrawn. The change in the institutional structure is having a feedback effect on the ethical integument: 'Markets leave their mark on social norms. Often, market incentives erode or crowd out non-market incentives' (Sandel, 2012: 64, 89). Exchange is an active ingredient and not merely a passive response. Wolfenschiessen is the proof.

Wolfenschiessen, freely translated, means 'we look after our own'. The name says it all. Wolfenschiessen is a small Swiss village which the Swiss government had identified as a storage centre for its nuclear waste. The locals knew the risk of contamination. They also knew that someone would have to make the sacrifice. In a poll, 50.8 per cent of the residents in Wolfenschiessen said that they were prepared to do their civic duty.

What happened next could not have been predicted on the assumption of an upward-sloping curve. The government offered to pay compensation.

As soon as it did so, however, popular support for the dump dropped to 24.6 per cent (Frey and Oberholzer-Gee, 1997: 749). Concealed preference may have been a consideration. Calculative locals may have been reacting strategically in order to secure a higher bribe. Yet the evidence proves otherwise. Only 4.9 per cent of the sample said that the money offered was not enough.

The monetisation of the activity had altered its perceived meaning. The nature of the frame had been subject to a radical displacement. Initially the appeal was to the duty of each to all. Later it was to the shopping trolley. Radiation is a serious matter. Once money had attenuated their attachment, the citizens of Wolfenschiessen went over to a whole new world-view. They were prepared to commit prostitution, but they also wanted their moral degradation to command its proper rent. The duty of each to all is a better deal: 'Social norms such as civic virtue and public-spiritedness are great bargains. They motivate socially useful behavior that would otherwise cost a lot to buy' (Sandel, 2012: 119). Intrinsic motivation is cost-effective. It is also affectual and emotive. It made the citizens of Wolfenschiessen feel good about themselves.

The citizens of Wolfenschiessen were expressing a felt need for organic integration. The same is true of the British blood-donors who gifted their blood in order that an unknown stranger might live: 'They were thus denying the Hobbesian thesis that men are devoid of any distinctively moral sense' (Titmuss, 1970: 239). In Britain, Titmuss contended, the blood banks are full, the risk of infection is low and the cost of blood is minimal. The blood budget is being freed up for irreducibly economic tradeables that cannot be made into a *quid* without a *quo*.

In Britain blood is gifted. It is not sold. The reason is that the community donor is the median citizen. Donors know that the National Health Service will not be reselling their free gift at the market-clearing price. Donors know that transfusions in Britain are allocated on the basis of medical need alone and not the ability to pay. The suppression of the cash nexus was the institutional precondition for the stranger gift. It gave British donors the freedom to call themselves stakeholders. They were proud to be a part of their community and their nation.

America is different. In America the blood relationship is objectified into supply and demand. In America, Titmuss reported, it is a subclass of mercenary donors, disproportionately black, unskilled, unemployed, alcoholic or addicted, who are keeping the transfusions on stream. The inner city sells. The leafy dormitories pay. The system is inequitable and expensive. It is also a threat to health. Unpaid volunteers have no incentive to conceal a history of malaria, syphilis, AIDS or hepatitis. Not so the 'blood proletariat'. Skid Row would truly be on the skids if the down-and-out behaved morally and told the truth. The commercial donor is led by an invisible hand to purchase his own freedom at the cost of an unknown stranger's freedom. Socialised blood is good blood. Commodified blood can kill.

The freedom to sell is qualitatively different from the freedom to share. The British system is the cause and effect of 'creative altruism' – 'creative in the sense that the self is realized with the help of anonymous others' (Titmuss, 1970: 212). It builds up the muscles that come from and lead to other stranger gifts. Stakeholders do not drop litter. They do not give short measure. They do not perform unnecessary surgery. They volunteer to be guinea pigs in a medical experiment. They agree to be educational tools for a sunrise cohort of medical students. These muscles would atrophy if the freedom to share were to be outsourced to Skid Row or the Third World. The muscles would atrophy if Britain were to adopt the American system of bought blood and profit-based belonging.

The unblocking of exchange is a slippery slope. Historically as well as sociologically, 'if the bonds of community giving are broken the result is not a state of value neutralism. The vacuum is likely to be filled by hostility and social conflict' (Titmuss, 1970: 199). A decline in altruism in one sphere may be accompanied by an encroaching selfishness in others. Money crowds out the other-regarding norms: 'Putting a price on the good things in life can corrupt them. That's because markets don't only allocate goods; they also express and promote certain attitudes toward the goods being exchanged' (Sandel, 2012: 9).

Transplant tourism removes the organ from the organism. It also removes the lonely isolate from the embedding mass: 'Transplant tourism embodies all that we associate today with neoliberal globalization . . . There's no *here* here – when the world is all "there there"' (Scheper-Hughes, 2011: 63). An organ has no body, no nation and no culture. Europeans secure body-parts from Brazilians in South Africa. They never meet or discuss their personhood. Market values are all the values they need.

Paying mercenaries to fight our enemies alters the nature of our citizenship nexus. Putting friendship, education and the rainforest through the cost–benefit filter conveys the hidden message that sociability, erudition and ecology are means but not ends. Paying children to lose weight, to brush their teeth or to give up smoking trains them to regard money rather than health as their primary incentive. When the money is withdrawn, the old habits return.

The new way of looking at things spreads. If it is acceptable to commoditise one's blood, one's womb and one's kidneys, then it might appear reasonable to claim insider bonuses from a vulnerable bank or to lend on subprime assets. If it is acceptable to avoid a one-class ward by going to a five-star foreign hospital, then it might be permissible to withdraw from communal space into fenced-off space where all guests must be vetted and some bounced away: 'The privately owned car upsets the whole urban structure and communications to the point that it eventually hampers the rational exploitation of public transport and militates against a great many forms of group and community leisure activity (notably by destroying the neighborhood as a living environment)' (Gorz, 1967 [1973]: 195).

10.2 THE PARADIGM SHIFT

As public transport decays, those who can buy a car. As the NHS decays, those who can go private. Those who can, do. Those who cannot, do without. Commodification increases the perceived distance between the buses and the Jaguars, the Royal Free and treatment abroad: 'Not only has the gap between rich and poor widened, the commodification of everything has sharpened the sting of inequality by making money matter more' (Sandel, 2012: 8–9).

The commodification of everything makes the relatively deprived less tolerant towards the relatively privileged. The meritocratic society promises an equal start and an open road. The market economy sells education and health to privileged contestants who can pay for a more probable win. The haves buy superior services. The have-nots are left with the pooled and the shared. The left-behind will not feel that enabling institutions have made good on the Enlightenment's promise of a fair race for all.

Yachts are a luxury. Threshold health is life or death. It makes a difference: 'Even where we may tolerate many other inequalities, inequalities in healthcare are of especial concern because such care is not merely another commodity to be allocated by the market' (Yamin, 2009: 3). Basic health is both a human right and the precondition for other human rights. It is also a social fact. It is embedded in social attitudes to poverty, discrimination, employment and promotion. It is what we as a nation want our government and not our market to do. Commodification transforms the framework of discourse.

Markets are an embodiment of values even as they are a mode of allocation. Rationality, efficiency and self-interest take the place of older words like compassion, justice and levelling-up. It is a slippery slope that ends in a self-fulfilling prophecy. Medical tourism reflects and perpetuates the new economism. If selfness is freedom, then togetherness is unfreedom. Because Bumrungrad is, therefore the Royal is no longer Free.

Marketisation leaves non-commodified provision in an unintended niche. State care, once a social obligation, becomes a safety net for the absolutely deprived. The hard cases are already stigmatised because they are shut out from citizenship consumption. They will suffer from additional stigma because they have no choice but the residual provider. Unable to pay for an alternative, they will be the greatest losers from the contraction in the subsidised sector. Money counts in the new liberal order. It is not demand but effectual demand that gets things done.

International public opinion is increasingly in sympathy with the paradigm shift. The World Trade Organization and the 'Washington Consensus' suggest that deregulation, competition, internal markets within public health systems, performance bonuses for budget-trimming managements, the operational autonomy of public sector trusts, outsourced tendering for ancillary services are all economical ways of squeezing efficient doctoring from a constrained resource base. Whatever is not in the rules is not supplied. Many people perceive the recommendations as science rather than ideology. It is hard to take issue with productivity.

Globalisation itself is a cause of intellectual convergence. 'Abroad' is not one country, one nuclear affiliation. There is no common culture, solidarity or collective memory in a world of strangers. There are no historical traditions, folk heroes or moral affinities. There is no seamless web. There is less 'love thy neighbour' if 'thy neighbour' is a faceless cipher half a world away. The new ethos is the market as an end in itself. This is not to say that the rights-based solidarism of the European social democracies stands no chance against the possessive individualism of the American Dream. The point is simply that microeconomics is something on which the disparate cultures can agree. The widening reference groups of inexorable cosmopolitanism force them to select their rules in a non-national way.

A foreign university that teaches values incompatible with the domestic mainstream must in a liberal economy be allowed to compete against state-run institutions that disseminate the national ideology. The position is the same in the marketplace for care: 'By limiting the power of the nation-state to discriminate against foreign-service suppliers, the GATS restricts the scope for public and democratic choice in matters of basic services' (Scherrer, 2011: 490). The new entrants are not foreign governments but foreign businesses. Internationalisation in that sense privatises the stock by skewing the flow: 'GATS is about the rights of capital *vis-à-vis* government' (Scherrer, 2011: 490). The GATS is sectors and not just nations. It is also all but irreversible.

The mode of delivery affects the character of the product. There is a qualitative transformation from public service to corporate profit. The state sector lacks the resources to match the private hospitals. Fiscal stringency exacerbates its problems. It is a one-way ratchet. Assets privatised in bad times are unlikely to be nationalised again when the crisis ends. McGuire and Burke use the evocative phrase 'raiding the medical commons' (McGuire and Burke, 2008: 2669) to describe the institutional transition. They feel that the commons can deliver a product which the factored-down neglects. It is being pushed out by the MBAs. Medical travel is the proof that some patients at least are willing to pay money to decide for themselves.

10.3 THE DOCTOR KNOWS BEST

Pineapples are for sale. It is not from the civic duty of the pineapple seller that we expect our pineapples. The debate is whether the doctor too is becoming a street stall-holder who sells and should sell whatever the paying customer most wants to buy.

Traditionally it was the professional oath and the national consensus that served as the compass. In the commoditised market, it is informed consent and effective demand. A contract is negotiated and signed. Pregnancy or suicide, the principal demands and the agent supplies. That is how business is done. Anyone who has ever bought a pineapple knows that.

Where medicine is commodified, the locus of control shifts from supply toward demand. Consumers become active: 'If their needs were dismissed or demeaned or they felt patronized by a doctor, they just went elsewhere' (Voigt and Laing, 2010: 255). The customer is always right. Surgeons experiment with 'radically new and potentially dangerous therapeutic interventions' (Song, 2010: 385) where their patients are unwilling to wait for the animal trials and the clinical tests. The doctors are not to blame. Because Costa Rica is just down the road, the providers know that they have to please their clients. Excessive altruism could cost them their bonuses and even their job.

Supplier-induced demand magnifies the consumer-led waste. Underoccupied doctors push products that are expensive, unneeded and in the limit risky. As medicine becomes profit-orientated, the practitioners and the institutions are tempted to sell peripheral add-ons. Frills and luxuries, unwarranted space and redundant staff are all selling points which waste resources but attract customers. Glamorous surroundings do wonders for the image. Medical websites become an exercise in rampant materialism: 'Given that medical tourism is fueled by increased commercialisation in the health sector, it is unsurprising that a number of sites provide information on commerce allied to medical tourism including: overseas property site sales; money saver, cost comparison sites and financial advice sites and travel insurance products available for medical tourism trips' (Lunt and Carrera, 2011: 59).

Health travel is primarily situated in the private sector. The private sector has to satisfy its shareholders. Hospitals are quoted on the stock exchange. Some have financial relationships with hotels and banks. Some executives are incomers who have made their career in neighbouring industries such as cars, restaurants and resort hotels. They talk like businessmen and not like healers. They know how to penetrate the best-buy leagues. Some give discounts to shareholders and to regular customers. State support contributes to the commodification bias. The state sponsors marketing campaigns. It represents domestic sellers at international fairs. Its investment in quality control, accreditation and audit is *de facto* a marketing tool. It reassures the foreigners and pulls in the currency.

It is not just the clinicians and the clinics that landmark the new commercialism. Health tourism is a joint product. Many find the combination of 'tourism' with 'health' at once distasteful and inappropriate. A triple bypass is served up with Universal Studios, the casino and the beach. A facelift is packaged with elephants, apes and a cookery class. Commercial advertising magnifies the money-making stance. Publicity may be inevitable where there is competition among the few. It is, however, often perceived as undignified. Phrases like 'McDoctoring' and 'Kentucky Fried Medicine' pick up the reservations that many people have towards treatment centres that market new hips and enhanced fertility as if they were fun restaurants and trendy bars.

The commodification of the supply chain can mean that no single doctor treats the whole human being. The liver is inspected in Colombia. The heart is screened in Taiwan. Specialisation and multinationalism can downgrade the role of the family doctor as a non-judgmental counsellor, a provider of information and a listening ear. Often the patient going abroad will not have a general practitioner at home. The patient will be on his own when he makes his choice.

Choice itself is an affirmation of personhood. Choice is self-actualisation, self-determination and self-worth. The market is intensely moral. It allows individuals to make their own mistakes. They proportion risk to their own appetite. They form their own expectations based on will and skill: 'Choice is essential to autonomy, which is absolutely fundamental to well-being. Healthy people want and need to direct their own lives' (Schwartz, 2004: 2). Medical travel is only more of the same.

Choice is personhood. In the case of medical attention, however, personhood will often mean the abdication of choice. In the medical market there can be too much technical information. The overload leads to anxiety, confusion, regret, cost and fear. It is no surprise that the majority of leaders turn into followers as soon as they fall ill. Schwartz reports that '65 per cent of people who didn't have cancer said that if they got it, they would prefer to choose their treatment. Of those who actually had cancer, 88 per cent said they would prefer *not* to choose' (Schwartz, 2004: 116). A mistake can cost the patient more than money alone. The consequence is that shoppers find it rational to be irrational. They hand over their proxy to a paternalist who knows best: 'We want our doctors to be weighting trade-offs before making treatment recommendations . . . We don't want to do it because it is emotionally unpleasant' (Schwartz, 2004: 131).

Spoiled image too is emotionally unpleasant. Many people feel guilty when they choose a doctor or a treatment. Rightly or wrongly, they feel that the pineapples are compatible with market allocation but that the intensely personal should not be bought and sold. As they see it, 'commodification is inherently "bad", something which leads to a materialistic, egoistic, and self-obsessed society. An insurmountable conflict is perceived to exist between the market and those things that are integral to personhood or intimate social relations (e.g., love, sex, parenthood, body parts)' (Voigt and Laing, 2010: 263).

Subjectively, they are drawing a line between market and personhood. Even if it is lawful to sell a part of a body to which the body-holder has unencumbered title, still they feel that the integrity of the body is a part of what it means to be a person. Slavery is banned because it fails to value human beings in the appropriate way. Then there are kidneys, hearts and corneas: 'Such markets promote a degrading, objectifying view of the human person, as a collection of spare parts' (Sandel, 2012: 110). How many pieces can be detached before the condition of indivisibility is violated?

John's kidney is inseparable from John. So is his look. Bariatric surgery makes John a superior package. First impressions count. Fat people count less. Presentation is not always a good predictor of performance but appointments committees are only human. It cannot be very satisfying to John to know that it was his stomach that swayed the balance. A bought prize is not an earned prize; and John's stomach is not an article of commerce. John is fully John. John is a human being. A human being is deserving of unquestioning respect. The aesthetics crowd out the ethics. But John gets the job.

It is the triumph of alienated man over the three-dimensional species-being that Marx describes as 'self-stupefaction', 'illusory satisfaction': 'The less you *are* . . . the more you *have*' (Marx, 1973 [1844]): 150, 153). Erich Fromm puts it as follows: '*Things* have no self and men who have become things can have no self' (Fromm, 1956: 143). Moral judgments go by the board since they no longer have any interpersonal reinforcement: 'Conscience exists only when man experiences himself as a man, not as a thing, as a commodity' (Fromm, 1956: 173).

The mentality is privatised along with the institutions. Some observers will regret the incorporation of the 'sacred' into the 'profane'. Others will welcome the transition as the abandonment of a functionless crutch. People want pineapples but need health. That is a fact. What is not a fact is that healthcare must be treated as a sacred cow. Neoliberals, describing the medical mystique as the ultimate irrationality, say that medicine is a tradeable thing like any other. Like it or not, exchange and economics are what we have become.

Capitalism need not be more obscene than rights talk and merit goods. Medical pragmatists would say that relative performance and not inflexible *a prioris* must be the primary consideration. If a body-works financed by debentures sold to venture capitalists produces a better outcome, if it is both more cost-effective and more successful in healing the sick, the intuition might be that capitalism is good because even the profit motive can make the difference between life and death. Reproductive tourism allows a childless couple to have a family. It cannot be corrosive of the ethical binding to have a child. A family too is a part of personhood and a marker of identity.

10.4 THE POLITICAL LEAD

Going abroad is a citizen's right. Yet so is not going abroad. Not every patient is prepared to put up with the inconvenience and discomfort of foreign travel: 'The duty of the state is not only to enable people to have treatment but to enable people to have treatment reasonably close to their home . . . Cross-border health care should be exceptional and cannot be the solution for a structural deficiency of the health care system' (Pennings, 2007: 506). Even if insurance is portable, some patients prefer to be treated where their relatives can visit.

Pennings warns that medical travel can be a facile stop-gap that retards the correction of fundamental flaws. Rare diseases are an exception: then patients will have no option but to go to the centre of excellence. Long waits, escalating costs and inadequate insurance are less easy to excuse. Politicians find it all too convenient to make medical tourism the convenient non-solution for state inaction at home. Weiss and his colleagues are right to call it 'an epiphenomenon of domestic health care failure': 'If affordable care were available domestically, then many fewer patients would seek care in foreign countries' (Weiss, Spataro, Kodner and Keune, 2010: 600).

People are educated by what is seen and what is done. When the role models go out of network, the rank and file may conclude that the previously unacceptable has become the new normal. At the same time a cash-starved government may be taking advantage of middle-class flight to cut back on the services it provides. The buffer is there. Medical tourism is the answer.

The affluent, cream-skimmed by the private sector, drop out. International commodification continues the detribalisation of what previously had been a blocked exchange. A contraction of state services will not affect patients who are making little use of them. The safety-valve deprives the public system of the articulate and the vocal, of the intellectual vanguard that would have campaigned vociferously for improved state facilities. In Britain the desertion of the lawyers, the journalists, the business and financial elite would deprive the NHS of its most demanding critics. The same, of course, cannot be said of the United States. There, 'the access constraints that prompt people to leave the country for care have never had any significant political impact on the perceived flaws of the domestic health care system' (Laugesen and Vargas-Bustamante, 2010: 229). The middle classes have already gone private. Medical travel for them is only the tropicalisation of the commodity that they are already enjoying at home.

When the middle classes withdraw from the public system, they put less pressure on the state budget. The risk profile in the public sector swings towards the destitute, the deprived, the uninsurable, the unemployed, the elderly, the chronically ill. State resourcing might be better able to accommodate the residual. What is more likely is that the publicly funded sector will be scaled down. The uncompensated drip-drip of care-cost inflation gives the politicians the chance to hide behind money illusion without having to cut the nominal values.

The simplest way to preserve the common entitlement would be to increase public funding. It is no violation of the GATS for money at home to be made so generous that few patients will want to jump ship. Contraction is more probable. Premiums go up. Taxes go up. Waits become longer. Quantity is cut back. Opening the floodgates may be taken as an excuse for fiscal tightening at home. Medical travel may make austerity economics more acceptable. Debasement triggers still more medical travel. The process is privatisation by the back door. Medical travel is not just a solution but also a cause of the shortfall which medical travel itself is making worse.

The state does less for the poor. The private sector does more for the rich. Whittaker believes that the transition 'exemplifies the commodification of the body' in a stratified world that 'places social costs upon those least willing to bear them: the poor and the dispossessed' (Whittaker, 2010: 404). The lower deciles cannot pay for organs or hire a surrogate. There is a global market in cut-up human pieces. They have little access to it.

The transition to the market will pass largely unnoticed. In the commodified world, the focus shifts from ideology and vision to technocracy and technique. André Gorz sees the movement from 'who gets what' to 'how to' as a direct consequence of commoditisation: 'The depoliticization of politics is the ideological weapon of corporate capital' (Gorz, 1967 [1973]: 45). The new politics is not the naked repression of a tyrannical police state. Rather, and more insidiously, it is the repressive tolerance of a new consensus that likes its affluence and is prepared to leave its principles to its bishops.

Medicalisation itself narrows the focus. Health is holistic. It is a function of housing, nutrition, alcohol, cigarettes and education as well as care. Commodification is sector-specific. Monads compare doctors and shop around. Decomposition flattens the dimensions into single-valued space. It is not enough. Public policy should be made on the basis of the whole and the interdependent. It should be more than individuals and prices, self-perceived.

Medical travel is a good servant but a bad master. So long as the Categorical Imperative and the Collective Conscience are respected, medical travel can safely be enlisted to contain cost, protect quality and facilitate differentiation. It can create jobs, balance the payments and open new windows. Commoditisation and marketisation lurk, however, in the global economy where the most familiar face is cash. If darkness is darkness and light is light, then the easy option cannot go through on the nod: 'The organ seller cannot choose to violate rights. If organ sale is wrong, it is so whether or not it is chosen' (Widdows, 2011: 90). Medical travel should let its cat out of the bag. Its friends and its enemies would like to find out what kind of a cat it is.

References

Abu Sneineh, H. (2011), 'The impact of applying international standards to quality services', *Medical Tourism Magazine*, 22, 72–74.

Adams, R.H. (2009), 'The determinants of international remittances in developing countries', *World Development*, 37, 93–103.

Adams, R.H. and J. Page (2005), 'Do international migration and remittances reduce poverty in developing countries?', *World Development*, 33, 1645–1669.

Adlung, R. and A. Carzaniga (2006), 'Update on GATS commitments and negotiations', in C. Blouin, N. Drager and R. Smith, eds, *International Trade in Health Services and the GATS: Current Issues and Debates*, Washington, DC: World Bank, 83–99.

Alleman, B.W., T. Luger, H.S. Reisinger, R. Martin, M.D. Horowitz and P. Cram (2010), 'Medical tourism services available to residents of the United States', *Journal of General Internal Medicine*, 26, 492–497.

Alonso-Garbayo, A. and J. Maben (2009), 'Internationally recruited nurses from India and the Philippines in the United Kingdom: the decision to emigrate', *Human Resources for Health*, 3, http://www.human-resources-health.com.content/7/1/37, accessed on 26 September 2012.

Alsharif, M.J., R. Labonté and Zuxun Lu (2010), 'Patients beyond borders: a study of medical tourists in four countries', *Global Social Policy*, 10, 315–335.

Amirthalingam, K. (2003), 'Judging doctors and diagnosing the law: *Bolam* rules in Singapore and Malaysia', *Singapore Journal of Legal Studies*, 22, 125–146.

Amiti, M. and S.-J. Wei (2004), *Fear of Service Outsourcing: Is It Justified?*, IMF Working Paper WP/04/186, Washington, DC: International Monetary Fund.

Aniza, I.M., R. Aidalina, M.C. Nirmalini, H. Inggit and T.E. Ajeng (2009), 'Health tourism in Malaysia: the strength and weaknesses', *Journal of Community Health*, 15, 7–15.

Apton, J. and R. Apton (2010), 'The role of the facilitator – dental tourism', *Medical Tourism Magazine*, 14, 40–42.

Arangkada Philippines (2009), *Tourism, Medical Travel and Retirement*,

http://www.investphilippines.ionfo/arangkada/tourism-medical-travel-retirement, accessed on 6 September 2012.
Arunanondchai, J. and C. Fink (2007), *Trade in Health Services in the ASEAN Region*, World Bank Policy Research Working Paper No. 4147, Washington, DC: World Bank.
Australian Society of Plastic Surgeons (2007), 'Holidays from hell – when bargain surgery goes wrong', Media Release, 1 May, http://plasticsurgery.org.au, accessed on 17 January 2012.
Bach, S. (2003), *International Migration of Health Workers: Labour and Social Issues*, Working Paper No. 209, Geneva: International Labour Organization.
Beecham, L. (2002), 'British patients willing to travel abroad for treatment', *British Medical Journal*, 325, 10.
Behrman, J. and E. Smith (2010), 'Top 7 issues in medical tourism: challenges, knowledge gaps, and future directions for research and policy development', *Global Journal of Health Science*, 2, 80–90.
Bergmark, R., D. Barr and R. Garcia (2008), 'Mexican immigrants in the USA living far from the border may return to Mexico for health services', *Journal of Immigrant and Minority Health*, 12, 610–614.
Berliner, H.S. and C. Regan (1987), 'Multinational operations of US for-profit hospital chains: trends and implications', *American Journal of Public Health*, 77, 1280–1284.
Bevan, A. (1958), Speech in the House of Commons, 30 July, in *Parliamentary Debates (Hansard)*, London: HMSO, Cols 1382–1398.
Bhagwati, J.N. (1979), 'International migration of the highly skilled: economics, ethics and taxes', *Third World Quarterly*, 1, 17–30.
Bhagwati, J.N., A. Panagariya and T.N. Srinivasan (2004), 'The muddles over outsourcing', *Journal of Economic Perspectives*, 18, 93–114.
Biggins, S.W., K. Bambha, N. Terrault, J. Inadomi, J.P. Roberts and N. Bass (2009), 'Transplant tourism to China: the impact on domestic patient-care decisions', *Critical Transplantation*, 23, 831–838.
Birch, J., R. Caulfield and V. Ramakrishnan (2007), 'The complications of "cosmetic tourism" – an avoidable burden on the NHS', *Journal of Plastic, Reconstructive and Aesthetic Surgery*, 60, 1075–1077.
Blinder, A.S. (2006), 'Offshoring: the next industrial revolution?', *Foreign Affairs*, 85, 113–128, reprinted at http://proquest.umi.com.ezlibproxy1, accessed on 15 January 2009.
Blyth, E. and A. Farrand (2008), 'Reproductive tourism – a price worth paying for reproductive autonomy?', *Critical Social Policy*, 25, 91–114.
Bollard, A., D. McKenzie, M. Morten and H. Rapoport (2011), 'Remittances and the brain drain revisited: the microdata show that the

more educated migrants remit more', *World Bank Economic Review*, 25, 132–156.

Bookman, M.Z. and K.R. Bookman (2007), *Medical Tourism in Developing Countries*, London: Palgrave Macmillan.

Boscher, L. (2009), 'A long trip', *Medical Tourism Magazine*, 12, 87–89.

Breinlich, H. and C. Criscuolo (2011), 'International trade in services: a portrait of importers and exporters', *Journal of International Economics*, 84, 188–206.

Brown, H.S., J.A. Pagan and E. Bastida (2009), 'International competition and the demand for health insurance in the US: evidence from the Texas–Mexico border region', *International Journal of Health Care Finance and Economics*, 9, 25–38.

Brush, B. and R. Vasupuram (2006), 'Nurses, nannies and caring work: importation, visibility and marketability', *Nursing Inquiry*, 13, 181–185.

Burkett, L. (2007), 'Medical tourism: concerns, benefits, and the American legal perspective', *Journal of Legal Medicine*, 28, 223–245.

Butler, S. (2009), 'Holidays for health', *Newsweek*, 11 May, 51.

Carrera, P.M. and J.F.P. Bridges (2006), 'Globalization and healthcare: understanding health and medical tourism', *Expert Review of Pharmacoeconomics Outcomes Research*, 6, 447–454.

Cattaneo, O. (2009), *Trade in Health Services: What's in it for Developing Countries?*, Policy Research Working Paper No. 5115, Washington, DC: World Bank.

Caves, R.E. (2007), *Multinational Enterprise and Economic Analysis*, 3rd edn, Cambridge: Cambridge University Press.

Chanda, R. (2002), 'Trade in health services', *Bulletin of the World Health Organization*, 80, 158–163.

Chanda, R. (2010), 'Constraints to foreign direct investment in Indian hospitals', *Journal of International Commerce, Economics and Policy*, 1, 121–143.

Chanda, R. (2011), 'India–EU relations in health services: prospects and challenges', *Globalization and Health*, 7, 1–13.

Chee, H.L. (2010), 'Medical tourism and the state in Malaysia and Singapore', *Critical Social Policy*, 10, 336–357.

Chioy, H.M., J.Y. Lee and L.W. Teo (2013), *National Income and Health Status: Health Tourism with a New Health Index*, Final Year Project HE_2AY1213_10, Singapore: Nanyang Technological University.

Coase, R.H. (1937), 'The nature of the firm', *Economica*, n.s., 4, 386–405.

Cohen, I.G. (2011), 'Medical tourism, access to health care, and global justice', *Virginia Journal of International Law*, 52, 1–56.

Cohen, I.G. (2012), 'How to regulate medical tourism (and why it matters for bioethics)', *Developing World Bioethics*, 12, 9–20.

Confucius (n.d. [1979]), *The Analects*, transl. by D.C. Lau, Harmondsworth: Penguin Books.
Connell, J. (2009), *The Global Health Care Chain: From the Pacific to the World*, London: Routledge.
Connell, J. (2010), *Migration and the Globalisation of Health Care: The Health Worker Exodus?*, Cheltenham, UK and Northampton, MA, USA: Edward Elgar.
Connell, J. (2011), *Medical Tourism*, Oxford: CABI.
Cortez, N. (2008), 'Patients without borders: the emerging global market for patients and the evolution of modern health care', *Indiana Law Journal*, 83, 71–132.
Cortez, N. (2012), 'Into the void: the legal ambiguities of an unregulated medical tourism market', in J.R. Hodges, L. Turner and A.M. Kimball, eds, *Risks and Challenges in Medical Tourism: Understanding the Global Market for Health Services*, Santa Barbara, CA: Praeger, 188–206.
Crooks, V.A. and J. Snyder (2010), 'Regulating medical tourism', *The Lancet*, 376, 1465–1466.
Crush, J., A. Chikanda and B. Maswikwa (forthcoming), 'South–South and North–South medical tourism: the case of South Africa', in R. Labonté, R. Deonandan, C. Packer and V. Runnels, eds, *Travelling Well: Essays in Medical Tourism*, Toronto: University of Toronto Press.
Daniels, N. (1985), *Just Health Care*, Cambridge: Cambridge University Press.
Declaration of Independence (US) (1776), http://www.ushistory.org/declaration/document, accessed on 6 November 2012.
de Haas, H. (2007), *Remittances, Migration and Social Development: A Conceptual Review of the Literature*, Social Policy and Development Programme Paper No. 34, Geneva: United Nations Research Institute for Social Development.
Deloitte (2008), *Medical Tourism: Consumers in Search of Value*, Washington, DC: Deloitte Center for Health Solutions.
Deloitte (2009), *Medical Tourism: Update and Implications*, Washington, DC: Deloitte Center for Health Solutions.
Deloitte (2010), *Evolving Medical Tourism in Canada: Exploring a New Frontier*, Washington, DC: Deloitte Center for Health Solutions.
Deloitte (2011), 2011 *Survey of the UAE Healthcare Sector: Opportunities and Challenges for Private Providers*, Washington, DC: Deloitte Center for Health Solutions.
Dollar, D. and A. Kraay (2004), 'Trade, growth, and poverty', *Economic Journal*, 114, F22–F49.
Dovlo, D. (2005), 'Wastage in the health workforce: some perspectives

from African countries', *Human Resources for Health*, 3, http://www.human-resources-health.com, accessed on 17 September 2012.

Doyle, M. (2013), 'Africans' remittances outweigh Western aid', *BBC News Africa*, http://www.bbc.co.uk/news/world-africa-22169474, accessed on 23 April 2013.

Durkheim, E. (1893 [1964]), *The Division of Labor in Society*, transl. by G. Simpson, London: Collier-Macmillan.

Durkheim, E. (1895 [1964]), *The Rules of Sociological Method*, transl. by S.A. Solvay and J.H. Muller, London: Collier-Macmillan.

Dussault, G. and M.C. Franceschini (2006), 'Not enough there, too many here: understanding geographical imbalances in the distribution of the health workforce', *Human Resources for Health*, 4:12, http://www.human-resources-health.com/content/4/1/12, accessed on 31 July 2012.

Eastwood, J.B., R.E. Conroy, S. Naicker, P.A. West, R.C. Tutt and J. Plange-Rhule (2005), 'Loss of health professionals from sub-Saharan Africa: the pivotal role of the UK', *The Lancet*, 365, 1893–2005.

The Economist (2008), 'Operating profit', 388, 16 August, http://web.ebscohost.com.ezlibproxy 1, accessed on 24 January 2012.

Eden, C. (2012), 'The rise of medical tourism in Bangkok', *BBC Travel*, 4 September, http://www.bbc.com/feature/20120828-the-rise-of-medical-tourism-in-bangkok, accessed on 21 January 2013.

Ehrbeck, T., C. Guevara and P.D. Mango (2008), 'Mapping the market for medical travel', *McKinsey Quarterly*, May, 1–11.

Einhorn, B. (2008), 'Hannaford's medical-tourism experiment', *Business Week*, 9 November, http://www.businessweek.com/globalbiz/content/nov.2008, accessed on 20 April 2012.

European Union (2011), *Directive of the European Parliament and of the Council on the Application of Patients' Rights in Cross-Border Healthcare*, Brussels: European Union.

Firhat, E. and D. Abratt (2011), 'Exceeding expectations: domestic and inbound medical tourism', *Medical TourismMagazine*, 22, 9–11.

Forgione, D. and P.C. Smith (2006), 'Medical tourism and its impact on the US health care system', *Journal of Health Care Finance*, 34, 27–35.

Frey, B.S. and F. Oberholzer-Gee (1997), 'The cost of price incentives: an empirical analysis of motivation crowding-out', *American Economic Review*, 87, 746–755.

Friedman, M. (1962), *Capitalism and Freedom*, Chicago, IL: University of Chicago Press.

Fromm, E. (1956), *The Sane Society*, London: Routledge & Kegan Paul.

Frost & Sullivan (2012), *Independent Market Research on the Global Healthcare Services (HCS) Industry: Final Report*, Singapore: Frost & Sullivan.

Galbraith, J.K. (1975), *Economics and the Public Purpose*, Harmondsworth: Penguin Books.
Gallup Organization (2007), *Cross-Border Health Services in the EU: Analytical Report*, Budapest: Gallup.
Gensler, H.J. (2011), *Ethics: A Contemporary Introduction*, 2nd edn, London: Routledge.
George, J.T., K.S. Rozario, J. Anthony, E.B. Jude and G.A. McKay (2007), 'Non-European Union doctors in the National Health Service: why, when and how do they come to the United Kingdom of Great Britain and Northern Ireland?', *Human Resources for Health*, 5:6, http://www.human-resources-health.com/content/2/1/17, accessed on 31 July 2012.
Gerein, N., A. Green and S. Pearson (2006), 'The implications of shortages of health professionals for maternal health in Sub-Saharan Africa', *Reproductive Health Matters*, 14, 40–50.
Gerl, R., L. Boscher, T. Mainil and H. Kunhardt (2009), 'European competence centers for health and medical tourism', *Medical Tourism Magazine*, 12, 66–69.
Glinos, I.A., R. Baeten and H. Maarse (2010), 'Purchasing health services abroad: practices of cross-border contracting and patient mobility in six European countries', *Health Policy*, 95, 103–112.
Goodrich, J.N. (1993), 'Socialist Cuba: a study of health tourism', *Journal of Travel Research*, 32, 36–41.
Gorz, A. (1967 [1973]), *Socialism and Revolution*, transl. by N. Denny, Garden City, NY: Anchor Books.
Gruskin, S., S. Ahmed, D. Bogecho, L. Ferguson, J. Hanefeld, S. MacCarthy, Z. Raad and R. Steiner (2012), 'Human rights in health systems frameworks: what is there, what is missing and why does it matter?', *Global Public Health*, 7, 337–351.
Gupta, I., B. Goldar and A. Mitra (1998), 'The case of India', in S. Zarrilli and C. Kinnon, eds, *International Trade in Health Services: A Development Perspective*, Geneva: United Nations Conference on Trade and Development / World Health Organization, 213–236.
Hagopian, A., M.J. Thompson, M. Fordyce, K.E. Johnson and L.G. Hart (2004), 'The migration of physicians from sub-Saharan Africa to the United States of America: measures of the African brain drain', *Human Resources for Health*, 2:17, http://www.human-resources-health.com/content/2/1/17, accessed on 30 July 2012.
Hamid, Z. (2010), 'Redefining the globalisation of healthcare', *International Medical Tourism Journal*, http://www.itmj.com/articles/2010, accessed on 6 December 2012.
Hanefeld, J., N. Lunt, D. Horsfall and R.D. Smith (2012), 'Discussion on

banning advertising of cosmetic surgery needs to consider medical tourists', *British Medical Journal*, 345, e7997.

Harling, R., D. Turbitt, M. Millar, I. Ushiro-Lumb, S. Lacey, G. Xavier, J. Pope, S. Ijaz and C.G. Teo (2007), 'Passage from India: an outbreak of hepatitis B linked to a patient who acquired infection from health care overseas', *Public Health*, 121, 734–741.

Haslam, C. (2007), 'Incisor trading', *Sunday Times*, 27 May, 4.

Hawkes, M., M. Kolenko, M. Shockness and K. Diwaker (2009), 'Nursing brain drain from India', *Human Resources for Health*, 7:5, http://www.human-resources-health.com/content/7/1/5, accessed on 24 September 2012.

Hay, C. (2011), 'Globalization's impact on states', in J. Ravenhill, ed., *Global Political Economy*, 3rd edn, Oxford: Oxford University Press, 312–343.

Hazarika, I. (2010), 'Medical tourism: its potential impact on the health workforce and health systems in India', *Health Policy and Planning*, 25, 248–251.

Herman, L. (2009), *Assessing International Trade in Healthcare Services*, ECIPE Working Paper No. 03/2009, Brussels: European Centre for International Political Economy.

Herrick, D. (2007), *Medical Tourism: Global Competition in Health Care*, Dallas: National Center for Policy Analysis, NCPA Policy Report No. 304.

Himmelstein, D.U., D. Thorne, E. Warren and S. Woolhandler (2007), 'Medical bankruptcy in the United States: results of a national study', *American Journal of Medicine*, 122, 741–746.

Hirshleifer, J. (1985), 'The expanding domain of economics', *American Economic Review*, 75, Supplement, 53–68.

Ho, D. (2008), 'When good organs go to bad people', *Bioethics*, 22, 77–83.

Ho, V. (2009), 'Korean healthcare at its finest', *Medical Tourism Magazine*, 13, 34–35.

Hodges, J.R. and A.M. Kimball (2012), 'Unseen travellers: medical tourism and the spread of infectious disease', in J.R. Hodges, L. Turner and A.M. Kimball, eds, *Risks and Challenges in Medical Tourism: Understanding the Global Market for Health Services*, Santa Barbara, CA: Praeger, 111–137.

Holy Bible (2001), English Standard Version (ESV), London: HarperCollins Religious.

Hopkins, L., R. Labonté, V. Runnels and C. Packer (2010), 'Medical tourism today: what is the state of existing knowledge?', *Journal of Public Health Policy*, 31, 185–198.

Howze, K.S. (2007), 'Medical tourism: symptom or cure?', *Georgia Law Review*, 41, 1013–1051.

Hudson, S. (2011), 'Domestic medical tourism: a neglected dimension of medical tourism research', *Medical Tourism Magazine*, 22, 43–45.

Humbyrd, C. (2009), 'Fair trade international surrogacy', *Developing World Bioethics*, 9, 111–118.

Hyo-Mi, P. Leong, E. Heob, C. Gaitz and B. Anderson (2009), 'Medical tourism from US to border region of Mexico', *Medical Tourism Magazine*, 12, 70–75.

IHH Healthcare Berhad (2012), *Prospectus* for an Initial Public Offering, Singapore, http://masnet.mas.gov.sg/opera/sdrprosp.nsf/936bad13609791c948256b3e001ed49f/7D25B8CD5027A75148257A2F00356284/$File/2.2.01%20Prospectus%20dated%202%20July%202012%20-%20Part%201.pdf, accessed on 10 October 2012.

International Medical Travel Journal (2013a), 'Thailand: New realistic medical tourism figures from Thailand', http://www.imtj.com/news/?entryid82=381992, accessed on 29 April 2013.

International Medical Travel Journal (2013b), 'Singapore: Singapore medical tourism is recovering', http://www.imtj.com/news/?entryid82=413890, accessed on 26 May 2013.

International Medical Travel Journal (2013c), 'Medical tourism destinations: Today Nigeria . . ., next stop . . . Mars?', http://www.imtj.com/blog/2013/nigeria-medical-tourism-destination-40182, accessed on 3 July 2013.

Jesse, M. and R. Kruuda (2006), 'Cross-border care in the north: Estonia, Finland and Latvia', in M. Rosenmöller, M. McKee and R. Baeten, eds, *Patient Mobility in the European Union: Learning from Experience*, Copenhagen: World Health Organization, 23–37.

Johnson, T.J. and A. Garman (2010), 'Impact of medical travel on imports and exports of medical services', *Health Policy*, 98, 171–177.

Johnston, R., V.A. Crooks, J. Snyder and P. Kingsbury (2010), 'What is known about the effects of medical tourism in destination and departure countries? A scoping review', *International Journal for Equity in Health*, 9, www.equityhealth.com/content/9/1/24, accessed on 31 January 2012.

Jose, R. and S. Sachdeva (2010), 'Keeping an eye on future: medical tourism', *Indian Journal of Community Medicine*, 35, 376–378.

Kaelin, L. (2011), 'A question of justice: assessing nurse migration from a philosophical perspective', *Developing World Bioethics*, 11, 30–39.

Kanchanachitra, C., C.-A. Pachanee, M.M. Dayrit and V. Tangcharoensathien (2012), 'Medical tourism in Southeast Asia: opportunities and challenges', in J.R. Hodges, L. Turner and A.M. Kimball, eds, *Risks and Challenges in Medical Tourism: Understanding the Global Market for Health Services*, Santa Barbara, CA: Praeger, 56–86.

Kangas, B. (2007), 'Hope from abroad in the international medical travel of Yemeni patients', *Anthropology and Medicine*, 14, 393–305.

Kangas, B. (2010), 'Travelling for medical care in a global world', *Medical Anthropology*, 29, 344–362.

Kant, I. (1785 [1961]), *Groundwork of the Metaphysic of Morals*, transl. by H.J. Paton, reprinted in H.J. Paton, ed., *The Moral Law*, London: Hutchinson, 53–148.

Kaushik, M., A. Jaiswal, N. Shah and A. Mahal (2008), 'High-end physician migration from India', *Bulletin of the World Health Organization*, 86, 40–45.

Kharas, H. (2010), *The Emerging Middle Class in Developing Countries*, OECD Development Centre, Working Paper No. 285, Paris: Organisation for Economic Co-operation and Development.

Kher, U. (2006), 'Outsourcing your heart', *Time Magazine*, 21 May, http://www.time.com/time/magazine/article/0,9171,1196429,00.html, accessed on 13 December 2011.

Khoury, C. (2009), 'Americans consider crossing borders for medical care', www.gallup.com/poll/118423/americans-consider-crossing-borders-medical-care.aspx, accessed on 23 January 2012.

Krugman, P., M. Obstfeld and M.J. Melitz (2012), *International Economics: Theory and Policy*, 9th edn, Boston, MA: Pearson.

Labonté, R. (2003), *Dying for Trade: Why Globalization Can Be Bad for Our Health*, Toronto: CSJ Foundation for Research and Education.

Laugesen, M.J. and A. Vargas-Bustamante (2010), 'A patient mobility framework that travels: European and United States–Mexican comparisons', *Health Policy*, 97, 225–231.

Lautier, M. (2008), 'Export of health services from developing countries: the case of Tunisia', *Social Science and Medicine*, 67, 101–110.

Lautier, M. (2013), *The Growth of International Trade in Health Services: Export Prospects in North Africa*, AfDB Economic Brief, Abidjan: African Development Bank.

Leach, B. and L. Donnelly (2013), 'Most "danger doctors" come from abroad', *Weekly Telegraph*, 219, 2–8 January, 1–2.

Lee, C. (2012), 'Socialized medicine meets private industry: medical tourism in Costa Rica', in J.R. Hodges, L. Turner and A.M. Kimball, eds, *Risks and Challenges in Medical Tourism: Understanding the Global Market for Health Services*, Santa Barbara, CA: Praeger, 87–108.

Lee, O.F. and T.R.V. Davis (2004), 'International patients: a lucrative market for US hospitals', *Health Marketing Quarterly*, 22, 41–56.

Lee, Tae-hoon (2010), 'Korea overlooks soaring medical fees on foreign-

ers', *Korea Times*, 22 February, http://www.koreatimes.co.kr/www/news/include/print.asp?newsIdx=61214, accessed on 18 October 2010.
Lee, W.L. (2008), 'Medical care is not a commodity', *Straits Times*, 15 October, A23.
Lee, Y., R.A. Kearns and W. Friesen (2010), 'Seeking affective health care: Korean immigrants' use of homeland medical services', *Health and Place*, 16, 108–115.
Leenhouts, P. (2009), 'Thank goodness for ladyboys. My (brief) experience with medical tourism', *Medical Tourism*, 1, 23–24.
Lennon, C. (2009), *Trade in Services and Trade in Goods: Differences and Complementarities*, Working Paper No. 53, Vienna: Vienna Institute for International Economic Studies.
Lori, J.R., S.D. Rominski, M. Gyakobo, E.W. Muriu, N.E. Kweku and P. Agyei-Baffour (2012), 'Perceived barriers and motivating factors influencing student midwives' acceptance of rural postings in Ghana', *Human Resources for Health*, 10:17, http://www.human-resources-health.com/content/4/1/24, accessed on 20 March 2013.
Lunt, N. and P. Carrera (2010), 'Medical tourism: assessing the evidence on treatment abroad', *Maturitas*, 66, 27–32.
Lunt, N. and P. Carrera (2011), 'Systematic review of web sites for prospective medical tourists', *Tourism Review*, 66, 57–67.
Lunt, N.T., R. Mannion and M. Exworthy (2013), 'A framework for exploring the policy implications of UK medical tourism and international patient flows', *Social Policy and Administration*, 47, 1–25.
Lunt, N.T., R.D. Smith, M. Exworthy, S.T. Green, D. Horsfall and R. Mannion (2011), *Medical Tourism: Treatments, Markets and Health System Implications*, Paris: Organisation for Economic Co-operation and Development.
MacIntyre, A. (1998), *A Short History of Ethics: A History of Moral Philosophy from the Homeric Age to the Twentieth Century*, 2nd edn, London: Routledge.
MacReady, N. (2007), 'Developing countries court medical tourists', *The Lancet*, 369, 1849–1850.
MacReady, N. (2009), 'The murky ethics of stem-cell tourism', *The Lancet Oncology*, 10, 317–318.
Mareckova, M. (2004), 'Exodus of Czech doctors leaves gaps in health care', *The Lancet*, 363, 1443–1446.
Marshall, A. (1890 [1949]), *Principles of Economics*, 8th edn, London: Macmillan.
Marshall, T.H. (1981 [1965]), 'The right to welfare', *Sociological Review*, 13, in *The Right to Welfare and Other Essays*, London: Heinemann Educational Books, 83–94.

Martinez Alvarez, M., R. Chanda and R.D. Smith (2011), 'How is telemedicine perceived? A qualitative study of perspectives from the UK and India', *Globalization and Health*, 6, http://www.globalizationandhealth.com/content/7/1/17, accessed on 16 April 2012.

Marx, K. (1973 [1844]), *Economic and Sociological Manuscripts of 1844*, transl. by M. Milligan, London: Lawrence and Wishart.

Maslow, A. (1970 [1954]), *Motivation and Personality*, 2nd edn, New York: Harper & Row.

Mathauer, I. and I. Imhoff (2006), 'Health worker motivation in Africa: the role of non-financial incentives and human resource management tools', *Human Resources for Health*, 4:24, http://www.human-resources-health.com/content/4/1/24, accessed on 31 July 2012.

Mattoo, A. and R. Rathindran (2005), *Does Health Insurance Impede Trade in Health Care Services?*, World Bank Policy Research Working Paper WPS3667, Washington, DC: World Bank.

Mattoo, A. and R. Rathindran (2006), 'How health insurance inhibits trade in health care', *Health Affairs*, 25, 358–368.

McGuire, A.L. and W. Burke (2008), 'Raiding the medical commons: an unwelcome side-effect of direct-to-consumer personal genome testing', *Journal of the American Medical Association*, 300, 10 December, 2669–2671.

McPake, B. (2012), 'Human resources and the health sector', in R.D. Smith and K. Hanson, eds, *Health Systems in Low- and Middle-Income Countries: An Economic and Policy Perspective*, Oxford: Oxford University Press, 124–145.

Medical Tourism Association (2009), 'MTA releases first patient surveys on medical tourism', *Medical Tourism Magazine*, 10, 34–36.

Medical Tourism Association (2011), *Medical Tourism Updates May 2011*, http://www. slideshow.net/reneemariestephano/mta-webinar-travel-update-may-2011, accessed on 11 June 2012.

Medical Tourism Association/Bumrungrad International (2010), 'Patient survey – Bumrungrad International', *Medical Tourism Magazine*, 14, 22–25.

Meghani, Z. (2011), 'A robust, particularist ethical assessment of medical tourism', *Developing World Bioethics*, 11, 16–29.

Mendoza, R.L. (2010), 'Kidney black markets and legal transplants: are they opposite sides of the same coin?', *Health Policy*, 94, 255–265.

Mendoza, R.U. (2013), 'Examining the risk of brain drain and lower remittances', *Singapore Economic Review*, 68, 1350006-1-13.

Mill, J.S. (1974 [1859]), *On Liberty*, ed. by G. Himmelfarb, Harmondsworth: Penguin Books.

Milstein, A. and M. Smith (2007), 'Will the surgical world become flat?', *Health Affairs*, 26, 137–141.

Miyagi, K., D. Auberson, A.J. Patel and C.M. Malata (2012), 'The unwritten price of cosmetic tourism: an observational study and cost analysis', *Journal of Plastic, Reconstructive and Aesthetic Surgery*, 65, 22–28.

Mortensen, J. (2008), *Emerging Multinationalists: The South African Hospital Industry Overseas*, DIIS Working Paper No. 2008/12, Copenhagen: Danish Institute for International Studies.

Murdoch, C.E. and C.T. Scott (2010), 'Stem cell tourism and the power of hope', *American Journal of Bioethics*, 10, 16–23.

NaRanong, A. and V. NaRanong (2011), 'The effects of medical tourism: Thailand's experience', *Bulletin of the World Health Organization*, 89, 336–344.

Nguyen, L., S. Ropers, E. Nderitu, A. Zuyderduin, S. Luboga and A. Hagopian (2008), 'Intent to migrate among nursing students in Uganda: measures of the brain drain in the next generation of health professionals', *Human Resources for Health*, 6:5, http://www.human-resources-health.com/content/6/1/5, accessed on 1 August 2012.

Nielsen, S.S., S. Yazici, S.G. Petersen, A.L. Blaakilde and A. Krasnik (2012), 'Use of cross-border healthcare services among ethnic Danes, Turkish immigrants and Turkish descendants in Denmark: a combined survey and registry study', *BMC Health Services Research*, 12, http://www.biomedcentral.com/1472-6963/12/390, accessed on 21 February 2013.

Oatley, T. (2012), *International Political Economy*, 5th edn, Boston, MA: Longman.

Oberholzer-Gee, F., T. Khanna and C-I. Knoop (2005), *Apollo Hospitals – First-World Health Care at Emerging-Market Prices*, Harvard Business School Case N9-705-442, Cambridge, MA: Harvard University.

O'Brien, P. and L.O. Gostin (2011), *Health Worker Shortages and Global Justice*, New York: Milbank Memorial Fund.

Office for National Statistics (UK) (2010), *International Passenger Survey*, http://www.ons.gov.uk/ons/datasets-and-tables/index.html?pageSize=50&sortBy=none&sortDirection=none&newquery=international+passenger+survey&content-type=Reference+table&content-type=Dataset, accessed on 24 May 2013.

Organisation for Economic Co-operation and Development (2011), *Health at a Glance 2011: OECD Indicators*, Paris: OECD.

Österle, A., P. Balázs and J. Delgado (2009), 'Travelling for teeth: characteristics and perspectives of dental care tourism in Hungary', *British Dental Journal*, 206, 425–428.

Outreville, J.F. (2007), 'Foreign direct investment in the health care sector

and most-favoured locations in developing countries', *European Journal of Health Economics*, 8, 305–312.
Pachanee, C.-A. and S. Wibulpolprasert (2006), 'Incoherent policies on universal coverage of health insurance and promotion of international trade in health services in Thailand', *Health Policy and Planning*, 21, 310–318.
Paffhausen, L., C. Peguero and L. Roche-Villareal (2010), *Medical Tourism: A Survey*, Washington, DC: United Nations Economic Commission for Latin America and the Caribbean.
Palmer, D. (2006), 'Tackling Malawi's human resources crisis', *Reproductive Health Matters*, 14, 27–39.
Patel, V. (2003), 'Recruiting doctors from poor countries: the great brain robbery?', *British Medical Journal*, 327, 926–928.
Pellegrino, E.D. (1999), 'The commodification of medical and health care: the moral consequences of a paradigm shift from a professional to a market ethic', *Journal of Medicine and Philosophy*, 24, 243–266.
Pennings, G. (2002), 'Reproductive tourism as moral pluralism in motion', *Journal of Medical Ethics*, 28, 337–341.
Pennings, G. (2004), 'Legal harmonization and reproductive tourism in Europe', *Human Reproduction*, 19, 2689–2694.
Pennings, G. (2007), 'Ethics without boundaries: medical tourism', in R.E. Ashcroft, A. Dawson, H. Draper and J.R. McMillan, eds, *Principles of Health Care Ethics*, Chichester: Wiley, 505–510.
Peters, D.H. and V.R. Muraleedharan (2008), 'Regulating India's health services: To what end? What future?', *Social Science and Medicine*, 66, 2133–2144.
Phillips, N. (2011), 'Globalization and development', in J. Ravenhill, ed., *Global Political Economy*, 3rd edn, Oxford: Oxford University Press, 416–449.
Pollard, K. (2011), 'The medical tourism numbers game . . . part 2', *International Medical Travel Journal*, http://www.imtojonline.com/articles/2011, accessed on 13 August 2012.
Pollard, K. (2012), 'Medical tourism: key facts', www.treatmentabroad.com, accessed on 5 December 2012.
Pond, R. and B. McPake (2006), 'The health migration crisis: the role of four Organisation for Economic Co-operation and Development countries', *The Lancet*, 367, 1448–1455.
Ramchandani, N. (2012), '4.3b revenue likely for Singapore from medical tourism this year', *Business Times*, 5 October, http://yourhealth.asiaone/com/content/43b-revenue-likely-singapore-medical-tourism-year, accessed on 26 May 2012.
Rao, K.D., A. Bhatnagar and P. Berman (2012), 'So many, yet few: human

resources for health in India', *Human Resources for Health*, 10:19, http://www.human-resources-health.com/content/10/1/19, accessed on 26 September 2012.

Rawls, J. (1971 [1999]), *A Theory of Justice*, revised edn, Cambridge, MA: Belknap Press.

Reddy, S.G., V.K. York and L.A. Brannon (2010), 'Travel for treatment: students' perspective on medical tourism', *International Journal of Tourism Research*, 12, 510–522.

Richman, B.D., K. Udayakumar, W. Mitchell and K.A. Schulman (2008), 'Lessons from India in organizational innovation: a tale of two heart hospitals', *Health Affairs*, 27, 1260–1270.

Roemer, M.I. and R. Roemer (1990), 'Global health, national development, and the role of government', *American Journal of Public Health*, 80, 1188–1192.

Rutten, M. (2009), 'The economic impact of medical migration: an overview of the literature', *World Economy*, 32, 291–325.

Sandel, M.J. (2012), *What Money Can't Buy: The Moral Limits of Markets*, New York: Farrar, Straus & Giroux.

Scheper-Hughes, N. (2002), 'The ends of the body: commodity fetishism and the global traffic in organs', *SAIS Review*, 22, 61–80.

Scheper-Hughes, N. (2003), 'Keeping an eye on the global traffic in human organs', *The Lancet*, 361, 1645–1648.

Scheper-Hughes, N. (2011), 'Mr Tati's holiday and João's safari – seeing the world through transplant tourism', *Body and Society*, 17:2–3, 55–92.

Scherrer, C. (2011), 'GATS: long-term strategy for the commodification of education', *Review of International Political Economy*, 12, 484–510.

Schwartz, B. (1994), *The Costs of Living: How Market Freedom Erodes the Best Things in Life*, New York: Norton.

Schwartz, B. (2004), *The Paradox of Choice: Why More is Less*, New York: HarperCollins.

Sengupta, A. and S. Nundy (2005), 'The private health sector in India is burgeoning, but at the cost of public health care', *British Medical Journal*, 331, 1157–1158.

Shetty, S. (2010), 'Medical tourism booms in India, but at what cost?', *The Lancet*, 376, 671–672.

Shimazono, Y. (2007), 'The state of the international organ trade: a provisional picture based on integration of available information', *Bulletin of the World Health Organization*, 85, 955–961.

Smith, A. (1759 [1966]), *The Theory of Moral Sentiments*, New York: Augustus M. Kelley.

Smith, A. (1776 [1961]), *The Wealth of Nations*, 2 vols, ed. by E. Cannan, London: Methuen.

Smith, R.D. (2004), 'Foreign direct investment and trade in health services: a review of the literature', *Social Science and Medicine*, 59, 2313–2323.
Smith, R.D. (2012), 'The health system and international trade', in R.D. Smith and K. Hanson, eds, *Health Systems in Low- and Middle-Income Countries: An Economic and Policy Perspective*, Oxford: Oxford University Press, 173–192.
Smith, R.D., R. Chanda and V. Tangcharoensathien (2009), 'Trade in health-related services', *The Lancet*, 373, 593–601.
Smith, R.D., C. Correa and C. Oh (2009), 'Trade, TRIPS and pharmaceuticals', *The Lancet*, 373, 684–691.
Smith, R.D., M. Lagarde, D. Blaauw, C. Goodman, M. English, K. Mullei, N. Pagaiya, V. Tangcharoensathien, E. Erasmus and K. Hanson (2012), 'Appealing to altruism: an alternative strategy to address the health workforce crisis in developing countries?', *Journal of Public Health*, 35, 164–170.
Smith, R.D., H. Legido-Quigley, N. Lunt and D. Horsfall (2012), 'Medical tourism the European way', in J.R. Hodges, L. Turner and A.M. Kimball, eds, *Risks and Challenges in Medical Tourism: Understanding the Global Market for Health Services*, Santa Barbara, CA: Praeger, 37–55.
Smith, R.D., M. Martinez Alvarez and R. Chanda (2011), 'Medical tourism: a review of the literature and analysis of a role for bi-lateral trade', *Health Policy*, 103, 276–282.
Snyder, J., V. Crooks, R. Johnston and P. Kingsbury (2013), 'Beyond sun, sand, and stitches: assigning responsibility for the harms of medical tourism', *Bioethics*, 27, 233–42.
Song, P. (2010), 'Biotech pilgrims and the transnational quest for stem cell cures', *Medical Anthropology*, 29, 384–402.
Spar, D. (2005), 'For love and money: the political economy of commercial surrogacy', *Review of International Political Economy*, 12, 287–309.
Stackpole & Associates (2010), *Inbound Medical Tourism: Survey of US International Patient Departments*, Brookline, MA: Stackpole & Associates.
Steering Committee of the Istanbul Summit (2008), *The Declaration of Istanbul on Organ Trafficking and Transplant Tourism*, www.declarationofistanbul.org.
Steiner, N. (2009), 'Israel's pioneer in medical tourism', *Medical Tourism Magazine*, 13, 126–7.
Straits Times (2012), Singapore, 'Young, urban workers drive Philippines' growth', 29 August, A15.
Straits Times (2013), Singapore, 'Foreign patients coming back to Singapore', 18 February, 1.

Tawney, R.H. (1939), 'Introduction to J.P. Mayer', in J.P. Mayer, *Political Thought: The European Tradition*, London: J.M. Dent & Sons, i–xxi.
Tawney, R.H. (1966 [1949]), *The Radical Tradition*, ed. by R. Hinden, Harmondsworth: Penguin Books.
Thun, E. (2011), 'The globalization of production', in J. Ravenhill, ed., *Global Political Economy*, 3rd edn, Oxford: Oxford University Press, 354–371.
Titmuss, R.M. (1970), *The Gift Relationship: From Human Blood to Social Policy*, London: George Allen & Unwin.
Todaro, M.P. and S.C. Smith (2009), *Economic Development*, 10th edn, Harlow: Pearson Education.
Tourism Research and Marketing (TRAM) (2006), *Report on the Global Medical Tourism Market*, http://www.atlas-euro-org/pages/content/pqpublications.htm, accessed on 6 September 2012.
Tourism-Review.com (2007), 'Tunisia: new medical tourism destination', http://www.tourism-review.com, accessed on 2 October 2012.
Treatment Abroad (2012), 'Cosmetic surgery tourism: keeping the patient satisfied', www.treatmentabroad.com/medical-tourism/medical-tourist-research-2012, accessed on 17 April 2013.
Tudor Hart, J. (1971), 'The inverse care law', *The Lancet*, 27 February, 405–412.
Turner, L. (2007), '"First world health care at third world prices": globalization, bioethics and medical tourism', *BioSocieties*, 2, 303–325.
Turner, L. (2011a), 'Quality in health care and globalization of health services: accreditation and regulatory oversight of medical tourism companies', *International Journal for Quality in Health Care*, 23, 1–7.
Turner, L. (2011b), 'Canadian medical tourism companies that have exited the marketplace: content analysis of websites used to market transnational medical travel', *Globalization and Health*, 7, http://globalizationandhealth.com/content/7/1/40, accessed on 25 March 2013.
Turner, L. (2012), 'News media reports of patient deaths following "medical tourism" for cosmetic surgery and bariatric surgery', *Developing World Bioethics*, 12, April, 21–34.
United Nations (1948 [1950]), *Universal Declaration of Human Rights*, http://www.un.org/rights/50/decla.htm, accessed on 1 November 2012.
United Nations Department of Economic and Social Affairs (2002), *Manual on Statistics of International Trade in Services*, Geneva: United Nations.
United Nations Economic and Social Commission for Asia and the Pacific (2007), *Medical Travel in Asia and the Pacific: Challenges and Opportunities*, Bangkok: United Nations.
United States Senate Special Committee on Ageing (2006), *The*

Globalization of Heath Care: Can Medical Tourism Reduce Health Care Costs?, Washington, DC: US Government Printing Office.
Unti, J.A. (2009), 'Medical and surgical tourism: the new world of health care globalization and what it means for the practicing surgeon', *Bulletin of the American College of Surgeons*, 94, 18–25.
Vijaya, R.M. (2010), 'Medical tourism: revenue generation or international transfer of healthcare problems?', *Journal of Economic Issues*, 44, 53–69.
Voigt, C. and J.H. Laing (2010), 'Journey into parenthood: commodification of reproduction as a new tourism niche market', *Journal of Travel and Tourism Marketing*, 27, 252–268.
Wagner, C., K. Dobrick and F. Verheyen (2011), *EU Cross-Border Health Care Survey 2010: Patient Satisfaction, Quality, Information and Potential*, Hamburg: Scientific Institute of Techniker Krankenkasse for the Benefit and Efficiency in Health Care.
Walzer, M. (1983), *Spheres of Justice: A Defense of Pluralism and Equality*, New York: Basic Books.
Walzer, M. (1994), *Thick and Thin: Moral Arguments at Home and Abroad*, Notre Dame: University of Notre Dame Press.
Wangberg, S., H. Andreassen, P. Kummervold, R. Wynn and T. Sørensen (2009), 'Use of the internet for health purposes: trends in Norway 2000–2010', *Scandinavian Journal of Caring Sciences*, 23, 691–696.
Warner, D. (2009), 'Trends and drivers of trade in health services: mode 2', World Health Organization Centre for Health Development, www.utexasa.edu/lbj/directory/faculty/david-warner, accessed on 6 December 2011.
Weekly Telegraph (2009), 'Immigrants send £4bn home a year', 4–10 June.
Weiner, R., G. Mitchell, and M. Price (1998), 'Wits medical graduates: where are they now?', *South African Journal of Science*, 94, 59–63.
Weiss, M.E., P.F. Spataro, I.J. Kodner and J.D. Keune (2010), 'Banding in Bangkok, CABG in Calcutta: the United States physician and the growing field of medical tourism', *Surgery*, 148, 597–601.
Whittaker, A. (2010), 'Challenges of medical travel to global regulation: a case study of reproductive travel in Asia', *Global Social Policy*, 10, 396–415.
Wibulpolprasert, S., C. Pachanee, S. Pitayarangsarit and P. Hempisut (2004), 'International service trade and its implications for human resources: a case study of Thailand', *Human Resources for Health*, 2:10, http://www.human-resources-health,com/content/2/1/10, accessed on 14 June 2012.
Wibulpolprasert, S. and P. Pengpaibon (2003), 'Integrated strategies to tackle the inequitable distribution of doctors in Thailand: four decades

of experience', *Human Resources for Health*, 1:12, http://www.human-resources-health.com/content/1/1/12, accessed on 31 July 2012.

Widdows, H. (2007), 'Is global ethics moral neo-colonialism? An investigation of the issue in the context of bioethics', *Bioethics*, 21, 305–315.

Widdows, H. (2011), 'Localized past, globalized future: towards an effective bioethical framework using examples from population genetics and medical tourism', *Bioethics*, 25, 83–91.

Williamson, O.E. (1981), 'The modern corporation: origins, evolution, attributes', *Journal of Economic Literature*, 19, 1537–1568.

Wiskow, C. (2006), *Health Worker Migration Flows in Europe: Overview and Case Studies in Selected CEE countries – Romania, Czech Republic, Serbia and Croatia*, Geneva: International Labour Office.

Wolff, J. (2007), 'Passport to cheaper health care?', *Good Housekeeping*, October, www.goodhousekeeping.com, accessed on 4 February 2013.

Woodward, D. (2005), 'The GATS and trade in health services: implications for health care in developing countries', *Review of International Political Economy*, 12, 511–534.

Woomer, J. (2011), 'The global healthcare provider shortage and medical tourism – impact and solutions', *Medical Tourism Magazine*, 22, 68–71.

World Bank (2011), *Migration and Remittances Factbook 2011*, Washington, DC: World Bank.

World Bank (2013), *World DataBank*, http://databank.worldbank.org/data/views/variableselection/selectvariables.aspx?source=world-development-indicators, accessed on 15 April 2013.

World Health Organization (1962 [1946]), *Constitution of the World Health Organization*, in WHO, *Basic Documents*, Geneva: WHO, 1–18.

World Health Organization (2005), *Methodological Approach to Assessing Trade in Health Services: A Guide to Conducting Country Studies*, Cairo: World Health Organization Regional Office for the Eastern Mediterranean.

World Health Organization (2006), *World Health Report 2006: Working Together for Health*, Geneva: World Health Organization.

World Health Organization (2012), *World Health Statistics*, Geneva: World Health Organization.

World Health Organization (2013), *Global Health Observatory Data Repository*, http://apps.who.int/gho/data/view.main.1910?lang=en, accessed on 21 April 2013.

World Trade Organization (1995), 'General Agreement on Trade in Services', in *WTO Legal Texts*, Geneva: World Trade Organization, 283–317.

World Trade Organization (2012), *Statistics Database*, http://stat.wto.

org/StatisticalProgram/WSDBStatProgramHome.aspx?Language=E, accessed on 15 April 2013.
Yach, D. and D. Bettcher (1998), 'The globalization of public health, II: the convergence of self-interest and altruism', *American Journal of Public Health*, 80, 738–741.
Yamin, A.E. (2009), 'Shades of dignity: exploring the demands of equality in applying human rights frameworks to health', *Health and Human Rights*, 11, 1–18.
Yap, J.C.H., (2006), 'Medical tourism/medical travel (Part One)', *SMA News*, 38, May, 17–21.
Yap, J.C.H., (2007), 'Singapore: medical travel and consumer driven health care', *AARP Journal*, http://www,aarpinternational.org/resource library/resourcelibrary_show.htm?doc_id=545751, accessed on 7 May 2012.
Youngman, I. (2009), 'Medical tourism statistics: why McKinsey got it wrong', *International Medical Travel Journal*, http://www.imtojonline.com/articles/2009, accessed on 19 April 2012.
Youngman, I. (2011), 'Good news . . . the medical tourism world is shrinking!', *International Medical Travel Journal*, http://www.imtojonline.com/articles/2011, accessed on 12 September 2012.
Youngman, I. (2012), 'How much has the world of medical tourism changed?', *International Medical Travel Journal*, http://www.imtojonline.com/articles/2012, accessed on 10 September 2012.

Index